A History of the Kings of England

𝔉LORENCE
of
𝔚ORCESTER

A
HISTORY
OF
THE
KINGS
OF
ENGLAND

Published by Llanerch Enterprises,
Felinfach, Lampeter, Dyfed.
SA48 8PJ.

ISBN 0947992227

A facsimile reprint.
Translated by Joseph Stevenson, and
first published by Seeleys in the series
'The Church Historians of England' (c.1860's).

PREFACE TO FLORENCE OF WORCESTER.

§ 1. THE Chronicle of Florence of Worcester has a double claim upon our attention. It is valuable historically, as a record of events, and critically, as contributing to a knowledge of the condition of the Saxon Chronicle at the time when that document supplied the monk of Worcester with the basis of the history which passes under his name. It is in the former of these capacities only that it claims our notice upon the present occasion.

§ 2. Of Florence himself we know very little. He is said to have been an inmate of the great Benedictine monastery of Worcester; and not only is there nothing in his Chronicle which militates against this statement, but there is much which establishes its credibility. The Continuation of this history states, that " upon the nones of July, Florence, the monk of Worcester, died; by whose skill, learning, and studious industry this Chronicle has the preeminence over all others."[1] In the preparation of this work, Florence adopted for his basis the Chronicle of Marianus Scotus,[2] into which he has interwoven a large body of information respecting England. The earlier portion of his work is borrowed from the Saxon Chronicle and the Ecclesiastical History of the Venerable Beda, interspersed, however, with a few extracts from the Lives of the English Saints. From 849 to 888 Asser's Life of Alfred forms the staple; but the narrative is slightly abridged, and occasionally transposed. After this last date he returns to the Saxon Chronicle once more; and from it by far the larger portion of the remainder of his work is derived. These several materials he employs with care and discretion; and although his narrative is without the slightest claim to artistic skill, it tells its tale simply and intelligibly.

[1] See also Wharton's Angl. Sacr. i. 475, for a note to the same effect.

[2] This Marianus, an Irishman, was born about A.D. 1028, and, like many of his countrymen, he spent the larger portion of his life upon the continent, residing successively at Cologne, Fulda, and Mentz. He died about 1082 or 1083, leaving behind him a Chronicle which extends from the creation of the world to his own time. The notices of British affairs which it contains are few and unimportant. The copy of Marianus which was used by Florence appears to have very closely resembled that in the Cottonian Library, marked Nero, C. v. An admirable edition has lately appeared in the fifth volume of Pertz's collection of German Historians, the text of which is founded upon a MS. in the Vatican, which claims to be the autograph of the author.

§ 3. The most important manuscripts of Florence which remain are the following :—

One in the library of Corpus Christi College at Oxford, written in folio, upon parchment, in double columns, about the middle of the twelfth century. It appears to have formerly belonged to the church of Worcester, and may be considered the most valuable copy which we have. It breaks off in the year 1140, having suffered mutilation at the end.

§ 4. One in the archiepiscopal library at Lambeth, in large folio, written upon vellum, in double columns. It contains the Continuation, ending in 1131. From the fact of it presenting some interpolated passages respecting the monastery of Abingdon, it is supposed, not unreasonably, to have formerly belonged to that foundation.

§ 5. One in the Bodleian Library, MS. Bodl. 297, in folio, on vellum, written in double columns, towards the end of the twelfth century. It also contains the Continuation, ending in 1131. It apparently belonged to the monastery of Bury St. Edmund's.

§ 6. One in the library of Corpus Christi College, Cambridge, marked XCII. in Nasmith's Catalogue, in folio, on vellum, written in double columns, towards the end of the twelfth century, or perhaps the beginning of the thirteenth. This copy formerly belonged to the monastery of Peterborough. It also contains the Continuation as far as 1131; and then a third annalist, named John de Taxter (of whom more hereafter), carries on the narrative to 1295.

§ 7. One in the library of Magdalen College, Oxford, number XXXVI., on vellum, in folio, written in the thirteenth century. It has the Continuation as far as 1131.

§ 8. One in the library of Trinity College, Dublin, in small quarto, on vellum, written in the thirteenth century, with a Continuation to 1137.

§ 9. A second in the same library, in duodecimo, on vellum, written in various hands. It is continued as far as the year 1141, where it concludes abruptly, being mutilated at the end.

§ 10. The Cottonian manuscript, Vitellius A. XIII., and that numbered CLXXXV. in the library of Corpus Christi, Cambridge, may be here mentioned, since they both contain copies of Florence of Worcester, although they are erroneously described as manuscripts of the Chronicle of Walter of Coventry.

§ 11. Three editions of the Chronicle of Florence of Worcester have appeared.

The first edition is that edited in quarto, at London, in 1592, from two manuscripts which then were in the possession of Lord William Howard, of Naworth,[1] and which afterwards became the property of Archbishop Ussher, and are now, with the rest of the collections of that eminent prelate, in the library of Trinity College, Dublin. (See §§ 8 and 9.) This edition was very carelessly reprinted at Frankfort in the year 1601.

§ 12. Mr. Petrie's first volume of the Materials for the History of Britain contains a carefully executed edition of the Chronicle of

---

[1] Dugd. Bar. ii. 281.

Florence as far as the year 1066. The text is revised by collation with the more important of the copies which we have described above.

§ 13. In 1848 and 1849 the English Historical Society published an edition of this work, which was edited by B. Thorpe, Esq. It is based upon the manuscript belonging to Corpus Christi College at Oxford, but with collations from some other copies. It also contains the several Continuations which we have specified in the course of our remarks upon the different manuscript copies of this author.

§ 14. The Continuation, which extends from the period of the death of Florence of Worcester to the year 1141, next claims our notice, since a translation of it into English is contained in the present volume. It would seem that this narrative was, in the first instance, carried no further than 1131, at which date it ceases in several copies, while in others it ends at various years between the last-mentioned period and 1141. These Continuations are certainly the productions of contemporary[1] writers, one of whom was called John;[2] and this portion of the work is entitled to especial notice as recording much valuable information upon the history of our nation during the period which it embraces.

§ 15. Prefixed to all the manuscript copies of Florence of Worcester, and probably compiled by himself, are lists of the archbishops and bishops of the several English sees, together with the succession of the sovereigns of the various kingdoms into which this realm was formerly divided. These are founded upon some very ancient lists still remaining. Translations of these have been appended to this edition. The text of Florence which has been used for this purpose, and for the Chronicle as far as 1066, is that of Petrie; from 1066 to the end of the work, the edition of the English Historical Society has been employed.

[1] He speaks of Henry, bishop of Winchester, as papal legate at the time when he wrote, (see A.D. 1134,) and from that prelate he had some information which he records A.D. 1137. Stephen is mentioned in the following year, as being upon the throne when the passage was written, (see also A.D. 1139.) In one place (A.D. 1139), an expression is employed which would seem to lead to the inference that it was written by a monk of the abbey of Gloucester: but when narrating the pillage of the city of Worcester, which occurred in the same year, the author speaks of himself as engaged, along with the other monks, in performing divine service within the quire of that cathedral. In 1141 he tells us that some of his information respecting the empress Matilda was derived immediately from Milo, earl of Hereford.

[2] See A.D. 1138.

LEIGHTON BUZZARD,
    17th November, 1853.

THE CHRONICLE

OF

FLORENCE OF WORCESTER.

In the year of our Lord 450, in the time of the emperor Martian, as Beda[1] testifies, the Anglo-Saxons came over to Britain in three long ships; they who came were of the three most powerful nations of Germany, that is to say, the Saxons, the Angles, and the Jutes. From the Jutes descend the inhabitants of Kent and the Isle of Wight; from the Saxons spring the East Saxons, the South Saxons, and the West Saxons; and from the Angles (that is, from the country which is called Angulus) have come the East Angles, the Mid-Angles, the Mercians, all the Northumbrian race, and the rest of the English people. Their two first leaders are said to have been two brothers named Hengst and Hors. They were the sons of Wictgisl, whose father was Witta, whose father was Wecta, whose father was Woden; from whose stock the royal families of many provinces deduce their origin.

A.D. 451—454.

A.D. 455. Hengst and Hors fought against Wyrtgeorne, king of the Britons, at a place which is called Aegelesthrep; and although Hors was slain in that battle, yet Hengst gained the victory: and after that, he began to reign with his son Aesc.

A.D. 456.

A.D. 457. Hengst and Aesc fought a battle with the Britons at a place called Creccanford, and slew four thousand of their men with the edge of the sword; the remainder entirely deserted Kent, and fled in great terror to London.

A.D. 458—464.

A.D. 465. Hengst and Aesc fought with the Britons near Wippedesfleote, that is, Wipped's passage; and slew twelve chiefs, and many others of the enemy, and only one of their own thanes named Wipped was killed.

A.D. 466—472.

A.D. 473. Hengst and Aesc fought for the fourth time against the Britons, and, gaining the victory, carried off booty beyond measure. In this battle the Britons fled from the Angles as from fire.

A.D. 474—476.

[1] Eccl. Hist. I. xv.

A.D. 477. Aelle and his three sons, Cimen, Wlencing, and Cissa, came over to Britain with three ships, and landed at a place called Cymenesore, and there slew many of the Britons, and drove the others into the forest called Andredeslea.

A.D. 478—484.

A.D. 485. Aelle, in a battle with the Britons near Mearcredes-Burn, that is, Mearcred's Brook, slew many of them, and put the rest to flight.

A.D. 486, 487.

A.D. 488. Hengst died, after having vigorously governed the kingdom of Kent for thirty-four years. His son Aesc succeeded him in the kingdom, and reigned twenty-four years.

A.D. 489, 490.

A.D. 491. Olibrius the younger was consul. In the same year the emperor Zeno died. Saint Patric, archbishop of Ireland, died in perfect peace, aged 122 years. Aelle and his son Cissa took Andred-cester after a long siege, and exterminated its inhabitants down to the very youngest.

A.D. 492—494.

A.D. 495. In this year, two chiefs, namely Cerdic and his son Cynric, came over to Britain with five ships, and landing at a place called Cerdicsore, fought on the same day against the Britons, defeated them, and put them to flight.

A.D. 496—500.

A.D. 501. Port, and his two sons, Bida and Meagla, arrived in Britain with his two ships, at a place called Portesmuth, and slew many Britons, among whom was a young man of very high birth.

A.D. 502—507.

A.D. 508. Cerdic, and his son Cynric, slew Natanleod, king of the Britons, and five thousand of his men with the edge of the sword; all the region, as far as Cerdicsford, was called Natanleod after his name.

A.D. 509—513.

A.D. 514. The West Saxons came over to Britain with three ships, and landed at a place called Cerdicsore. Their chiefs, Stuf and Wihtgar, were the nephews of Cerdic. They shortly afterwards attacked the Britons, and slew some, and put the rest to flight.

A.D. 515—518.

A.D. 519. Cerdic and Cynric began to reign, and in the same year they fought against, and overcame the Britons at the place called Cerdicsford.

A.D. 520.

A.D. 521. Simmachus and Boetius were consuls. Saint Brigid, the Scotch virgin, died in Ireland.

A.D. 522—526.

A.D. 527. Cerdic and Cynric fought for the fourth time against the Britons at the place called Cerdicsleage.

A.D. 528, 529.

A.D. 530. Cerdic and Cynric took the Isle of Wight and gave it to their nephews Stuf and Wihtgar, and slew a few men at Wihtgarabirig [Carisbrook].

A.D. 531—533.

A.D. 534.   Cerdic, the first king of the West Saxons, died, and his son Cynric reigned after him by himself for twenty-six years.

A.D. 535—537.

A.D. 538.   An eclipse of the sun took place on the 14th of the kalends of March [15th Feb.], and lasted from the first until the third hour.

A.D. 539.

A.D. 540.   An eclipse of the sun took place on the 12th of the kalends of July [20th June], and the stars showed themselves full nigh half-an-hour after the third hour of the day.

A.D. 541—543.

A.D. 544.   Wihtgar, the nephew of Cerdic, king of the West Saxons, died, and was buried in Wihtgarabirig, that is, the city of Wihtgar.

A.D. 545, 546.

A.D. 547.   Ida began to reign in the province of Bernicia, and he reigned twelve years.   He had, by his queens, six sons, namely, Adda, Baelric, Theodric, Aethelric, Theodher, and Osmer ; and six by his concubines, namely, Occ, Alric, Ecca, Oswold, Sogor, and Sogether.   From these descended the royal line of the North-humbrians.   Ida was the son of Eoppa, who was the son of Esa, who was the son of Ingui, who was the son of Angenwit, who was the son of Aloc, who was the son of Benoc, who was the son of Brand, who was the son of Bealdeag, who was the son of Woden, who was the son of Frithelaf, who was the son of Frithulf, who was the son of Finn, who was the son of Godulf, who was the son of Geata.

A.D. 548—551.

A.D. 552.   Cynric, king of the West Saxons, fought against the Britons, at a place called Searesbirig, and put them to flight.   His father was Cerdic, who was the son of Elesa, who was the son of Esla, who was the son of Gewis, who was the son of Wig, who was the son of Freawine, who was the son of Freothegar, who was the son of Brand, who was the son of Bealdeag, who was the son of Woden.

A.D. 553—555.

A.D. 556.   Cynric and Ceaulin fought against the Britons at Beranbyrig and put them to flight.

A.D. 557, 558.

A.D. 559.   Aelle began to reign in the province of Deira, and he governed it vigorously for nearly thirty years.   When Saint Gregory saw some English youths set for sale in the market-place at Rome, he said, in allusion to the name of this province, " Alleluiah, the praise of God the Creator must be sung in those parts."   During Aelle's lifetime, Adda, the eldest son of Ida, reigned over the Bernicians seven years ; Clappa, five years ; Theoduulf, one year ; Freothulf, seven years ; Theodric, seven years ; and Aethelric, two years : the latter, on the death of Aelle, and the expulsion from the kingdom of his son Edwin, reigned five years over both provinces. Aelle was the son of Iffi, whose father was Wuscfrea, whose father was Wilgels, whose father was Westorwalcna, whose father was Seomel, whose father was Suearta, whose father was Saefugel, whose father was Seabald, whose father was Siggeot, whose father was Suuebdeag, whose father was Siggar, whose father was Weagdeag, whose father was Woden.

A.D. 560.   Ceaulin, the son of Cynric, began to reign over the West Saxons, and he reigned thirty-three years.

A.D. 561.   Aethelbriht, king of Kent, began to reign, and according to Beda,[1] he reigned fifty-six years.

A.D. 562—564.

A.D. 565.   Columba, priest and abbot, came from Ireland into Britain, the most potent king Bridius being king of the Picts, and converted the Northern Picts to Christianity.   Hence he obtained from them the Island of Hii, for the purpose of building a monastery.

A.D. 566, 567.

A.D. 568.   While Aethelbriht, king of Kent, was waging war against Ceaulin, king of the West Saxons, and Cutha his brother, he was driven by them into Kent ; and Oslaf and Cnebba, two of his ealdormen, were killed at Wibbandun.

A.D. 569, 570.

A.D. 571.   Cuthulf, the brother of king Ceaulin, fought with the Britons, at a place called Bedanford ; and gaining the victory, took from them four royal vills, namely, Liganburh, Egelesburh, Bensingtun, and Eignesham ; and he died in the same year.

A.D. 572—576.

A.D. 577.   Ceaulin, king of the West Saxons, and his son Cuthwine, fought with the Britons at a place called Deorham, and slew their three kings, Conmeail, Condidan, and Farinmeil, and many other men ; and took from them three cities, namely, Glauwecester, Cirenceaster, and Bathanceaster.

A.D. 578—583.

A.D. 584.   Ceaulin, king of the West Saxons, and his son Cutha, fought with the Britons at a place called Fethanleah.   In this battle Cutha fell, fighting bravely in the thickest of the strife.   But king Ceaulin gained the victory, and took from them much booty and many vills.

A.D. 585—587.

A.D. 588.   Aelle, king of Deira, died in the thirtieth year of his reign, and after him, Aethelric, the son of Ida, reigned five years over both provinces.

A.D. 589.   The holy father Columba,[2] with Saint Gall and other tried disciples, came from Ireland, the island of saints, into Burgundy ; and there, by the permission of king Theodoric, he built the monastery of Luxeu.   Driven thence by Brunihilda, he went into Germany, and left Saint Gall there : but he himself passed over into Italy and founded the monastery of Bobbio, where he became the head of a large congregation of monks.

A.D. 590.

---

[1] Eccl. Hist. II. v.
[2] On the history of St. Columba and his various ecclesiastical foundations, see Mabill. Annal. Ord. S. Bened. lib. viii. § 1.

A.D. 591.   Ceol, the son of Cuthulf, who was the brother of king Ceaulin, began to reign, and he reigned five years over the West Saxons.

A.D. 592.   There was a battle at a place called Wodnesbeorh, that is, Woden's Mount, and king Ceaulin was driven from his kingdom with great slaughter in the thirty-third year of his reign.

A.D. 593.   Ceaulin, Cuíchelm, and Crida perished.   Aethelric, king of Northumbria died : Aethelfrith, his son, assumed the reins of government and held them twenty-four years : he had seven sons, namely, Eanfrith, Oswald, Oslaf, [1] Oswiu, Offa, Osuudu, and Oslac, and one daughter, named Aebbe.

A.D. 594, 595.

A.D. 596.   In the 147th year after the arrival of the Angles in Britain, and the fourteenth indiction, pope Gregory, moved by divine inspiration, sent Augustine, the servant of God, and several God-fearing monks with him, to preach the word of God to the English nation.

A.D. 597.   The aforesaid teachers arrived in Britain this year, as Beda[2] testifies, and converted Aethelbriht, king of Kent, to Christianity, in the thirty-fifth year[3] of his reign.   It was not long before the king advanced his teacher Augustine to the episcopal see of Canterbury, the metropolis of his kingdom.   Supported by the king, Augustine obtained possession of a church which had been formerly built there by the Roman Christians, and consecrated it in the name of the Saviour.   Ceolulf, son of Cutha, who was the brother of king Ceaulin, succeeded to the kingdom of the West Saxons, and he held it fourteen years : he was always at war either with the Angles, or Britons, or Picts, or Scots.   He was the son of Cutha, who was the son of Cenric, who was the son of Cerdic.

A.D. 598, 599.

A.D. 600.   Ivo, the apostolic doctor, and truly an ambassador from heaven, and a renowned prelate, died; born, like the Star of the East, in Persia, he was destined by God for the western limits of Britain.

A.D. 601.   In the nineteenth year of the reign of the emperor Mauritius, the fourth indiction, Gregory, in a letter to Augustine, decided that the bishops of London and York should alike receive the pall from Rome and be metropolitans.

A.D. 602.

A.D. 603.   Aethelfrith, a very brave king, and most greedy of glory, did more damage to the Britons than any former English ruler.   Large tracts of their country, the natives being either exterminated or subdued, he either made tributary to, or fit for the habitation of the Angles.   Indignant at these successes, Aedan, king of the Scots, came with an immense army against him, but was defeated, and fled with only a few survivors.   Aethelfrith put an end to this war at a place called Degsastan, in the eleventh year of his reign, and the first of that of the emperor Phocas.

---

[1] See the Royal Genealogies.
[2] Eccl. Hist. I. xxv. and xxvi.
[3] We should perhaps rather read xxxvii.

A long time 'afterwards he collected an army at Chester, called by the Britons Carlegion, and by the just judgment of God, and in accordance with the prophecy of the archbishop St. Augustine, he slew 1,200 of the British priests who had met to offer up prayers for the success of the enemy. And thus he destroyed the remainder of their wicked army.

A.D. 604.   Augustine ordained as bishops Mellitus and Justus. Mellitus was to preach to the province of the East Saxons. When the East Saxons, with their king Sebert, the nephew of king Aethelberht, had received the word of truth by the preaching of Mellitus, the said king Aethelberht built the church of the apostle in London, which city was his metropolis.   As for Justus, Augustine ordained him bishop in the city of Dorubrevum, called by the English Hroveceaster.   He also consecrated the presbyter Laurence to be archbishop in his stead; and shortly afterwards, to wit, on Tuesday, the 7th of the kalends of June [26th May], he departed to the heavenly kingdom.

A.D. 605.   The blessed pope Gregory, apostle of the Angles, and pride of the Romans, after having most gloriously governed the see of the Roman and Apostolic Church for thirteen years, six months, and ten days, was translated to the eternal see of the kingdom, on Friday, the 4th of the ides of March [12th March].

A.D. 606.

A.D. 607.   Ceoluulf, king of the West Saxons, waged war against the South Saxons.[2]

A.D. 608—610.

A.D. 611.   King Ceoluulf died.   Cynegils, the son of his brother Ceol, succeeded him, and reigned thirty-two years.   He was the son of Ceol, who was the son of Cutha, [3]who was the son of Kenric, who was the son of Cerdic.

A.D. 612, 613.

A.D. 614.   Cynegils and his son Cuichelm marched against the Britons at Beandune, engaged with them, and slew two thousand and forty-six of them.

A.D. 615.

A.D. 616.   Aethelbert, king of Kent, the son of Irmenric, whose father was Octa, whose father was Oric, surnamed Oisc, whose father was Hengst, entered on the joys of the heavenly kingdom, on the twenty-fourth day of February, in the fifty-sixth year of his reign, and the twenty-first of his conversion to the faith.   He was succeeded by his son Aedbold, who not only refused to embrace the Christian faith, but even married his father's widow.   Redwald, king of the East Angles, slew Aethelfrid, king of Deira and Bernicia, in a battle near the river called Idle.   Edwin, in accordance with the prediction which he had received, succeeded him, and drove out the seven sons of Aethelfrid.   Sebert, king of the East Saxons, departing to the heavenly kingdom, left his three sons,

---

[1] According to the Annals of Cambria, in 613. See the Saxon Chron. A.D. 607.
[2] A later hand here inserts in A. the following passage :—" St. David, also called Dewi, bishop of St. David's in Wales, departed to the Lord."
[3] This link in the pedigree is omitted in B.

who obstinately remained pagans, to inherit his earthly kingdom. They immediately began to profess idolatry, and drove Mellitus, bishop of London, from their kingdom : he, however, went to Kent, and, after consulting with archbishop Laurence, withdrew into Gaul with Justus, bishop of Rochester. But the kings who had driven from them this messenger of truth did not long exercise their devilish rites unpunished ; for, going out to battle against the Gewissi, [West Saxons,] they and all their army perished. When Laurence was about to follow Mellitus and Justus, Peter, the chief of the apostles, appeared to him by night, and inflicted severe stripes on him. The next morning he repaired to king Eadbald, and showed him the heavy flagellation which he had received. When the king saw it, great fear came upon him ; he forbad all idolatrous worship, renounced his unlawful marriage, embraced the faith of Christ, and sent over into Gaul, and recalled Mellitus and Justus.

A.D. 617—620.

A.D. 621. During the reign of Eadbald, and on the 4th of the nones of February [2d Feb.], the blessed archbishop Laurence departed to the Lord. Mellitus, bishop of London, succeeded him in the see of Canterbury, and was the third archbishop from Augustine. Cedd, the brother of Ceadda, succeeded Mellitus in the bishopric of London.

A.D. 622—624.

A.D. 625. On the 8th of the kalends of May [24th April], Eadbald being king, archbishop Mellitus died, having ruled over the church for five years. He was succeeded by Justus, bishop of Rochester, who consecrated Romanus to be bishop of that see in his own stead.

A.D. 626. Paulinus,[1] a man beloved of God, who had been sent with others by the blessed Gregory to preach the Gospel in England, and who was the third bishop of Rochester, was by archbishop Justus consecrated archbishop of the Northumbrians, and was sent to Edwin, the king of that province, with his intended wife, a daughter of king Aethelbert, by king Eadbald, brother of the said virgin.

A.D. 627. An[2] assassin named Eomer, sent by Cuichelm, king of the West Saxons, came to king Edwin on the first day of Easter, and drawing a dagger from under his garment, made a stab at the king. But a certain guard named Lilla, who was most devoted to the king, interposed his body to the blow ; yet so fierce a thrust had the assailant made, that he wounded the king through the body of this soldier, whom he slew. On the night of that Easter-Sunday, the queen bore to the king a daughter, who was baptized (the first among the Northumbrians to be so) by bishop Paulinus, on the day of Pentecost, and was named Eanfled.

In the fiftieth year of his age, Penda succeeded to the Mercian kingdom, and he reigned thirty years : he was the son of Pibba, who was the son of Crida, who was the son of Cynewald, who was the son of Cnebba, who was the son of Icel, who was the son of

[1] A.D. 625. Beda, Eccl. Hist. II. ix. [2] A.D. 626. Beda, ibid.

Eomer, who was the son of Angengeat, who was the son of Offa, who was the son of Weremund, who was the son of Wightleag, who was the son of Waga, who was the son of Wothelgeat, who was the son of Woden.

A.D. 628. [1]In the sixteenth year of the emperor Heraclius, and the fifteenth indiction, Edwin, the most renowned king of the northern Trans-Humbrian nation, and all his people, accepted the message of salvation through the preaching of bishop Paulinus, whom archbishop Justus had sent from Kent. This took place in the eleventh year of his reign, and about the two hundred and thirtieth year after the arrival of the Angles in Britain. It was he who gave to Paulinus the episcopal see of York. This king received an increase of temporal power in anticipation of his approaching conversion, and as an earnest of his share in the heavenly kingdom : for he, first of all the Angles, subjected to his power the whole of Britain, Kent only excepted.

At this time pope Honorius refuted by his epistle the error of the Quartodecimans concerning the observance of Easter, which had originated with the Hibernian Scots. John, also, who succeeded his (Honorius's) successor, Severinus, contested the same point with them ; for before he was elected pope, he wrote to them on the subject of Easter, and on the Pelagian heresy, which had revived among them.

Kinegils and his son Cuichelm, kings of the West Saxons, fought with Penda, king of the Mercians, near Cirenceaster, and afterwards, having made peace and confirmed it, retired.

A.D. 629[2]—631.

A.D. 632. Eorpwald, son of king Redwald, whose father was Titell, whose father was Vuffa, was prevailed on by king Edwin to renounce idolatry, and with all his province received the Christian faith and sacraments ; but a short time afterwards he was slain by a pagan named Ricbert.

A.D. 633. On the 4th of the ides of October [12th Oct.], the noble king Edwin, after reigning gloriously for seventeen years over the Angles and the Britons, was, in the forty-eighth year of his age, slain by that very brave man, Penda, the pagan king of the Mercians, and by Cedwal, king of the Britons, a still worse pagan, in a very fierce battle fought at Heathfeld. The affairs of the Northumbrians falling into confusion, Paulinus, in company with queen Aethelburge, returned by sea to Kent, and was honourably received by archbishop Honorius and king Eadbald.

A.D. 634. Ceadwala, king of the Britons, destroyed king Osric, the cousin of king Edwin, with his whole army, and then slew king Eanfrith, the son of king Ethelfrith, as he was coming to him to sue for peace : on whose death, his brother Oswald advanced with an army, small indeed, but strong in their faith in Christ, and slew the infamous British chief, together with his immense army,

---

[1] A.D. 627. Beda, Eccl. Hist. II. xiv.
[2] In A. a different hand has added the following passage :—" Pope Honorius sent the pall to Paulinus, who afterwards, in the province of Lindissi, consecrated Honorius, the successor of Justus, as archbishop of Canterbury."

which he boasted nothing could resist, and assumed the government of both kingdoms ; and he afterwards received the submission of all the nations and provinces of Britain.   At that time the nation of the West Saxons, Cinegils being their king, embraced Christianity, the word of God being preached to them by bishop Birin. Saint Wilfrid was born.

A.D. 635.   King Oswald sent to the elders of the Scots, requesting that they would send bishops to him.   Bishop Aidan was sent ; by whom, and the said most renowned and holy king Oswald, the church of Christ was first founded and established in the province of Bernicia.   By means of the preaching of Birin (who was sent into England for that purpose by pope Honorius) in the West-Saxon province, king Cinegils and all his people became believers : the most victorious king Oswald was his sponsor at the baptismal font.   From those kings the said bishop received the city of Dorcic [Dorchester] for the purpose of making it an episcopal see.

A.D. 636.   Sigebert, brother of Eorpwald, king of the East Angles, a man in all respects most christian and most learned, soon after he began to reign, was careful to make his whole province participate in the faith and sacraments.   Bishop Felix, a Burgundian, who had become very intimate with Sigebert, king of the East Angles, while he was an exile in Gaul, and had come over to England with him after the death of Eorpwald, and was made bishop of the East Angles, encouraged his designs, and brought the province over to the faith of Christ ; and receiving an episcopal see in the city of Dummoc [Dunwich], presided for a long time over that race.

At that time there came from Ireland to the province of the East Angles a most holy man named Fursey, who, being honourably entertained by the aforesaid king, preached there the word of life, and turned many unbelievers to Christ ; and he afterwards built a splendid monastery.

Meanwhile, the king, having abandoned the cares of state to his kinsman Egric, retired to the monastery which he had prepared for himself, and receiving the tonsure, was for a long time a devout soldier of the eternal King.   But when Penda, the pagan king of Mercia, marched to battle against the East Angles, he was most reluctantly drawn out of the monastery, and against his will led to the engagement, where, with a staff in his hands, he was slain, as was also king Egric.   They were succeeded in the kingdom by Anna, the son of Eni.   Quichelm, the son of king Cinegils, was baptized by bishop Birin, in the city of Dorcic [Dorchester], and died in the same year.

A.D. 637, 638.

A.D. 639.   Bishop Birin baptized Cuthred, the son of king Cuichelm, in the city of Dorcic [Dorchester], and stood sponsor for him at the font of regeneration.

A.D. 640.   Eadbald, king of Kent, departed this life in the twenty-fifth year of his reign, leaving his kingdom to his son Erconbert.   He was the first of the English kings who ordered the idols to be abandoned and destroyed throughout his kingdom, and the fast of Lent to be observed.   His daughter Ercongota, by his queen, Saint Sexburg, was a virgin of pre-eminent virtue.

A.D. 641.

A.D. 642. The most Christian king Oswald, nephew[1] of king Edwin, and son of king Aethelfrith, was slain in the thirty-eighth year of his age, and the ninth of his reign, by Penda, the pagan king of Mercia, in a severe battle fought at a place called Maserfeld : he was humble and courteous, and generous to strangers and the poor.

A.D. 643. His brother Osuiu, a young man about thirty years of age, succeeded to his kingdom shortly afterwards, and by dint of great exertion, retained it for twenty-eight years. In the same year, Cenwalch, son of king Cinegils, assumed the government of the West-Saxon kingdom, and retained it for thirty-one years. He built the cathedral church at Winchester.

A.D. 644. On the 6th of the ides of October [10th Oct.], Paulinus, who had been formerly bishop of York, but was then bishop of Rochester, died, having held the bishopric eighteen years, two months, and twenty-one days. Ithamar was ordained in his place by archbishop Honorius, the successor of Justus.

A.D. 645. Cenwalch, king of the West Saxons, being attacked and dethroned by Penda, king of the Mercians, for having repudiated his wife, who was Penda's sister, fled to Anna, king of the East Angles. In this year, too, king Oswine, son of Osric, who was Edwin's cousin, began to reign in the province of Deira, and he reigned seven years. He was of a handsome countenance, and tall, pleasant of speech, courteous in his manners, openhanded to all ; as a king most humble, and beloved of all men.

A.D. 646. King Cenwalch was baptized by bishop Felix in East Anglia.

A.D. 647. Felix, the first bishop of the East Angles, died. His deacon, Thomas, was ordained in his stead, by archbishop Honorius. On the death of Thomas, in the fifth year of his bishopric, his place was filled by Boniface.

A.D. 648. King Cenwalch returned from East Anglia to West Saxony, and in the same year made a grant of a large portion of his territory to his nephew, Cuthred, son of king Cuichelm.

A.D. 649.

A.D. 650. Aegelberht, a Gaul by birth, was on the death of Birin made bishop of the West-Saxon province by king Cenwalch, and he presided over it as bishop for many years.

A.D. 651. Saint Cuthbert entered the monastery of Mailrose, being received by the most holy man Eata, abbot of that church. On the 13th of the kalends of September [20th Aug.], in the seventh year of his reign, Oswine, king of Deira, a man of the deepest humility and great piety, having been betrayed by earl Hunwald, whom he had considered a trustworthy friend, was slain in a detestable manner by order of king Osuiu, and by the hands of his ealdorman Aethelwin. He was succeeded by Aethelwald, son of king Oswald. After Oswiu's death, and on the 2d of the kalends of September [31st Aug.], bishop Aidan died. Cuthbert, an

---

[1] See the genealogy of the Northumbrian kings.

ingenuous youth, saw his spirit borne to heaven by angels. Finan, who was ordained and sent by the Scots, was made bishop in his stead.

A.D. 652.

A.D. 653. In the twenty-fifth year of his age, Benedict, surnamed Biscop, an Englishman of noble birth, and minister of king Oswiu, leaving his home, his kindred, his possessions, and his native country, went to Rome and returned full of learning. Honorius, archbishop of Canterbury, died on the 2d of the kalends of Oct. [30th Sept.] A year and six months afterwards, Deusdedit, the sixth from Augustine, succeeded him in the archbishopric, being ordained thereto by Ithamar, bishop of Rochester, on the 7th of the kalends of April [26th March], and ruled over the church for nine years, four months, and two days. The Midland Angles, under their prince Peada, son of Penda, king of the Mercians, received the faith and sacraments of Christ; the prince himself first of all, with his attendants who had come with him, being baptized by bishop Finan, in Northumbria, in the presence of king Oswiu. Afterwards, on his return home, the rest of his people were baptized by Cedd, Adda, Betti, and Diuma, four priests whom he had brought with him from that province. At that time, Sigebert, king of the East Saxons, successor of Sebert, surnamed the Little, was baptized by Finan, bishop of the Northumbrians, having been converted to Christianity by the arguments of king Oswiu, while on a visit to him in the province of Bernicia. On his departure home, king Oswi sent with him that man of God, Cedd, the priest, to preach the word to the East Saxons. There he gathered together a large church to the Lord. Afterwards, on the suggestion of bishop Finan, he went home and was ordained bishop by him, and then returned to the province [of the East Saxons], and carried out with more ample authority the work which he had begun. Once when he was on a visit to the Northumbrian province for the purpose of preaching, Aethelwald, king of Deira, son of king Oswald, requested him to accept a grant of land for the purpose of building a monastery. In accordance with the king's wish, he chose a site for a monastery in a place now called Leastingaig, and when it was built he furnished it with religious institutions. In the meantime, king Sigebert, at the instigation of the enemy of all good men, was slain by his own kindred; the reason given being that he was too much in the habit of sparing his enemies, and ready on their own petition easily to forgive their offences. He was succeeded by Suithelm, the son of Sexbald.

A.D. 654. Anna, king of the East Angles, was slain by king Penda, and was succeeded by his brother Aethelhere. St. Botulph built a monastery at a place called Ikanho.

A.D. 655. Penda, the perfidious king of Mercia, the slayer of Sigebert, Egric, and Anna, kings of the East Angles, and also of Edwin and Oswald, kings of the Northumbrians, invaded Bernicia at the head of thirty legions, commanded by as many noblemen, for the purpose of crushing king Oswiu. With only one legion, but

trusting in Christ as their leader, Oswiu and his son Alhfrid met
them at a place called Winwidfeld. The battle commenced, and
the pagans were routed and cut to pieces, and nearly all the thirty
auxiliary chiefs were slain: among these was Aethelhere, brother
and successor of Anna, king of the East Angles, who was the mover
of the war: his brother Aethelwald succeeded to the kingdom.
King Oswiu having obtained the victory, made an offering to God
of endowments for building twelve monasteries, and also of
his daughter Aelfleda, devoting her to perpetual virginity. She
entered the monastery of Heortesig, whereof Hild was then abbess.
King Oswiu fought this battle in the district of Loidis, on the
17th of the kalends of December [15th Nov.], in the thirteenth
year of his reign, and he converted the Mercians to Christianity.
In his reign Diuma, whom we have mentioned before, was made
first bishop of the province of Mercia, and of the Lindisfaras and
the Middle Angles; the second was Ceollach, a Scot. Oswiu
reigned three years over this nation [the Mercians], and the other
people of the southern provinces. He brought the Picts under the
dominion of the Angles, and gave the kingdom of the southern
Mercians to his kinsman, Peada, the son of king Penda.

A.D. 656. At the feast of Easter, king Peada was foully slain
by the treacherous connivance of his wife.

A.D. 657.

A.D. 658. Cenwalch, king of the West Saxons, fought against
the Britons, at Peonn, and drove them defeated as far as Pedrida
[the Parret]. The blessed abbess Hild began to build a monastery
at a place called Streoneshalh [Whitby]: the daughter of king
Oswiu was a nun there, and afterwards became superior thereof.
Her mother, queen Eanfleda, built a monastery known as In
Getling, on the spot where king Oswine, the son of her cousin
king Osric's father, was unrighteously slain, and made the godly
Trumhere, who was a relative of the deceased king, abbot thereof.

A.D. 659. Immin, Eaba, and Eadberht, ealdormen of the
Mercians, rebelled against king Oswiu, setting up as king Wulfer,
the son of Penda, a youth whom they had kept in concealment;
and so together with their king they joyfully became servants of
Christ. This king's first bishop was the aforesaid Trumhere, the
second was Jarumann, the third was Cedd, and the fourth
Winfrid.

A.D. 660. King Cenwalch divided the West-Saxon province
into two dioceses, and gave the city of Winchester as bishop
Wina's episcopal see. Bishop Agelbert was grievously offended
at this, and retiring into Gaul, was made bishop of Paris. King
Egfrid, son of king Oswiu, married Atheldritha, daughter of Anna,
king of the East Angles.

A.D. 661. Cuthred, son of king Cuichelm, and grandson of
king Cinegils, and also nephew of the kings Cenwalch, and
Centuuin, and the under-king Cenbriht, who was the great grandson of king Ceaulin, and father of king Ceadwala, died. Wulfer,
king of the Mercians, laid waste Ascesdun, and afterwards took
the Isle of Wight. The latter he gave to his godson Aethelwold.

king of the South Saxons, and also the province of the Mavori [Meanvara] in the nation of the West Saxons. Finan, bishop of the Northumbrians, died, and was succeeded by Colmann, who was also sent from Ireland.

A.D. 662, 663.

A.D. 664. In the thirtieth year from the foundation of the Scotch bishoprics which existed in the Northumbrian province, and in the twenty-second year of the reign of king Oswiu, a controversy having arisen in that province concerning Easter, and the tonsure, and other ecclesiastical affairs, it was arranged that a synod should be held in the monastery of Streoneshealh, of which Hild was then the abbess. The following persons came to the synod :—King Oswiu and his son Alhfrid, who succeeded king Aethelwald, the son of king Oswald, bishop Colman and his clerks, Agelbert, bishop of the West Saxons, with the elders Agatho and Wilfrid, Cedda, bishop of the East Saxons, and the abbess Hild with her attendants. The debate between them was long, but at last all, both high and low, renounced the less accurate observances of the Scots, and hastened to conform themselves to what they had ascertained to be better. The dispute being ended, and the differences being determined, Agelbert returned home, and Cedda, forsaking the observances of the Scots, returned to his see. Colman, whom all the orthodox considered as vanquished, returned to Scotland to his own people. On his departure homewards, Tuda was made bishop of the Northumbrians in his place, but he held the office only for a short time. Eata, a most reverend man, abbot of the monastery of Mailrose, and who at the request of king Alhfrid had founded the monastery of Ripon, was made abbot of the brethren of Lindisfarn, and removed the blessed Cuthbert from the monastery of Mailrose to the island of Lindisfarn. In this year, about the tenth hour of the third day of May, occurred an eclipse of the sun. A sudden pestilence followed, which snatched from the world Tuda, the priest of the Lord. King Alhfrid, with the advice and consent of his father, king Oswiu, sent the venerable presbyter Wilfrid, abbot of the monastery of Ripon, to the king of France, requesting that he might be ordained a bishop, he being at that time about thirty years of age. But the king sent him to be ordained by Agelbert, who had left Britain and been made bishop of Paris ; and Agelbert and eleven other bishops met together for the purpose of consecrating him a bishop, and performed the ceremony with great honour. Deusdedit, sixth archbishop, counting from Augustine, died on the second of the ides of July [14th July]. Erconbert, king of Kent, died on the same day of the same year, leaving the kingdom to his son Egbert. The holy Ceadda, brother of the holy bishop Cedda, and abbot of the monastery of Leastingaeig, was by command of king Oswiu consecrated bishop of York by Wine, bishop of Winchester, Wilfrid being still absent beyond sea. On the [1]fifth of the ides of October [11th Oct.], Athelburg, the God-beloved mother of the monastery of Bercing, subsequently first abbess of the same place, was

[1] This date does not occur in Beda.

delivered from the bondage of the flesh : she was the sister of the wonderfully holy man, Erconwald, afterwards bishop of London ; her conversation was such that no one who knew her could doubt that when she departed this life she entered into the heavenly kingdom. Heldilith, a handmaid well beloved of God, succeeded her as abbess. A short time after this, Cedd, bishop of the East Saxons, went to his monastery of Leastingaig, and falling ill there died on the seventh of the kalends of November [26th Oct.]. Aethelwald, king of the East Angles, having died, was succeeded by Aldulf, whose mother was Hereswith, sister of St. Hild the abbess : their father was Hereric, whose father was Eadfrith, whose father was Edwine. Bosilius, abbot of the monastery of Mailrose, a monk of exalted virtue, a man of prophetic spirit, and a priest beloved of God, borne down by a deadly disease, entered on the splendours of eternal day. Sigere, king of the East Saxons, and a portion of his people, apostatised from the faith. When Wulfere, king of the Mercians, heard this, he sent bishop Jarumann, Trumhere's successor, to correct the error. However, Sebbi, the king's associate, and coheir in the kingdom, together with all his people, preserved the faith which he had embraced.

A.D. 665. Benedict, surnamed Biscop, went again to Rome in the time of pope Vitalian, and some months afterwards came to the island of Lerins. He devoted himself to the monks, received the tonsure, and under the guidance of the abbot served God for two years according to the regular discipline.

A.D. 666. Saint Aldelm was ordained abbot of Malmsbury, in the church of the apostles Peter and Paul, by the blessed Leutherius, fourth bishop of the West Saxons. Wina, bishop of Winchester, was driven from his see by king Cenwalch, and retiring to Wulfer, king of the Mercians, was by him made bishop of London, and he remained so during the rest of his life.

A.D. 667. The most noble English kings, Oswiu, of the province of Northumbria, and Ecgberht, of Kent, with the approbation of the holy English church, sent a priest named Wihard, one of the clergy of archbishop Deusdedit, to Rome for the purpose of being ordained bishop. But on his arrival at Rome, death snatched him away before he could be consecrated to the episcopate. Ceadda, bishop of York, governed the church with power for the space of three years. He afterwards withdrew to the superintendence of his monastery at Leastingaig, and Wilfrid was appointed to the bishopric of the entire province of Northumbria.

A.D. 668. Biscop, surnamed Benedict, went to Rome for the third time. There was at that time in Rome a monk named Theodore, born at Tarsus in Cilicia, a man well versed both in secular and ecclesiastical learning, thoroughly conversant in Greek and Latin, of unspotted character, and sixty-six years old; having been ordained archbishop on Sunday[1] the 7th of the kalends of April [26th March], he was by pope Vitalian sent into Britain, in company with abbot Adrian, and under the care of Biscop, the latter being a wise and energetic man.

[1] Namely, the fifth Sunday in Lent.

A.D. 669. On Sunday the 6th of the kalends of June [27th May] archbishop Theodore arrived in Kent, and committed the abbatial care of the abbacy of the monastery of St. Peter the apostle to Benedict, surnamed Biscop. Soon afterwards he made a progress through the whole island, ordained bishops in proper places, and at length completed what was defective in Ceadda's ordination after the catholic manner. In the city of Rochester, where the see had been long vacant by the death of Damianus, he ordained Putta, a man skilled in ecclesiastical discipline; and on the death of Jarumann not long afterwards, he, at the request of king Wulfer and with the consent of king Oswiu, appointed Ceadda to be bishop over the Mercians and the Lindisfaras; Ceadda obediently undertook the office, and devoted himself to the administration of it in rectitude of life. Moreover, king Wulfer gave him fifty hides of land for the purpose of building a monastery at a place called At Bearuwe.

A.D. 670. Oswiu, king of the Northumbrians, fell sick, and died on the 15th of the kalends of March [15th Feb.], in the fifty-eighth year of his age, leaving his son Egfrid heir to the kingdom. King Cenwalch and the West Saxons requested Theodore, archbishop of Canterbury, to consecrate as their bishop Leutherius, nephew of Agilbert, bishop of Paris; he was accordingly consecrated at Winchester, and was sole bishop for seven years.

A.D. 671. There was a very great destruction amongst the birds. The venerable abbot Benedict, surnamed Biscop, having been for two years abbot of the monastery of St. Peter the apostle, went for the third time from Britain to Rome, with the permission of archbishop Theodore. He was succeeded in the government of the monastery by abbot Adrian (whom we have before noticed), an African by birth, deeply versed in sacred literature, and a perfect master of Latin and Greek.

A.D. 672. Cenwalch, king of the West Saxons, died in the thirtieth year of his reign, according to the English Chronicle; his wife queen Sexburg reigned after him for the space of one year; but according to [1]Beda " subreguli" held the kingdom, which was divided between them for about ten years. Aetheldrith, queen of the Northumbrians, for a long time earnestly importuned king Egfrid to allow her to abandon the cares of the world, and to serve Christ her King in some monastery; her request being at last, though with difficulty, complied with, she entered the monastery[2] of the holy abbess Aebba, sister of kings Oswald and Oswiu, and aunt of king Egfrid, and received the veil at the hands of bishop Wilfrid. Bishop Ceadda, being much debilitated, but prepared for death by receiving the Body and Blood of our Lord, entered his eternal rest on the 6th of the nones of March [2d March], having presided over the church in the province of Mercia with great glory for two years and a half. As he was passing out of the world, the most reverend father Egberht, who had been his fellow-scholar in Ireland, saw the spirit of bishop Cedd, Ceadda's brother, descend from heaven with a company of angels, and

[1] See Eccl. Hist. IV. xii.   [2] Namely, at Coldingham, in Berwickshire.

return thither, bearing with them his spirit. His deacon, Winfrid, was ordained by Theodore to be bishop in his stead. Benedict Biscop returned from Rome, and on his arrival in Britain went to his own province and native place. He visited Egfrid, king of the Northumbrians, who immediately granted him seventy hides of land, in order that he might build a monastery at the mouth of the river Wir.

A.D. 673. Egbriht, king of Kent, died in the month of July, in the ninth year of his reign; he was succeeded by his brother Hlothere, who reigned eleven years and seven months. On the 24th day of September, the first indiction, Theodore, archbishop of Canterbury, convened a council at a place called Heortford. To this council Wilfrid, bishop of the Northumbrians, sent deputies; Putta, bishop of Rochester, Leutherius, bishop of the West Saxons, and Winfrid, bishop of the Mercian province, came in person; they were joined by Bisi, bishop of the East Angles, and successor of Boniface, whom we have mentioned before; he was a very holy and devout man, and had been ordained by Theodore not long previously; being prevented by his great infirmities from fulfilling the duties of his office, two bishops, Aecci and Badwine, were in his lifetime consecrated in his stead. Saint Aetheldrith was made abbess in the district called Elge [Ely], where having built a monastery, she commenced, as the virgin mother of virgins dedicated to God, a life of heavenly doctrine and practice.

A.D. 674. In this year, according to the English Chronicle, Aescuuine began to reign over the West Saxons; he was the son of Cenfus, who was the son of Cenferth, who was the son of Cuthgils, who was the son of Ceolwulf, who was the son of Cynric, who was the son of Cerdic. [1]Ireland, the island of saints, was considered to be entirely full of holy and remarkable men. Biscop [[2]built a monastery] at the mouth of the river Wir in the second indiction.

A.D. 675. Wulfere, king of the Mercians, and Aescuuine, king of the West Saxons, fought a battle at a place called Bidanheafd. In the same year, being the seventeenth of his reign, the said Wulfere entered the heavenly kingdom; he was the first of the Mercian kings who received the faith and the washing of holy regeneration; he abolished and thoroughly eradicated the worship of idols from all parts of his dominions, caused the name of Christ to be preached in every corner of his kingdom, and built churches in many places. His queen was Saint Eormengild, the daughter of Erconberht, king of Kent, and of his queen, Saint Sexburg, the latter being daughter of Anna, king of the East Angles, and sister of Saint Aetheldrith; by her he had a daughter, Saint Werburg, a virgin of exemplary virtues, who on her father's death renounced the world, and became a nun in the monastery of St. Aetheldrith, her mother's aunt, where by the help of God she wrought many miracles. When the report of her sanctity reached the ears of her uncle, king Aethelred, he made her abbess over several monas-

---

[1] This sentence is from Marianus Scotus.
[2] These words, necessary to complete the sense, are added from Beda.

teries of virgins devoted to God; living with and among these according to the rule, and devoutly providing for their necessities in all things, she passed the rest of her days as a good soldier of Christ; and dying in one of her monasteries called Triccingeham, as a sanctified virgin, she was thus embraced and espoused by the heavenly Bridegroom. Her corpse was taken, pursuant to her desire, to the monastery called Heanbirig, and there buried with great pomp; it remained uncorrupted up to the time when the pagan Danes with cruel slaughter barbarously depopulated and laid waste the English provinces. King Wulfer's brothers were, Aethelred, who succeeded to his kingdom; Peada, who (as we briefly mentioned) was king of the South Mercians; and Merewald, who reigned in the western division of Mercia. Merewald's queen was Saint Eormenburg, a daughter of king Ermenred; she bore him three daughters, namely Milburg, saint Mildrith, and saint Milgith, and one son named Merefin, a youth of transcendent piety.

Archbishop Theodore being offended with Winfrid, bishop of the Mercians, on account of some act of disobedience, deposed him from his bishopric, and appointed in his stead bishop Saxulf, the builder and abbot of the monastery of Burh, in the Girwian territory; the deposed Winfrid retired to his monastery of Bearuue, and there ended his days in a most exemplary manner. He then also appointed Erconwald to be bishop in the city of London over the East Saxons, at that time presided over by Saebba and Sighere; the see of his predecessor Wine was also in that same place. Erconwald's life and conversation, both before and after he was made bishop, are reputed to have been most saintly. He built two monasteries, one for himself and the other for his sister; his own was called Chertsey monastery, which with the generous assistance of the "subregulus" Frithewold, he filled with monks and richly endowed; his sister's was called Barking, and she was made its first abbess. Waldhere succeeded Erconwald, and he was succeeded by Inguald, who is the last bishop of London noticed by Beda[1] in his History of the Angles. Hildelith succeeded Aethelburg, the sister of saint Erconwald, to whom saint Aldelm addressed his book "On Virginity." In king Edgar's time Hildelith was succeeded by abbess Wulfhedis.

A.D. 676. Benedict Biscop went to Rome for the fourth time, accompanied by the monk Ceolfrid; at the request, and with the permission and consent of king Egfrid, he brought back with him a bull of privileges from pope Agatho, by which he secured for ever the security and immunities of his monastery. He also brought into Britain John, chief chanter of St. Peter the apostle, to teach in his monastery the course of singing for the whole year.

Escuuine, king of the West Saxons, died, and was succeeded by Centuuine, the son of Cynegils, who was the son of Ceol. Aethelred, king of the Mercians, devastated Kent, and involved the city of Rochester in the general destruction; when Putta, its bishop, heard thereof, he went to Saxulf, bishop of the Mercians, and

[1] See Eccl. Hist. V. xxiii.

being presented by him to a certain church, ended his days there in peace. Theodore consecrated Quichelm to be bishop in Putta's place, but on Quichelm leaving the bishopric shortly afterwards on account of its poverty, he substituted Gebmund as its bishop. Leutherius, bishop of the West Saxons, dying, Haeddi was consecrated by Theodore in the city of London, and succeeded him as bishop. Saint Cuthbert betook himself to an anchoret's life of meditation.

A.D. [1]677. In the month of August, in the eighth year of Egfrid's reign, a comet appeared. The same year a dissension arose between king Egfrid and the most reverend bishop Wilfrid, and the bishop was expelled from his see ; and two bishops were appointed in his place ; namely Bosa, a reverend monk of the monastery of the abbess Hild, to preside over the province of Deira ; and Eata, the venerable abbot of the monastery of Mailrose, to preside over the province of Bernicia; the former having his episcopal seat in the city of York, and the latter in the church of Hagustald [Hexham], or else of Lindisfarne ; they were both promoted from their monasteries to the dignity of the episcopate. Eathed also was ordained with them to be bishop in the province of the Lindisfaras, of which king Egfrid had very lately obtained possession, having defeated and put to flight Wulfere; he was the first separate bishop which this province had ; the second was Aethelwine ; the third was Eadgar ; the fourth Cynebert : before Eathed its bishop was Saxulf, who was at the same time bishop of the Mercians and Midland Angles; so that after his expulsion from Lindsey, he continued to preside over those provinces. Eathed, Bosa, and Eata, were ordained at York by archbishop Theodore.

On his expulsion from the bishopric, Wilfrid set out on his journey to Rome, but while at sea the west wind drove him over to Friesland, where he was the first to preach the Gospel, and converted many thousand barbarians to the faith, passing the winter there to his great satisfaction in the midst of God's newly acquired subjects.

A.D. 678. The holy Beda was born.

A.D. 679. A severe battle was fought near the river Trent, between Egfrid, king of the Northumbrians, and Aethelred, king of the Mercians ; and king Alfwine, brother of king Egfrid (whose sister Ostrith was king Aethelred's wife), was killed there.

Bishop Wilfrid left Friesland and went to Rome ; and having been by the sentence of pope Benedict and several bishops declared innocent, and worthy of his bishopric, he returned to Britain and converted the province of the South Saxons to Christianity. On the 9th of the kalends of July [23d June] the holy virgin Aetheldrith, abbess of the monastery of Ely, was taken away to the Lord, while she was in the midst of her flock; her sister Sexburg succeeded her in her office.

A.D. 680. In the sixth year of the reign of Aethelred, king of the Mercians, and the eighth indiction, archbishop Theodore convened an assembly of very many bishops and learned men at a

[1] According to Beda (Eccl. Hist. IV. xii.) this occurred in 678.

place called Haethfeld, in order that he might become acquainted with their several doctrines ; this he did in obedience to the commands of pope Agatho, transmitted by John the chief chanter, who was present at the synod. Under this king, Mercia was divided into five dioceses, and Tadfrith, a very learned man, belonging to the monastery of the abbess Hild, was chosen bishop of the province of the Hwiccas, but he died suddenly before he could be ordained; wherefore the reverend man Bosel was shortly afterwards ordained bishop of that province. Hild, the devout servant of Christ, abbess of the monastery of Streoneshalh [Whitby], and daughter of king Edwin's grandson Haereric, having finished her heavenly labours upon earth, was removed from this world to receive the reward of eternal life ; she passed from death to the Lord on the 15th of the kalends of December [17th Nov.], in the sixty-sixth year of her age. She was the builder of the two monasteries of Streoneshealh [Whitby] and Hacanos [Hackness], wherein she inculcated the observance of justice, piety, chastity, and other virtues ; but especially peace and charity. In this abbess's monastery dwelt Cedmon, that celebrated monk, who was a poet, not through human instruction, but by God's inspiration. The "subregulus" Oshere, by the permission of his lord Aethelred, the renowned king of the Mercians, gave to Frithewald, a monk under bishop Winfrid, whom we have mentioned before, thirty manors at a place called Rippel, in order that he might there build a monastery according to ecclesiastical discipline.

A.D. 681. When the ingenious boy Beda was seven years of age, he was delivered by his relations to the reverend abbot Biscop, for the purpose of being educated. Three years after the removal of Wilfrid, archbishop Theodore ordained Tunbert to the church of Hexham (Eata remaining at that of Lindisfarne), and Trumwine in the territory of the Picts. Eathed having returned from Lindsey, because king Aethelred had recovered possession of that province, he appointed him to the church of Ripon.

A.D. 682. Centwine, king of the West Saxons, drove the West Britons at the sword's-point as far as the sea. The most reverend abbot Benedict Biscop selected from his monastery his cousin Easterwini, a priest of great holiness, and appointed him to be abbot of the said monastery. For the redemption of his soul, king Egfrid gave forty more hides of land to abbot Benedict. Twenty-two monks being sent there under the government of abbot Ceolfrid, who was in everything his firm coadjutor, he, at the king's command, built the monastery of St. Paul the apostle at a place called Girvum [Jarrow].

A.D. 683.

A.D. 684. Egfrid, king of the Northumbrians, sending his general Berht into Ireland with an army, cruelly pillaged that harmless nation. At a synod, assembled in the presence of king Egfrid, at a place called Twiford, near the river Alne, archbishop Theodore presiding, Cuthberht was unanimously chosen to the bishopric of the church of Hexham ; but inasmuch as he preferred the appointment to the church of Lindisfarne, he was permitted to assume it, Eata returning to Hexham. For the fifth time, Benedict Biscop left Britain for Rome.

A.D. 685.   Lothere, king of Kent, was wounded in a battle against the South Saxons, and died while his wounds were being cured, on the second day of the week, on the eighth of the ides of February [6th Feb.], in the twelfth year of his reign.   He was succeeded by Eadric, his brother Ecgbert's son, who reigned one year and a half.   Britain was visited by a wide-spreading and very deadly pestilence ; on the nones of March [7th March], it carried off abbot Easterwini, beloved of God; in whose stead, the brethren, under the advice of abbot Ceolfrid, chose for their abbot Sigefrid, deacon of the said monastery, a man of wonderful piety, and deeply versed in the knowledge of the Scripture.   Biscop returned from Rome, laden, as usual, with presents of things to be used in the ceremonies of the church, and with foreign acquisitions.   At the feast of Easter [26th March], the ordination of St. Cuthberht was completed at York, in the presence of king Ecgfrid ; seven bishops, with archbishop Theodore at their head, assisting at his conse- cration.   On Saturday, the 13th of the kalends of June [20th May], in the fortieth year of his age, and fifteenth of his reign, king Ecgfrid was slain, while rashly leading an army to lay waste the territory of the Picts.   He was succeeded by his brother Alhfrid, a man deeply read in the Scriptures : the most holy bishop Eata dying at the commencement of this reign, John, a man of holiness, was appointed to the bishopric of Hexham.   Bishop Trumwine, one of the holiest of God's servants, retired with his people from the territory of the Picts, and took up his abode at Streoneshealh [Whitby], where he resided many years, to the great benefit not only of himself, but of many others : there too he died and entered the kingdom of heaven.   Ceadwalla, a very brave youth of the royal race of the Gewissi [West Saxons], came unexpectedly with his army upon ¹Aethelwalh, king of the South Saxons, and slew him; but was shortly afterwards driven back by the king's generals, Berthun and Aethelhun, who thenceforth ruled the province. Centwine, king of the West Saxons, departed this life, and was succeeded in the kingdom by the aforesaid Ceadwalla, who was the son of Cynebriht, who was the son of Cedde, who was the son of Cutha, who was the son of Ceaulin, who was the son of Cynric, who was the son of Cerdic.

A.D. 686.   Bishop Wilfrid, after having been long exiled, re- sumed his see and bishopric of the church of Hexham, at the invitation of king Alhfrid.   On the death of the holy and humble Bosa, John succeeded him as bishop of York.   Ceadwalla, king of the Gewissi [West Saxons], slew Beorthun, leader of the South Saxons, and reduced that province to a state of servitude ; after- wards, he and his brother Mul devastated Kent.   The same king Ceadwalla afterwards took the Isle of Wight, which, up to that time, had been wholly and entirely given up to idolatry ; and although he himself was not yet regenerated in Christ, yet he gave one-fourth part of the island, consisting of three hundred hides of

¹ This is the reading of A. ; the printed editions and B. read Æthelwald.

land, to bishop Wilfrid for the Lord's service; Wilfrid accepted the
donation, and, entrusting the management of it to his nephew,
¹ Berwin, appointed ministers of the Word in the island.

The godly bishop, Cuthbert, after having passed two years in his
bishopric, returned to the island of Farne, by the direction of a
message from God.   On the death of Edric, king of Kent, that
kingdom was for some time wasted by kings of doubtful title, or by
foreigners.

A.D. 687.   In Kent, the people of that province most in-
humanly threw Mul, brother of Ceadwalla, king of the West
Saxons, and twelve of his soldiers, into the fire, and burnt them:
thereat, king Ceadwalla being enraged, again devastated Kent.   On
the fourth day of the week, in the 13th of the kalends of April
[Wednesday, 20th March], the fifteenth indiction, the most reverend
father Cuthbert died in the island of Farne; but his body was
taken to the island of Lindisfarne, and buried in the church;
the duties of his episcopal office were performed by Wilfrid, bishop
of Hexham, for the space of one year.   The venerable Aethelwald
succeeded the godly Cuthbert in his life of solitude: how worthy
he was, and how excellent was his life, is shown by the numberless
miracles wrought at his hands.   ²At this time flourished St. Kilian,
bishop of Wurtzburg, a Scot of Irish birth.

A.D. 688.   On the departure of Ceadwalla to Rome, he was
succeeded in the kingdom by Ini of the royal race, ³who built the
monastery of Glaestingabirig [Glastonbury].   His father was Cenred,
whose father was Ceolwald, whose father was Cutha, whose father
was Cuthwine, whose father was Ceaulin.

Eadberht was ordained in the place of Cuthbert; he was a man
remarkable for his acquaintance with the sacred Scriptures, and his
obedience to the divine ordinances, and especially celebrated for his
almsgiving.   Abbots Benedict Biscop and Sigefrid, worn out by
long-continued sickness, both became bed-ridden.   Shortly afterwards, Benedict took counsel with the brethren, and summoned
Ceolfrid, abbot of the monastery of St. Paul the apostle, and on the
4th of the ides of May [12th May], in the first indiction, made him
abbot of both monasteries.   On ⁴Saturday, the 11th of the kalends
of September [22d Aug.], in the same year, the venerable and
God-beloved abbot, Sigefrid, was introduced into the enjoyment of
eternal rest, and entered the mansions of the heavenly kingdom
amid the sacrifices of perpetual praise.

A.D. 689.   On the 2d of the ides of January [12th Jan.],
Benedict Biscop, a repressor of vice, and a notable example of
virtue, entered into the repose and splendour of eternal life, after
having endured the purification of a long illness, during which he
was always offering his thanksgiving to God.   On the holy Saturday
before Easter Sunday [10th April], Ceadwalla, king of the West

---

¹ An error for "Bernuin."   ² This passage is from Marianus.
³ In the MS. B. the passage reads thus:—" Who completed the monastery
called Abingdon, which had been begun by Cissa, a noble, and king Ceadwala."
⁴ This word "Saturday," omitted in the editions, is now given from A.   The
dates correspond.

Saxons, was baptized, Sergius being then pope : and he died on the third day of the week [1][Tuesday], the [2]12th of the kalends of May [20th April], the second indiction, being about thirty years of age. His epitaph, written at the command of pope Sergius, runs in this wise :—

" Culmen, opes, sobolem pollentia regna, triumphos."[3]

A.D. 690. Archbishop Theodore, of blessed memory, died on the second [4]day of the week [Monday], the 13th of the kalends of October [19th Sept.], in the eighty-eighth year of his age, and the twenty-second of his bishopric.

[5] " Gladly he joined the spotless fellowship
Of angels, citizens of highest heaven."

Up to this time the archbishops of Canterbury were Romans, but from this time they were English.

A.D. 691. Wilfrid, bishop of Hexham, being again accused, was driven from his bishopric by king Alhfrid and several bishops : he withdrew shortly afterwards to Aethelred, king of the Mercians, and was by him appointed bishop of the Midland Angles. At this time, Bosel, bishop of the province of the Hwiccas, became so infirm, that he was unable personally to fulfil his episcopal duties ; in consequence of which, Oftfor, a man of singular merit and great holiness, who, for a long time, had discharged the office of the priesthood in the monastery of the abbess Hild, but was after- wards a preacher of the Word in the aforesaid province, was unani- mously elected bishop in his stead, and, at the king's command, was ordained by bishop Wilfrid of blessed memory ; for archbishop Theodore was then dead, and no one had been ordained to the episcopate in his stead. Wihtred, son of Ecgbert, king of Kent, being settled in his kingdom, by his piety and zeal delivered his subjects from foreign invasion. Suebheard governed a portion of the kingdom conjointly with him.

A.D. 692. The venerable Ecgbert, an Englishman by birth, (whose name is always to be mentioned with the greatest reverence,) having led a pilgrim's life in Ireland, in order to obtain a country in heaven, was desirous of going to preach in Germany ; but his wish not being granted by God, he sent over there holy and in- dustrious men to propagate the word ; among whom, the priest Willebrord deservedly shone preeminent, no less by office than by merit. Pepin the elder, chief of the Franks, received them joy- fully, and sent them to preach in Hither Friesland. Following their example, two priests, named Hewald, English by birth, went to the province of Old Saxony, there, by preaching, to win souls to Christ. But when the barbarians found that they were of a different religion, they seized them, and on the 5th of the nones of October [3d Oct.], martyred them. Willebrord, having received from prince Pepin permission to preach, went to Rome, in order that he might obtain from pope Sergius leave to begin the work of

---

[1] The day of the week, omitted in B. and the editions, is given from A.
[2] B. The editions incorrectly give xiv.   [3] See Eccl. Hist. V. vii.
[4] A. supplies the day of the week (correctly), which is not found in B. nor the editions.   [5] See Eccl. Hist. V. viii.

preaching the Gospel: and having accomplished his object, he returned to preach.

Brihtwald, abbot of the monastery of Raculfe, situate near the northern mouth of the river Genlade, a man well versed in the knowledge of the Scriptures, and thoroughly acquainted with ecclesiastical and monastic discipline, was chosen bishop in the place of Theodore. Oftfor, bishop of the Hwiccas, dying, was succeeded by St. Ecgwin, who, in the course of a few years, with the permission and assistance of king Aethelred, began the building of the monastery which is called Eovesham.

A.D. 693. On Sunday, the 3d of the kalends of July [29th June], Brihtwald was ordained by Godwin, metropolitan bishop of France : among the many other bishops whom he ordained, was Tobias, whom, on the death of Gebmund, bishop of Rochester, he consecrated bishop in his stead. The monk, Beda, obtained the rank of the diaconate from John, bishop of York.

A.D. 694. The men of Kent made peace with Ina, king of the West Saxons, and paid [1]three thousand seven hundred and fifty pounds, because they had burned his brother Mull, as before-mentioned.

A.D. 695. The body of the blessed virgin Aetheldrith, and the garment in which she was wrapped, were found uncorrupted, after having been buried sixteen years.

A.D. 696. On the anniversary of the nativity of the most blessed virgin Cecilia [22d Nov.], St. Willebrord, an Englishman born in Britain, was, at the request of Pepin, chief of the Franks, ordained archbishop of the Frisians by pope Sergius.

A.D. 697. St. Guthlac, at the age of twenty-four years, renouncing the pomps of the world, and abandoning all his property, entered the monastery of Hrepandun [Repton], and received the tonsure and clerical habit there under abbess Alfthrith. Ostrith, the queen of Aethelred, king of the Mercians, was slain by the South-Humbrians.

A.D. 698. The body of St. Cuthbert was, on the eleventh anniversary of his burial, found uncorrupted, as though he were just dead, and also the robe in which he was wrapped : so he was exhumed and put in a new shroud, and deposited in a new coffin on the pavement of the sanctuary. Shortly afterwards, bishop Eadbert, the friend of God, was attacked with a severe illness, and soon afterwards, to wit, on the 2d of the nones of May [6th May], he departed to the Lord : his body was deposited in the sepulchre of St. Cuthbert, on the top of the cist in which the corpse of that father had remained uncorrupted. The godly Eadfrid succeeded Eadbert in the bishopric.

A.D. 699. On the 8th of the kalends of September [25th Aug.], the most holy Guthlac came to the island of Cruland, and there began to lead an anchoret's life.

A.D. 700—702.

A.D. 703. [2]Beda, in his book "De Temporibus," thus writes,

---

[1] See the Saxon Chronicle, A.D. 694, (p. 25,) and the note there.
[2] This extract is from Marianus.

in the year in which he composed it : " If you wish to know how
many years, according to the computation of Dionysius, have
elapsed since our Lord's incarnation, take the number of indictions
since the fifth year of Tiberius, which in this present year will be
forty-six; multiply that number by fifteen; the product is six
hundred and ninety; always add the regular number twelve,
(because, according to Dionysius, our Lord was born in the fourth
indiction,) and also the indiction of the year for which you are
making your calculation, which in the present year is one; the
total result is seven hundred and three. This is the year of our
Lord according to Dionysius." These are Beda's words.

A.D. 704. Ethelred, king of the Mercians, turned monk in
the thirtieth year of his reign, and gave up the kingdom to his
nephew Cynred. The venerable monk Beda, in obedience to the
command of his abbot Ceolfrid, took priest's orders at the hands
of the holy John, bishop of York.

A.D. 705. On the 19th of the kalends of January [14th
Dec.], Alhfrid, king of the Northumbrians, died at Driffeld,
having reigned not quite twenty years. His son Osred, a boy
about eight years old, succeeded him, and reigned eleven years.
At the commencement of his reign, Haedda, bishop of the West
Saxons, departed to the life which is in heaven; and thereupon,
the bishopric of that province was divided into two sees, one of
which was assigned to Daniel, and the other to Aldelm, abbot of
the monastery of the city of Maildulf [Malmesbury]; both men
well versed in ecclesiastical matters and in the Scriptures. Saxulf,
bishop of the Mercians, departed this life. St. Aldelm was ordained
bishop by the holy Brihtwald, archbishop of Canterbury.

A.D. 706.

A.D. 707. In the thirtieth year of his age, Beda, having taken
priest's orders, began to write his books, in the composition of
which he spent twenty-nine years.

A.D. ¹708. Cynred, king of the Mercians, and Offa, king of the
East Saxons, son of king Sigher, leaving their wives, their lands,
their kindred, and their country, for Christ's sake and the Gospel's,
went to Rome, and received the tonsure, and became monks there :
they spent their whole lives at the seat of the apostles, in prayer,
fasting, and almsgiving, and thus joined the company of the
saints in heaven, for which they had so long sought. At their
request, St. Ecgwin, bishop of the Hwiccas, accompanied them to
Rome, and asked for and obtained from pope Constantine a bull,
whereby the monastery which he had built in the Worcestershire
territory was secured from spoliation of wicked persons.

A.D. 709. Cynred was succeeded in the kingdom by Ceolred :
he was the son of king Aethelred, and had preceded Cynred in the
government of the kingdom. St. Aldelm, bishop of the West-
Saxon province, an universally learned man, departed to the Lord :
he was succeeded in the bishopric by Forthred, who was also very
learned in the Scriptures.

> " Wilfrid, renown'd in name and saintly life,
> Through many years endured the world's fierce strife;
> Thrice fifteen years he fill'd a bishop's place,
> Then full of joy beheld his Maker's face."

His remains were buried with great ceremony in the church of St. Peter the apostle, in his original monastery of Ripon. After his death, Acca his priest was made bishop of the church of Hexham : he was a man of great energy, praised of God and of men ; a most skilful singer ; of consummate biblical learning ; most correct in his confession of the catholic faith ; of unblemished chastity ; intimately acquainted with the rules of ecclesiastical life. He had been formerly a pupil of the God-favoured Bosa, bishop of York.

A.D. 710. Berhfrid, the prefect of king Osred, fought against and overcame the Picts. Ine, the warlike king of the Gewissi [West Saxons], and his [1]kinsman Nun, waged war against Gerent, king of the Britons, routed and put him to flight. The very reverend father Adrian, abbot of the monastery of St. Peter the apostle, died, and was buried in the same monastery. He was succeeded by his disciple Albinus, who was as perfect in Greek and Latin as in English, which was his native language.[2]

A.D. 711—713.

A.D. 714. On the 3d of the ides of April [11th April], being the fourth day of Easter, the twelfth indiction, Guthlac, that most laudable anchoret, and most faithful priest of God, brother of Christ's dear virgin, Pegia, and exhibitor of countless virtues, died ; his spirit becoming a partaker of the joys of everlasting happiness : he was succeeded by Cissa, who was for a long time an idolater, but who had afterwards been baptized in Britain.

A.D. 715. [3]Gregory, the eighty-eighth pope, succeeded to the papacy, and held it for seventeen years and ten months. He was a chaste and learned man, and ordained as bishop of Mentz Boniface, an [4]Englishman by birth, from whom Germany received the word of salvation. Ine, king of the West Saxons, and Ceolred, king of the Mercians, fought a battle, at a place called Wodnes-beorh.

A.D. 716. The godly Egbert (whom we have mentioned before) brought over the monks of Hii to the catholic mode of observing Easter, and to the adoption of the ecclesiastical tonsure. Osred being slain, Cenred, son of the renowned Cuthwin, succeeded to the government of the Northumbrian kingdom. Ceolred, king of the Mercians, died, and was buried at Licetfeld. He was succeeded as king, in accordance with St. Guthlac's prophecy, by his cousin Aethelbald, who was the son of Alweon, who was the cousin of his father, king Aethelred. Aethelred, formerly king of the Mercians, but afterwards abbot of the monastery of Bardney, which he had built, departed this life, and entered on the joys of everlasting happiness, purity, and day. On the sixth day of the

---

[1] This reading is from B.; the editions read "his neighbour."
[2] A. here adds, "On the death of Tyrhtell, bishop of Hereford, he was succeeded by Forhtere."
[3] From Marianus.   [4] "An Irishman," N.

week [Friday], the 7th of the kalends of October [25th Sept.], the eminently holy and religious abbot Ceolfrid died, while on a pilgrimage, at the city of Langres, in Burgundy, and was buried in the church of the holy fellow-martyrs, Speusippus, Eleusippus, and Meleusippus : he was seventy-four years old when he died, and had been a priest for forty-seven years, and thirty-five years an abbot.

A.D. 717.   On the fifth day of the week [Thursday], the 3d of the kalends of January [30th Dec.], the fifteenth indiction, St. Ecgwin, the third bishop of the Hwiccas, died.   Wilfrid, a man of great piety, succeeded to the bishopric of Worcester, having been elected thereto in Ecgwin's lifetime.

A.D. 718.   Coenred, king of the Northumbrians, died, and Osric was exalted to the throne.   Ingels, brother of Ina, king of the West Saxons, died.   His sisters were Saints Quenburg and Cuthburg, the latter of whom built a monastery for holy virgins at a place called Winburn.   Aldfrid, king of the Northumbrians, married Cuthburg ; but before her death, both renounced connubial intercourse for the love of God.

A.D. 719, 720.

A.D. 721.   Daniel, bishop of Winchester, went to Rome.   In the same year king Ine slew Cyneulf the etheling.   The holy John, bishop of York, not being able to fulfil the duties of his bishopric, by reason of his great age, ordained his priest Wilfrid to succeed him, and retired to his monastery which was called In Derewood, and died there on the nones of May [7th May], having passed his life in godly conversation.   Eadfrid, bishop of Lindisfarne, died, and was succeeded by Aethelwald, priest and abbot of Mailrose.

A.D. 722.   Queen Aethelburg utterly destroyed the castle called Taunton, which had been previously built by king Ine : the latter in the same year fought a battle with the South Saxons.

A.D. 723, 724.

A.D. 725.   On the 9th of the kalends of May [23d April], Wihtred, king of Kent, son of Ecgbert, died, leaving three sons, Aethelbert, Eadbert, and Alric, heirs to his kingdom, which he had held thirty-four years and a half.   King Ine fought again with the South Saxons, and slew the etheling Aldbriht, whom he had previously driven from West Saxony.   [1]In this year the chronologist Beda composed his smaller book of computation ; for he thus writes : " If you wish to know the epact for any given year, take the year of our Lord, according to Dionysius, as, for instance, in the present eighth indiction, seven hundred and twenty-five, and divide by nineteen : nineteen multiplied by thirty produces five hundred and seventy, and nineteen multiplied by eight produces one hundred and fifty-two : subtracting these, there remain three : multiply the three by [2]nineteen ; the produce is thirty-three : subtract thirty, and three remain : three is the epact for the present year."   These are Beda's own words.

A.D. 726.   Tobias, bishop of Rochester, died : he had studied Greek and Latin so well as to understand and employ them as

---

[1] This passage is from Marianus.   [2] Read " eleven."

easily as his native English.   He was succeeded in the bishopric by Alduulf, who was consecrated thereto by Berhtwald, archbishop of Canterbury.

A.D. 727.

A.D. 728.   King Ine having abdicated, and transferred his throne to Aethelhard, one of the descendants of king Cerdic, went to Rome during the time of pope Gregory [II.], being desirous of spending some portion of his pilgrimage upon earth in the vicinity of the holy places, so that he might thereby earn a better reception of the saints in heaven.   In the same year, king Aethelhard and Oswold the etheling fought a battle: Oswold was the son of Aethelbald, who was the son of Cinebald, who was the son of Cuthwin, who was the son of Ceaulin.

A.D. 729.   In the month of January, two comets appeared near the sun, and remained nearly two weeks.   On Easter-day of the same year, which fell on the 8th of the kalends of May [24th April], the holy Egbert, whom we have often noticed before, departed to the Lord.   When Easter was over, that is to say, on the 7th of the ides of May [9th May], Osric, king of the Northumbrians, died, having appointed that Ceoluulf, brother of his predecessor, king Kenred, should be his heir.   To Ceoluulf, Beda, the servant of Christ, a priest and monk, addressed his Ecclesiastical History of the English nation.   Ceoluulf was the son of Cutha, who was the son of Cuthwin, who was the son of Ecgwald, who was the son of Aldhelm, who was the son of [1] Occa, who was the son of Ida, who was the son of Eoppa.

A.D. 730.   This year died the etheling Oswald, a very brave man.

A.D. 731.   On the 5th of the ides of January [9th Jan.], archbishop Brihtwald died, worn out with extreme old age.   Pope Gregory died on the 3d of the ides of February [11th Feb.].   On Sunday[2] the 10th day of the month of June, Tatwine, a priest of the monastery of Briudun, in the province of Mercia, was by bishops Daniel of Winchester, Inguald of London, Aldwin of Litchfield, and Adulf of Rochester, consecrated at Canterbury, to be archbishop in the place of Brihtwald.   He was a religious and prudent man, and eminently well read in sacred literature.   In about the two hundred and eighty-second year from the arrival of the Angles in Britain, Tatwine and Aldulf were bishops over the Kentish churches.   Moreover, Inguald was bishop of the province of the East Saxons; Eadbert and Hathulac were bishops of the province of the East Angles; and Daniel and Forthere of the province of the West Saxons: Aldwine was bishop of the Mercian province; Walhstod of those people[3] who live westward beyond the river Severn; Wilfrid of the Wiccian province,[4] and Kynebert of the province of the Lindisfari.   The bishopric of the Isle of Wight belongs to Daniel, bishop of Winchester.   The province of the South Saxons having been now for some years without a

---

[1] So MS. A.   The editions read "Osca."
[2] Namely, the second Sunday after Trinity.
[3] Of Hereford.   [4] Of Worcester.

bishop, requested the bishop of the West Saxons to exercise the episcopal office over them. These and the other southern provinces, as far as the river Humber, with their respective kings, were all subject to Aethelbald, king of the Mercians. But in the province of the Northumbrians, of which Ceolulf was king, there were four bishops, to wit, Wilfrid in the church of York, Athelwold in that of Lindisfarne, Acca in that of Hexham, and Pectelm in that which is called Candida Casa [Whiterne]. The Britons were to a great extent brought in subjection to the Angles.

A.D. 732.

A.D. 733. On the [1]18th of the kalends of September [14th Aug.], about the third hour of the day, the sun was eclipsed to such an extent that nearly the whole of its disc seemed to be covered with a dreadful deep black shield. Acca, bishop of Hexham, was driven from his bishopric.

A.D. 734. On the [2]2d of the kalends of February [24th Jan.], at about cock-crow, the moon became of a blood-red colour, and remained so for fully an hour, then turned black, and afterwards returned to its natural colour. On the 3d of the kalends of August [30th July], Tatwine, archbishop of Canterbury, died. His successor in the archbishopric was Nothelm, a priest of the church of London. On the fourth day of the week [Wednesday], before Ascension Sunday, that is, on the 8th of the kalends of June [25th May, 735], about the tenth hour of the day, the most holy Beda, a venerable priest, a monk praiseworthy in all things, and a wonderful calculator, breathed his last sigh, and thus in joy entered the kingdom of heaven. His death took place in this year according to the English chronicles; but in the following year, according to his disciple Cuthbert, who has given an account of his death, and who with many others was present at his departure. He composed an elegant and extensive history of his own people down to this period, and concluded his life and his history at the same time. And we, by God's assistance, have thought that events which have occurred subsequently to his happy departure, both as we find them recorded in the English chronicles, and as we have heard from trustworthy authority, as well as the undoubted facts which we have heard and seen, being chronicled from this period, are worthy of being bequeathed to the memory of the men of veracity who shall come after us.

A.D. 735. Pectelm, bishop of Whitherne, died, and was succeeded in the bishopric by Frithowald.

A.D. 736. Nothelm, archbishop of Canterbury, received the pall from Gregory [the Third], who was the eighty-ninth pope.

A.D. 737. Forther, bishop of Shireburn, and Frithogith, queen of the West Saxons, went to Rome.

A.D. 738. Ceolulf, king of the Northumbrians, became a monk, having abdicated his kingdom and bestowed in it Eadbriht, his cousin-german, son of Eata.

---

[1] We should here read " the nineteenth."
[2] Here also is an error; we should read "the ninth."

A.D. [1]739.   Athelwald, bishop of Lindisfarne, and Acca, bishop of Hexham, paid the debt of nature.   Cyneulf succeeded Aethelwald, and Acca was succeeded by Frithebert.

A.D. 740.

A.D. 741.   Aethelhard, king of the West Saxons, died, and was succeeded by his kinsman Cuthred, who perpetually harassed in war Aethelbald, king of the Mercians.   Nothelm, archbishop of Canterbury, dying on the 16th of the kalends of November [17th Oct.], Cuthbert, the fifth bishop of Hereford, succeeded as archbishop.[2]   Aldulf, bishop of Rochester, also died, and Dunn was consecrated in his stead.

A.D. 742.

A.D. 743.   Aethelbald, king of the Mercians, and Cuthred, king of the West Saxons, fought against the Britons.   Wilfrid, bishop of the Hwiccas died, and Milred succeeded.   [3] St. Boniface, archbishop of Mentz, flourished.   Stars[4] were seen falling as it were from heaven.

A.D. 744.   [5]St. Boniface began to build the monastery of Fulda, in the desert of Bochon.   Wilfrid the younger,[6] archbishop of York, died on the 3d of the kalends of May [29th April], and Ecgbert, brother of king Aedbert, was raised to the dignity of the archbishopric.   Daniel, bishop of Winchester, venerable for his great age, voluntarily gave up his office, and came to reside in that city, and Hunfrid was appointed bishop in his stead.

A.D. 745.   Daniel, in the forty-third year from his appointment to the office of the bishopric, and after many battles as a heavenly soldier, entered on his everlasting reward.

A.D. 746.   Selred, king of the East Saxons, was slain.

A.D. 747.

A.D. 748.   Kenric, the etheling of the West Saxons, was slain. Eadbert, king of Kent, died, and his brother Aethelbert was made king.

A.D. 749.

A.D. 750.   [7]Pepin, by order of pope Zachary, was anointed emperor by Boniface, archbishop of Mentz, in consequence of which the bishop of Mentz is considered as next in dignity to the pope.   Cuthred, king of the West Saxons, fought a battle with that very fierce earldorman Aethelhun.

A.D. 751.

A.D. 752.   In the twelfth year of the reign of Cuthred, king of the West Saxons, he and Aethelbald, king of the Mercians, fought a severe battle near Beorhtford.

A.D. 753.   King Cuthred fought again with the Britons, and slew many of them.

A.D. 754.   Cuthred, king of the West Saxons, died, and his

---

[1] A.D. 738, A.   See Saxon Chronicle, A.D. 737.
[2] "Podda succeeded him in the bishopric of Hereford."   A., in another hand.
[3] This sentence is from Marianus.   [4] See Saxon Chronicle, A.D. 744.
[5] From Marianus.
[6] Here is an error, arising from a confusion between Wilfrid of Worcester and Wilfrid the second, archbishop of York.   See the Saxon Chronicle, A.D. 734, 766.
[7] This sentence is from Marianus.

kinsman Sigebert, son of Sigeric, succeeded him.   On the death of
Hunferth, bishop of Winchester, Kinehard took his place as bishop.
Canterbury was destroyed by fire.

A.D. 755.   [1]On the nones of June [5th June], St. Boniface, the
archbishop, while preaching the word of God in Friesland, suffered
martyrdom in company with many other martyrs.   Kineulf, who
was descended from the line of king Cerdic, with the aid of the
West-Saxon nobles, drove their king Sigebert from his dominions
on account of the multitude of his evil deeds, and reigned in his
stead ; but he granted to Sigebert one province called Hampshire,
which he continued to hold until he had unjustly slain Cumbra,
the earldorman, who had followed him longer than any other person.   After that he was attacked by king Kineulf himself and was
driven into a wood which the English call Andred.   After
remaining there for a long time, a certain herdsman ran him
through with a spear, in revenge for the death of the aforesaid
earldorman, at a place called Privet's-flood.   The same king
Kineulf very frequently and utterly routed the Britons in severe
battles.   Aethelbald, king of the Mercians, was slain at Seges-
walde, and his corpse was taken to Repton and there buried.   His
kingdom was usurped by the tyrant Beornred, who held it for a
short time with neither peace nor comfort, and then lost his
throne and life together.   Beornred was succeeded in the kingdom
by Offa, grandson of a cousin of Aethelbald, king of the Mercians,
being a son of Thingferth, who was the son of Eanulf, who was the
son of Osmod, who was the son of Eoppa, who was the son of
Pybba,[2] the father of king Penda.[3]

A.D. 756.   Lullus succeeded as archbishop [of Mentz] after
Boniface, and held the see for thirty-two years.

A.D. 757.   Eadbert, king of the Northumbrians, abdicated his
kingdom out of love for the heavenly country, and received the
tonsure of St. Peter the apostle ; and his son Osulf assumed the
government of the realm, and after a reign of one year was slain by
the Northumbrians on the 9th of the kalends of August [24th
July].

A.D. 758.   On the 7th of the kalends of November [26th Oct.],
Cuthbert, archbishop of Canterbury, died.   At this period Swithred
was king of the East Saxons, Osmund of the South Saxons, and
Beorn of the East Angles.

A.D. 759.   Breogwin, Cuthbert's successor, was ordained archbishop on the festival of Michaelmas-day [29th Sept.].   Moll Aethelwold succeeded to the kingdom of Northumbria.

A.D. 760.   Aethelbert, king of Kent, died ; and that most religious monk Ceolulf, formerly the most glorious king of Northumbria, entered on the joys of eternal day.[4]

A.D. 761.   This year the winter was very severe ; and on the

---

[1] This first sentence is copied from Marianus.

[2] So A.   The editions read "Wibba."

[3] A. here adds, " On the death of Wita, bishop of Litchfield, he was succeeded
by Hemele."

[4] " On the death of Hemele, bishop of Litchfield, Cuthfrid succeeded."   A.,
addition.

8th of the ides of August [6th Aug.], Moll, king of the Northumbrians, slew a most noble etheling named Oswin, near Edwinscliff.

A.D. 762. Breogwin, archbishop of Canterbury, died on the 9th of the kalends of September [24th Aug.]. He was succeeded by Jainbert, abbot of St. Augustine's monastery.

A.D. 763. On the feast-day of the purification of St. Mary [2d Feb.], Jainbert was advanced to the archbishopric. On the nones of May [7th May], in the same year, Frithewold, bishop of Whiterne, died. Pechtwine succeeded him as bishop, being consecrated on the 16th of the kalends of August[1] [17th July], in the district called Aelfete.

A.D. 764. Archbishop Jainberht received the pall from pope Paul, brother of his predecessor pope Stephen.

A.D. 765. Moll abdicated the kingdom of Northumbria, and was succeeded by Alhred, son of Eanwin, who was the son of Birnhom, who was the son of Bofa,[2] who was the son of Bleocman, who was the son of Ailric,[3] who was the son of Ida.

A.D. 766. Ecgbert, archbishop of York, died on the 13th[4] of the kalends of December [19th Nov.], at York, and was succeeded by Aethelbert. Frithobert, bishop of Hexham, died, and was succeeded by Alhmund.

A.D. 767.

A.D. 768. That exquisitely pious monk, Eadbriht, formerly the most noble king of Northumbria, died on the 13th of the kalends of September [20th Oct.], and was buried in the same porch in which his brother archbishop Egbert lies.

A.D. 769[5]—773.[6]

A.D. 774. A red figure like a cross appeared in the sky after sunset. The Mercians and the men of Kent fought a battle at Otford. Frightful and exceeding wonderful serpents appeared in the province of the South Saxons. On the feast of Easter [3d April], the Northumbrians expelled their king Alhred, who had succeeded king Moll, from York, and raised Moll's son, Aethelbert, to the throne.

A.D. 775. Milred,[7] bishop of the Hwicca's, died, and was succeeded in the office of bishop by Weremund.

A.D. '776. Pechtwine, bishop of Whiterne, died 'on the 13th of the kalends of October [19th Sept.].

A.D. 777.

A.D. 778. Alfwold succeeded to the kingdom of Northumbria, after the natives had expelled Aethelbert therefrom. Kineulf,[10] king

---

[1] This date, indicating the seventh Sunday after Trinity, is probably correct.
[2] So A. B. The editions read " Bosa."   [3] Ealric, A.; Earic, B.
[4] So A. The editions read " xiv."
[5] "On the death of Cuthfrid, bishop of Litchfield, Berhtun succeeded." A., an addition by another hand.
[6] " A.D. 772. Sigga, bishop of the church of Sealsey, having died, Alubriht succeeded." An addition in A. by a second hand.
[7] See Saxon Chronicle, A.D. 772.
[8] The date is from B. A.D. 777, edd.
[9] This date is from A. B., and does not occur in the editions.
[10] See the Saxon Chronicle, A.D. 777.

of the West Saxons, and Offa, king of Mercia, fought a great battle near Bensington; but Offa gained the victory, and took and kept possession of the town. Weremund, bishop of the Hwiccas, died, and was succeeded by abbot Tilher. Aethelbert was ordained bishop of York at Whiterne on the 17th of the kalends of July[1] [15th June].

A.D. 779. Alhmund, [2]bishop of Hexham, died on the 7th of the ides of September [7th Sept.], and on the 6th of the nones of October [2d Oct.], Tilbert was ordained in his stead: and Higbald was consecrated bishop of Lindisfarne, at Soccabury, in the place of Kineulf. King Alfwold sent messengers to Rome to ask pope Adrian for the pall for Eanbald.

A.D. 780.

A.D. 781. Tilher, bishop of the Hwiccas, died, and Heathored succeeded him in the bishopric. Aethelbert, archbishop of York, Egbert's successor, died, and was succeeded by Eanbald.[3] A synod was held at Aclea [Ockley?]: and Kineulf, bishop of Lindisfarne, and Wereburg, queen of Ceolred, formerly king of the Mercians, died.

A.D. 782,[4] 783.[5]

A.D. 784. As Kineulf,[6] king of the West Saxons, was meditating the expulsion from his kingdom of the etheling Cynehard, brother of king Sigebert, he came to a vill, called by the English, Meretun, for the purpose of visiting a certain woman, and, as it happened, accompanied with very few attendants. On hearing this, the etheling assembled his friends from all quarters, and with great glee hastened to the town. On his arrival he found that every one was sound asleep; and he caused the chamber where the king lay sleeping to be closely surrounded. When the king was made aware of this, he rose up in haste from his couch, seized his arms, opened the door of the chamber, and fought manfully against his assailants. Catching sight at length of the etheling, he rushed headlong at him and wounded him very severely: seeing this, all the etheling's soldiers made a simultaneous attack on the king, and, having disabled, slew him. The woman cried out with fear and grief, and filled the room with her lamentations. The king's few guards rushed to the spot; and found the king, whom a short time previously they had left alive, lying dead. At this they became furious, and drawing their swords, made a fierce slaughter on his murderers. But the etheling addresses them in a most specious manner, promises a large sum of money to each, and also to spare their lives, if they will desist: they, however, reject his offers, and still press on; but all perish except one British hostage, who was

---

[1] As the 15th of June fell upon a Sunday in A.D. 777 (and not in 778), we may conclude that the chronology of Florence is here faulty by one year.

[2] See Saxon Chronicle, A.D. 780.

[3] " He was the scholar of Alchwin, the master of the emperor Charles." A., addition.

[4] "On the death of Herewald, bishop of the church of Sherburn, Ethelmod succeeded." A., from William of Malmesbury.

[5] Totta, bishop of Middle-Anglia, having died, Eadberht succeeded." A., in a second hand.   [6] See Saxon Chronicle, A.D. 755.

seriously wounded. The next morning the king's ealdorman, Osric, with whom he was most intimate, and Wiverth, a most trusty thane, hastened to the place, with all those whom the king had left behind the day before; but they find the gates all barred. While they are endeavouring to break in, the etheling comes out boldly, and promises that he will willingly grant to each person whatever he may desire, gold, silver, and honours, if they will exalt him to the regal throne; he hints, too, that very many of his relations are with him, who will on no account abandon, but are ready to live and die with him. But they too disdain his offers, and peremptorily summon his relations to quit their lord, and depart unharmed to their homes as soon as possible. The latter replied thus: " What you offer to us is the same as that which we previously offered to the king's companions, who were slain with him; but as they would not acquiesce in our request, so we too in this matter will not attend to yours." On hearing this the king's party advance, force open the gates, break through the enclosures, and slay the etheling and all his men, to the number of eighty-four, save only the etheling's little son, who was nevertheless dreadfully wounded. The king's corpse was carried to Winchester to be buried; that of the etheling was buried in the monastery of Axminster.

A.D. 785. A very boisterous synod was held at a place called in the English tongue Cealchithe, and thereby archbishop Iainbert lost a small portion of his diocese. Berthun, bishop of Dorchester, dying, Higebriht was chosen by Offa, king of Mercia, to succeed him in the bishopric; and Offa's son, Egferth, was consecrated king.

A.D. 786.[1]

A.D. 787. Brihtric, king of the West Saxons, married Eadburg, daughter of king Offa: in his time the Danish pirates came to England with three ships. When the king's reeve heard of their arrival, he advanced hastily against them with a small company. Being entirely ignorant who they were, or whence they came, he endeavoured to drive them against their will into the king's town; but they presently slew him. These were the first Danes who came to England.[2]

A.D. 788. On the 4th of the nones of September [2d Sept.], a synod was held at Pincanhale, in Northumbria.[3]

A.D. 789. On the 9th of the kalends of October [23d Sept.], Alfwold, king of the Northumbrians, was wickedly slain by a man named Siga, and was buried in St. Peter's church, at Hexham. A brilliant celestial light frequently appeared at the spot where he was slain. He was succeeded in the kingdom by his nephew, Osred, son of king Alhred.

A.D. 790. On the 2d of the ides of August [12th Aug.], Iainbert, archbishop of Canterbury, died; and abbot Aethelhard

[1] " On the death of Podda, bishop of Hereford, Ecca succeeded." A. in another hand.
[2] " On the death of Higberht, bishop of Litchfield, Aldulf succeeded." A. in a second hand.
[3] " Kynehard, bishop of Winchester, dying, was succeeded by Aethelhard, abbot of Malmesbury." A. in another hand.

was elected to succeed him. The Northumbrians drove Osred from his kingdom, who was succeeded therein by Aethelred's brother, Alfwold.

A.D. 791. On the 16th of the kalends of August[1] [17th July], Beadwulf was ordained bishop of Whiterne.

A.D. 792. Osred, whom the Northumbrians had driven from his kingdom, was taken captive, and on the 18th of the kalends of October [14th Sept.], unrighteously put to death, and was buried in the monastery at the mouth of the river Tine.

A.D. 793. Aegelbriht,[2] the most glorious and holy king of the East Angles, courteous of speech to all, and acceptable to Christ, the true King, by reason of his virtues, lost at once his kingdom and his life, being beheaded by the detestable commands of Offa, the very potent king of the Mercians, and the wicked incitement of his wife, queen Cynethrith : but, although wickedly deprived of his kingdom and slain, the martyr-king entered the courts of the blessed angels amid the great rejoicings of holy spirits. The ordination of archbishop Aethelhard took place on the 12th of the kalends of August [21st July].[3]

A.D. 794. On the 3d of the kalends of May [29th April], Aethelred, king of the Northumbrians, was slain by his subjects; wherefore Ceolulf, bishop of Lindisfarne, and bishop Aedbold, left that kingdom. Eadbert, also called Pren, began to reign over the Kentish people. Offa, king of the Mercians, dying on the 4th of the kalends of August [29th July], his son Egferth succeeded to his splendid kingdom, and died in the same year, having reigned one hundred and forty-one days. The glorious Kenulf, happy in a saintly progeny, succeeded him, and governed the kingdom in peace, justice, and piety.

A.D. 795.[4]

A.D. 796. Kenulf, king of the Mercians, laid waste nearly the whole of Kent, took captive its king Pren, and carried him in chains to Mercia.[5]

A.D. 797.

A.D. 798. The body of the holy virgin Wihtburg[6] (daughter of Anna, king of the East Angles, and sister of the holy virgins, Sexburg, Aethelburg, and Aetheldrith) was found uncorrupted, near fifty-five years having elapsed since it had been buried in the town of Dirham. Heathored, bishop of the Hwiccas, died, and Denebert was chosen and consecrated in his stead.

A.D. 799. Aethelhard, archbishop of Canterbury, and Kinebert, bishop of Winchester, went to Rome.

A.D. 800. Brihtric, king of the West Saxons, died, and was succeeded by Ecgbert. In the year when king Brihtric died, Aethelmund, ealdorman of the Mercians, led out his men and crossed over the ford, which is called in English Cymeresford.

---

[1] This falling on the eighth Sunday after Trinity, is probably correct.
[2] See Saxon Chronicle, A.D. 792.   [3] The seventh Sunday after Trinity.
[4] "Alubriht, bishop of Selsey, having died, was succeeded by Bosa," &c. A. from William of Malmesbury.
[5] "On the death of Eadbert, bishop of Middle Anglia, Unwona succeeded to the bishopric." A. in another hand.   [6] See Saxon Chronicle, A.D. 797.

On hearing of his advance, Weolhstan, ealdorman of Wiltshire, went up against him with the men of that county : a stubborn engagement ensued, many on both sides were slain, and both the leaders fell, but the men of Wiltshire gained the victory. Alhmund, son of Alhred, king of the Northumbrians, was slain.

A.D. 801.

A.D. 802.   Higebald, bishop of Lindisfarne, died, and Egbert, who was chosen to succeed him, was consecrated by Eanbald, archbishop of York, on the 3d of the ides of June [11th June]. Weremund, bishop of Rochester, dying, Beornmod was consecrated in his stead.

A.D. 803.   Aethelhard, archbishop of Canterbury, died, and was succeeded by Wulfred.

A.D. 804.   Archbishop Wulfred received the pall from pope Leo.

A.D. 805.   Cuthred, king of Kent, and Heabriht the earldorman, and Ceolburg, [1] abbess of Berkeley, died.

A.D. 806—811.

A.D. 812.   Wulfred, archbishop of Canterbury, and Wibert, bishop of Sherborne, went to Rome.

A.D. 813.   Archbishop Wulfred, having received the benediction of the holy pope Leo, returned to his see.   In the same year Ecgbert, king of the West Saxons, laid waste [the territory of] the West Britons [2] from the eastern boundary.

A.D. 814, 815.

A.D. 816.   The English school at Rome was burned. [3]

A.D. 817, 818.

A.D. 819.   St. Kenulph, king of the Mercians, after a life spent in good deeds, passed away to the everlasting joys of heaven, leaving his son [4] Kenelm, then seven years of age, the heir to his kingdom.   But after the lapse of a few months, he was, through the traitorous contrivance of his sister, Quendrith, whose fierce mind was swayed by an outrageous lust for supreme power, and by the hand of his barbarous tutor Ascebert, cruelly and secretly slain under a thorn-tree, in a vast and darksome wood : but as heaven alone was witness to his murder, so heaven afterwards revealed the deed by means of a column of light.   Milk-white in innocence, and pure as when born, fell the head of Kenelm : from it a milk-white dove, with golden pinions, soared to heaven. After his blessed martyrdom, Ceolulf succeeded to the Mercian kingdom.   Egbert, bishop of Lindisfarne, died, and was succeeded by Heathored.

A.D. 820.

A.D. 821.   Ceolulf, king of the Mercians, was driven from his kingdom ; and was succeeded in the realm by Beornulf.

A.D. 822.   The stalwart ealdormen Burhelm and Muca were slain, and a synod was held at a place called Clovesho.   Denebert, bishop of the Hwiccas, died, and was succeeded by Heaberht.

---

[1] Her designation, wanting in the editions, is supplied from A.
[2] Supplied from A. and B., and wanting in the editions.
[3] " On the death of Wigberht, bishop of Salisbury, Alhstan succeeded." A. in another hand.
[4] B. designates him " Saint" Kenelm.

A.D. 823.   The Britons were slaughtered at a place called Gafulford, by the men of Devonshire.   Ecgbert, king of the West Saxons, and Beornulf, king of the Mercians, fought a battle at Ellandune, that is, Ealla's hill; and, after a great slaughter, Ecgbert gained the victory.   This induced him soon afterwards to send his son Aetheluulf, and Alhstan, bishop of Sherborne, and his ealdorman Wulfhard, with a large army into Kent.   Immediately on their arrival they drove Baldred, king of that province,. from his dominions.   After these events, the inhabitants of Kent and Surrey, and the South Saxons and East Angles, submitted spontaneously to king Ecgbert: they had been previously violently withdrawn from the dominion of his kindred, and had been for some years most unwilling subjects of foreign kings.   The East Angles with their king sent ambassadors to Ecgbert, king of the West Saxons, intreating him to be their supporter and strong defence against the inroads and attacks of the Mercians; he acceded to their request, and promised that he would willingly assist them in all things.   But Beornulf, king of the Mercians, counted this promise for nought, and collecting a large army, entered their territories in a hostile manner, and began to put all the chief inhabitants to death.   Their king opposed him with his forces, and joining battle, slew him and almost all his army: his relation Ludecan succeeded him in the kingdom.[1]

A.D. 824.

A.D. 825.   Ludecan, king of the Mercians, mustered his forces and led an army into the province of the East Angles, for the purpose of taking vengeance for the death of king Beornulf, his predecessor.   He was quickly met by the natives and their king, who in a severe battle slew him and five of his ealdormen, and very many of his troops, and put to flight the remainder.   Wiglaf succeeded to his splendid kingdom.

A.D. 826.[2]

A.D. 827.   On the holy night of the day of our Lord's Nativity [25th Dec. 828], there was an eclipse of the moon.   In the same year Ecgbert, king of the West Saxons, brought the Mercian kingdom under his own rule, its king, Wiglaf, having been driven out. Then he led an expedition beyond the river Humber.   The Northumbrians met him at a place called Dore in a peaceful manner, and tendered their alliance and humble submission; so both parties separated, being mutually very well pleased.   This Ecgbert was the eighth king of the English nation who ruled over all the southern provinces, and those which are separated from the northern by the river Humber.

[3]For the first whose kingdom extended so far was Aelle, king of the South Saxons; the second was Celin, king of the West Saxons, called in their dialect Ceaulin; the third was Aethelbert, king of Kent; the fourth was Redwald, king of the East Angles, who in

---

[1] "On the death of Aldulf, bishop of Lichfield, Herewin succeeded." A. in a second hand.
[2] "Ceadda succeeded to the bishopric of Hereford on the death of Ecca." Id.
[3] See Beda, Eccl. Hist. II. v.

Aethelbert's life-time was ealdorman of that people ; the fifth was Edwin, king of the Northumbrians, that is, those who dwelt north of the river Humber, the most powerful of all the inhabitants of Britain—he ruled over all the English and British, the natives of Kent only excepted—he also brought under the English sway the Mevanian British Islands [Man and Anglesey], which are situated between Ireland and Britain ; the sixth was Oswald, also the most Christian king of the Northumbrians, who kept up to their full extent the boundaries of the kingdom ; the seventh was Oswiu his brother, who for some time kept up the kingdom to nearly the same magnitude—he, also, to a very great extent subdued the Picts and Scots, who inhabit the northern extremities of Britain, and made them tributary to himself ; the eighth, as we have said, was king Ecgbert. In his time (as is reported) was born St. Swithun, of noble ancestry: he, when his years of youth were passed, was invested with holy orders by St. Helmstan, bishop of Winchester. Moreover king Ecgbert entrusted his son Aethelwulf to his care, for the purpose of instructing him in sacred literature.

A.D. 828.   King Wiglaf succeeded to the Mercian kingdom. Heathored, bishop of Lindisfarne, died, and was succeeded by Ecgred. Ecgbert, king of the West Saxons, led an army into the territory of the Northern Britons ; and, notwithstanding their resistance, brought them under his dominion.

A.D. 829.   Wulfred, archbishop of Canterbury, died.

A.D. 830.   Ceolnoth was chosen and consecrated archbishop.

A.D. 831.   Archbishop Ceolnoth received the pall from pope Gregory.

A.D. 832.   The Danish pirates, those vultures of prey, plundered Sheppey.

A.D. 833.   Ecgbert, king of the West Saxons, attacked thirty-five of the pirates' ships at Carrum ; but after a great carnage, the Danes got the victory.

A.D. 834.

A.D. 835.   The Danes, with a large fleet, made a descent upon the territory of the West Britons, which is called Curvalia [Cornwall]; the Britons made a treaty with them, and in conjunction with them laid waste the boundaries of king Ecgbert's dominions. When that king heard of it, he collected his forces in haste, and engaged with the enemy at a place called Hengestesdune, which means Hengst's mount ; he slew many of them, and put the rest to flight.[1]

A.D. 836.   Ecgbert, king of the West Saxons, died. Before he became king, Offa, king of the Mercians, and Brihtric, king of the West Saxons, drave him out of England ; whereupon he went over to France, and there remained for three years : then he returned to England, and on Brihtric's death, succeeded to the government of the kingdom, as we have before mentioned. After his death, his son Aethelwulf began to reign in West Saxony, and made his own

---

[1] " On the death of Unwona, bishop of Chester, Warenberht succeeded." A. in a second hand.

son Aethelstan king over the men of Kent, the East Saxons, the inhabitants of Surrey, and the South Saxons.

A.D. 837. Wulfhard, the ealdorman, attacked thirty-four of the pirates' ships at Hamton [Southampton], made great havoc among them, and gained the victory : he died shortly afterwards. Athelm, the ealdorman, assisted by the people of Dorsetshire, attacked the Danes in the district called Port, and compelled them to make a long-continued retreat ; he, however, received a wound from them in the course of the retreat, and died in consequence, and the Danes got the victory. During the reign of king Aetheluulf, St. Helmstan the bishop departed this life, and St. Swithun was appointed by the king to succeed him.

A.D. 838. Herebriht the ealdorman, and with him very many of the Mercians, were slain by the pagan Danes. In the same year many were slain by the same horde, in the province of Lindsey, in East Anglia, and in Kent. Wiglaf, king of the Mercians, died : Beorhtulf succeeded to his kingdom.

A.D. 839. Between the eighth and ninth hour of the 3d of the nones of May,[1] being the vigil of our Lord's ascension, there was an eclipse of the sun. The Pagans, whom we have so often mentioned, slew great numbers in London, and in Cwentawic, and in the city of Rochester.

A.D. 840. Aetheluulf, king of the West Saxons, engaged thirty-five of the Danish ships at Carrum, but the Danish good-fortune overthrew the Saxons.

A.D. 841—[2]844.

A.D. 845. Eanulf the ealdorman, with the people of Somersetshire, Ealhstan, bishop of Sherborne, and Osric the ealdorman, with the men of Dorsetshire, fought at the mouth of the river Parret against the Danish army, made great havoc among them, and obtained the victory. Ecgred, bishop of Lindisfarne, died, and was succeeded by [3]Eanbert.

A.D. 846, 847.

A.D. 848. [4]Heaberht, the bishop of the Hwiccas, died ; and Athun succeeded.

A.D. 849. [5]Alfred, king of the Anglo-Saxons, was born at the royal town of Wanating [Wantage], in the region called Berkshire, so called from the wood of Berroc, where the box-tree grows in abundance. His [6]genealogy is thus deduced. Alfred was the son of king Aethelwulf, who was the son of Ecgbert, who was the son of Alhmund, who was the son of Eafa, who was the son of Eoppe, who was the son of Ingils ; Ingils and Ine, that famous king of the West Saxons, were brothers ; Ine went to Rome, and closing there in glory his earthly life, departed to the heavenly country, there to reign with Christ. Those two were the sons of Coenred, who was

---

[1] 5th May, A.D. 840.
[2] "A.D. 843. On the death of Herewin, bishop of Lichfield, Oethelwald succeeded." A. in a second hand.   [3] A. Eadbert, B. Egbert, edd.
[4] Eanbert, edd.
[5] From this point to A.D. 887, compare Asser's Life of King Alfred.
[6] The proper names are corrected by A., whose readings are here followed.

the son of Ceolwald, who was the son of Cutha, who was the son
of Cuthwin, who was the son of Ceaulin, who was the son of
Kenric, [1]who was the son of Creod, who was the son of Cerdic,
who was the son of Elis, who was the son of Esle, who was the son
of Gewis, (after whom the Britons gave to the whole tribe the
name of Gewis,) who was the son of Wig, who was the son of
Freawine, who was the son of Freodegar, who was the son of Brand,
who was the son of Bealdeag, who was the son of Woden, who was
the son of Frithewald, who was the son of Frealaf, who was the son
of Fritheulf, who was the son of Finn, who was the son of Godulf,
who was the son of Gaeta, (which Gaeta the Pagans formerly
worshipped as a god,) who was the son of Cetwa, who was the son
of Beawa, who was the son of Sceldwa, who was the son o
Heremod, who was the son of Itermod, who was the son o
Hathra, who was the son of Wala, who was the son of Bedwig, who
was the son of Seth, who was the son of Noa, who was the son of
Lamech, who was the son of Matusala, who was the son of Enoch,
who was the son of Jared, who was the son of Malaliel, who was
the son of Cainan, who was the son of Enos, who was the son of
Seth, who was the son of Adam. His mother's name was Osburg;
she was a woman of exceeding piety, noble in disposition, and
noble by descent, a daughter of Oslac, king Aethelwulf's celebrated
cup-bearer, which Oslac was a Goth by nation. He was descended
from the Goths and Jutes, through the two brothers and earls,
Stuf and Wihtgar, who being put in possession of the Isle of
Wight by their uncle Cerdic, and his son Cynric, their cousin, put
to death the few native British whom they could find there, at a
place called Wihtgarabirig. The rest of the natives of the island
had previously either been slain or had fled into exile.

A.D. 850. On the eve of Pentecost, being the kalends of June
[1st June],[2] Berhtferth, son of Berhtulf, king of the Mercians,
unjustly put to death his kinsman, St. Wistan. He was the grandson of two of the Mercian kings; for his father, Wigmund, was
the son of king Wiglaf, and his mother, Aelfled, was the daughter
of king Ceoluulf. His corpse was carried to the monastery of
Repton, which was then very celebrated, and was buried in the
mausoleum of his grandfather, king Wiglaf. But miracles from
heaven were not wanting at the place of his martyrdom; for, from
the spot where he was slain in his innocence, a column of light
shot up to heaven, and remained visible to the inhabitants of that
place for thirty days.[3]

A.D. 851. Ceorl, earldorman of Devonshire, along with the men
of that county, fought against the Pagans, at a place called Wicgan-
beorh, and the Christians gained the victory. In the same year, the
Pagans wintered for the first time in the island called Sheppey,
which means, the island of sheep. It is situated in the river
Thames, between Essex and Kent, but nearer Kent than Essex,

---

[1] This link in the pedigree, here supplied from A. and B., is wanting in the
editions.   [2] This concurrence of dates indicates the year 849.
[3] " On the death of Waerenbert, bishop of Chester, Rethun succeeded." A. in
another hand.

and contains a splendid monastery.[1] In the same year, too, a great army of the Pagans, with 350 ships, came to the mouth of the river Thames, and laid waste Dorubernia [Canterbury], that is, the chief city of Kent, and London, which is situated on the north bank of the river Thames, on the boundary of Essex and Middlesex, though, in fact, this city belongs to Essex; and put to flight Beorhtuulf, king of the Mercians, who with all his army had come up to war against them. After this the same pagan army advanced into Surrey, a district situated on the south bank of the river Thames, and to the eastward of Kent; and Aetheluulf, king of the West Saxons, and his son Aethelbald fought a long-contested battle with the whole of that army at a place called Ockley, which means Oak's field. After both sides had fought fiercely and courageously for a long time, the greater part of the pagan army was utterly routed and put to the sword, so much so that we have heard that there were never so many of them slain in that region in one day either before or after; and the Christians gained a splendid victory, and remained masters of the field of carnage. In the same year, king Aethelstan, and Ealhere, the ealdorman, destroyed a large army of the Pagans, at a place in Kent called Sandwich, and took nine of their ships; the remainder escaped by flight.

A.D. 852. Beorhtwulf, king of the Mercians, died, and Burhred succeeded him in the kingdom.

A.D. 853. Burhred, king of the Mercians, sent messengers to Aethelwulf, king of the West Saxons, entreating him to assist in bringing under his dominion the Western Britons, who dwell between Mercia and the western sea, and who were in high rebellion against him. Having received the embassy, king Aethelwulf quickly set his army in motion, and entered the territory of the Britons in company with king Burhred, and immediately thereon laid waste that people, and subdued them to Burhred's dominion : having done this he returned home.

In this year, king Aetheluulf sent his before-mentioned son Alfred, accompanied by a number of the nobles and also of the common people, in great splendour to Rome. Pope Leo, at his father's request, appointed him to all his dignities, anointed him king, received him as a son by adoption, and confirmed him.

In this year, also, Ealhere, the ealdorman, and the men of Kent, and Huda, with the men of Surrey, fought bravely and stubbornly against the army of the Pagans, in the island which is called in the Saxon language Tenet, but in the British, Ruim. At the first, the Christians were victorious. The battle lasted for a long time, and many on both sides were slain there, and driven into the water and drowned; and both of the ealdormen were killed there. In the same year, also, after Easter, Aethelwulf, king of the West Saxons, gave his daughter as queen to Burhred, king of the Mercians, in the royal vill called Cippenham, and the nuptials were very splendid.

A.D. 854. Eanbert,[2] bishop of Lindesfarne, died, and was succeeded by Eardulf.

---

[1] Namely, Minster.   [2] So the MSS. A. B.; the editions read "Egbert."

A.D. 855. A large army of the Pagans passed the whole winter in the aforesaid Isle of Sheppey. In this year, king Aetheluulf exonerated the tenth part of all his kingdom from all royal service and tribute, and by a charter, marked with the cross of Christ, dedicated it for ever to the indivisible and triune God, in order to obtain redemption of the souls of himself and his ancestors. Thus, with great honour, he went to Rome, taking with him again his favourite son Alfred, and remained there for a whole year. At the end of that period he returned to his own country, bringing with him Judith, daughter of Charles, king of the Franks. But in the meanwhile, during the short time that king Aetheluulf was absent beyond sea, a scandalous transaction, and contrary to all christian behaviour, occurred at Selwood, in the western part of the kingdom : for king Aethelbald and Ealhstan, bishop of Sherborne, and Eanwulf, ealdorman of Somersetshire, are reported to have conspired to prevent king Aetheluulf from ever resuming his kingdom when he returned from Rome. This piece of mischief, unheard of in any former age, is by very many attributed to, and considered to have been concocted by, the bishop and the ealdorman only ; but many say that the king's haughtiness alone caused it ; for, as we have heard from certain persons, the king was very offensive, both in that respect and in many other pieces of frowardness, and the issue of the affair proves this. For when he returned from Rome, the before-named son of king Aetheluulf, together with all his advisers, or rather plunderers, were tempted to commit the great crime of repelling the king from his own dominions. But God did not permit it, nor would the Saxon nobles consent thereunto ; for in order that there might not accrue to Saxony the irremediable danger of (as it were) a civil war, growing fiercer and more cruel day by day—the father and son fighting against each other, and, moreover, the whole nation in rebellion against both—the kingdom, hitherto entire, was by the unspeakable condescension of the father, and the consent of all the nobles, divided between the father and the son, the eastern parts being assigned to the father, and the western to the son. Where the father ought by lawful right to reign, there the wicked and aspiring son was to hold rule ; for the western part of Saxony was always superior to the eastern. So, when king Aetheluulf returned from Rome, all that people were so rejoiced (and properly) at the return of the old man, that they were desirous, if he would permit it, to deprive his rebellious son Aethelbald and all his counsellors of any share of the kingdom. But he, as we have related, would not allow this—showing great clemency, and adopting prudent counsel, so that the kingdom might not be endangered : and he made Judith, daughter of king Charles, whom he had received in marriage from her father, to sit beside him on the throne of state as long as she lived, without any controversy or opposition on the part of his nobles, although this was done in contravention to a preposterous custom of that nation : for the West-Saxon nation does not allow the queen to sit by the king's side, or even endure to call her the queen, but only the king's consort. The origin of this contest (or rather indignity), which arose on account of a certain froward and wicked queen of that nation, is thus related by our elders:—There was in recent times, in Mercia, a powerful king named Offa, whose daughter Eadburh was taken to wife by Brihtric, king of the West Saxons, as we have before mentioned. She very soon began to act tyrannically, committed all possible enormities against God and man, made accusations to the king against every person she could, and thus treacherously tried to deprive them of their life or their station; and when the king would not thereto consent, she endeavoured to take them off by poison. This is shown in the case of a youth who was a great favourite with the king, and whom, when she was unable to criminate him in the king's eyes, she poisoned. The said king, Brihtric, is reported to have drank some of this poison by mistake. She did not mix the poison for the king, but for the youth, but the king took the cup first, and so both perished. On account of this queen's atrocities, all the inhabitants of that country swore that they would never suffer any king to reign over them who would make his queen to sit beside him on the throne. On the death of king Brihtric, the queen, being no longer able to remain among the Saxons, went beyond sea with countless treasures, and came to Charles, that most renowned king of the Franks. As she was standing before the throne, offering many presents to the king, Charles said to her, "Choose, Eadburh, which you prefer—me or my son, who is standing with me on this royal seat." She returned a quick but foolish answer, saying, "If the choice is open to me, I take your son, because he is younger than you." Charles smiled, and replied, "If you had chosen me you should have had my son; but inasmuch as you have chosen my son, you shall have neither me nor him." However, he gave to her an extensive monastery of nuns, where she laid aside her secular dress, and assumed a nun's habit, but remained abbess thereof for only a very few years; for having committed fornication with a certain layman, and being expelled from the monastery by order of king Charles, she passed the remainder of her life in a state of poverty and misery.

King Aetheluulf lived two years after his return from Rome, during which period, among many other deeds of good intent with respect to this life, and having in contemplation the period when he should go the way of all flesh, he caused a testamentary epistle to be drawn up, lest his sons might causelessly quarrel after their father's death; and by this he divided his kingdom equally between his sons Aethelbald and Aethelbert, and his private domains between his sons and his daughter, and also his relations; and the money which he might leave behind him he disposed, in equal proportions, for the good of his own soul, and the benefit of his sons and his nobles. For the good of his soul, about which from the first bloom of youth he had been careful above all things, he enjoined that his successors should, from his death until the last day of doom, furnish, out of every tenth hide of his hereditary lands, one poor man, either native or a foreigner, with meat, drink, and clothing, provided that the land was inhabited and stocked with cattle, and not waste. He ordered, moreover, that the sum of 300 mancuses in money should be annually carried to Rome, to be divided there in the following manner, that is to say—100 mancuses in honour of St. Peter specially, for the purpose of buying oil to supply all the lamps in his apostolic church on Easter eve, and likewise at cock-crowing ; and 100 mancuses in honour of St. Paul the apostle, for the same purpose ; and 100 mancuses to the catholic and apostolic pope.

After his death, which took place on the ides of January[1] [Jan. 13], and his burial at Winchester, his son Aethelbald invaded his father's marriage-bed, in defiance of God's commands and the dignity of Christians, yea, and of the customs of all pagan nations, and married Judith, the daughter of Charles, king of the Franks; and, for two years and a half after his father's death, he held with an unsteady hand the kingdom of the West Saxons.

Eadmund, a most holy man, and accepted of God, descended from the Old Saxons, a most exact observer of the Christian faith, affable and kindly-spoken to all, eminent for the grace of humility, a liberal entertainer of the needy, a most fostering parent to orphans and widows, obtained the kingdom of East Anglia.

A.D. 856, 857[2]—859[3].

A.D. 860. King Aethelbald died, and was buried at Sherborne ; and Aethelbert, his brother, added Kent, Surrey and Sussex to his own kingdom, as was proper. In his days, a great army of the Pagans landed and assaulted Winchester, and laid it waste. As they were returning to their ships with great booty, they were manfully opposed by Osric, ealdorman of Hampshire, and his men, and by Aethelulf, the ealdorman, with the men of Berkshire. They joined battle, and the Pagans were cut down on all sides; and when they could no longer resist, like women they began to flee, and the Christians remained masters of the field of carnage.

Aethelbert having governed the kingdom for five years in peace, and love, and honour, went the way of all flesh, to the great grief of his people, and rests at Sherborne, being honourably buried by the side of his brother.[4]

A.D. 861.

A.D. 862. On the fifth day of the week, on the 6th of the nones of July [Thursday, 2d July], in the tenth indiction, St. Swithun passed away to heaven.[5]

A.D. 863.

A.D. 864. The Pagans wintered in the Isle of Thanet, and made a firm compact of peace with the people of Kent, who promised them money if they would observe the treaty. Nevertheless the Pagans, like foxes, stole out of their camp by night, and breaking

---

[1] In B. (erroneously) "June."

[2] "On the death of Ceadd, bishop of Hereford, Aldbert succeeded." A. in a second hand.

[3] "Oethelwald, bishop of Lichfield, having died, was succeeded by Hunberht." Id.

[4] He died, A.D. 866. The later hand in A. here adds, "On the death of Rethun, bishop of Chester, Aldred succeeded."

[5] "This pearl of God lay ingloriously hidden for nearly one hundred years: he was succeeded in the bishopric by Alfrith, Dunberht." A. from William of Malmesbury.

the treaty and contemning the promise of money (for they knew that they could obtain greater wealth by clandestine plunder than in peace), laid waste the whole of the eastern part of Kent.

A.D. 865.[1]

A.D. 866. Aethered,[2] the brother of king Aethelbert, succeeded to the kingdom of the West Saxons. In the same year a large fleet of the Pagans from the Danube arrived in Britain, and wintered in the kingdom of the East Angles (called in the Saxon tongue East Engle), where the greater part of their army was converted into cavalry.

A.D. 867. The aforesaid army of Pagans changed its quarters in East Anglia for the city of York, situate on the northern bank of the river Humber. At that time a very great discord among the Northumbrians had arisen by means of diabolical agency, as usually happens to a people which are under the wrath of God. For the Northumbrians had then, as we have related, expelled from the kingdom their lawful king, named Osbriht, and had elevated to the throne a certain tyrant named Aella, who was not of the royal race : but by divine counsel, and the cooperation of their nobles, that discord was on the arrival of the Pagans somewhat appeased, and Osbriht and Aella joined their forces, and with the united army marched to the town of York. When they arrived there, the Pagans immediately took to flight, and took care to defend themselves within the walls of the city. When the Christians saw their flight and fear, they began to pursue them even within the city walls, and to make breaches in the wall : this they effected, for that city had not then strong and well-built fortifications. When the Christians had, as they intended, made a breach in the wall, and a great number of them had entered the city along with the Pagans, the latter, driven to it by despair and necessity, made a ferocious attack upon them, slew, routed, and overthrew them, both within and without the city. Of the Northumbrian army the greater part, including the two kings, was slain : those who escaped made peace with the Pagans.

In that year, also, Ealhstan, bishop of Sherborne, went the way of all flesh, after having held the bishopric with honour for fifty years, and was buried in peace at Sherborne.

A.D. 868. A comet was seen very distinctly in this year.

The venerable king Alfred, who then held the second place in the kingdom, obtained in marriage a Mercian lady of noble descent, she being the daughter of Aethelred, surnamed Mucil, ealdorman of the Gaini. His wife's mother was named Eadburh, descended from the royal race of the kings of the Mercians, a most venerable woman, who for many years after the death of his father, and until her own decease, remained a chaste widow.

In the same year, the before-mentioned pagan army left the Northumbrians, and came to Mercia, and marched to Nottingham, called in the British tongue Tigguocobauc, and in the Latin The house of caves, and there they passed the winter of that year.

---

[1] "On the death of Hunberht, bishop of Lichfield, Cineferth succeeded." A. in a later hand.

[2] Such is the constant orthography of A.; the editions read "Ethelred."

Immediately after their coming, Burhred, king of the Mercians, and all the chief men of that tribe, sent messengers to Aethered, king of the West Saxons, and to his brother Alfred, earnestly soliciting all the aid they could render in giving battle to the said army : and they easily obtained what they requested ; for the two brothers, not slow to fulfil their promise, assembled from every part of their dominions an immense army, and came into Mercia, and went as far as Nottingham, being unanimous in desiring a battle. But as the Pagans, rendered strong by the defences of the citadel, declined the engagement, and the Christians could not make a breach in the wall, a peace was concluded between the Mercians and the Pagans, and the two brothers, king Aethered and Alfred, returned home with their troops.   [1] The oratory of St. Andrew the apostle, at Kemsege, was built and dedicated by Alhun, bishop of Worcester.

A.D. 869.   The aforesaid army of Pagans again rode into Northumbria, and came to the city of York, and remained there for a whole year.

A.D. 870.   The above-mentioned army of the Pagans passed through Mercia into East Anglia, and wintered there, at a place called Thetford.

In the same year Eadmund, the most saintly and glorious king of the East Angles, was on [2]Sunday, the 12th of the kalends of December [20th Nov.], in the second indiction, martyred by king Inguar, a thorough pagan, as is related in the history of his passion. In this year, also, Ceolnoth archbishop of Canterbury died, and was buried in peace in that city.   He was succeeded by the venerable Aethelred.[3]

A.D. 871.   The pagan army, of detestable memory, quitted East Anglia, and marching into the kingdom of the West Saxons, came to the royal vill of Reading, situate on the southern bank of the river Thames, in the country called Berkshire; and on the third day after their arrival, two of their earls rode out to plunder, accompanied by a great number of their troops, while another portion made a trench on the right of the said royal vill, between the rivers Thames and Kennet.   Aethelulf, ealdorman of Berkshire, and his men, went up against them, at a place called in the English tongue Englafeld, and in the Latin The field of the Angles : there the battle was contested stoutly on both sides.   The two armies maintained their ground for a long time, when one of the pagan earls being slain, and the greater part of the army destroyed, and the rest running away, the Christians gained the victory, and remained masters of the field of carnage.   Four days afterwards, king Aethered and his brother Alfred, joining their forces and marshalling the army, came to Reading.   When they had succeeded in getting to the gate of the citadel, by slaying and putting to rout all the Pagans whom they found outside, the Pagans did not exert them-

---

[1] This passage occurs neither in Asser nor the Saxon Chronicle, and is one of those which Florence must have obtained from local information.

[2] These concurrents point to the previous year, A.D. 869.

[3] Here and elsewhere B. reads " Aethered."

selves the less, rushing out like wolves from all the gates, and doing
battle with all their might; and both sides fought long and fiercely.
But, oh misery! the Christians at last turned their backs, and the
Pagans gained the victory, and remained masters of the field of
death. The said ealdorman Aethelulf was among the number of
the slain. Full of grief and shame at this defeat, the Christians,
four days afterwards, with all their forces and with right good will,
renewed the battle against the before-mentioned host, at a place
called Aescesdun [Ashdown], the Latin interpretation whereof
is "mons fraxini," or the hill of the ash. The Pagans divided
their army into two bodies, and put both in battle array, for
they had with them two kings and several earls, placing one-half of
the army under the two kings, and the other half under the earls.
When the Christians saw this, they too divided their army into two
parts, and as quickly put them in battle array. Alfred brought up
his men sooner and more promptly to the field : for his brother,
king Aethered, was then praying and hearing mass in his tent, and
positively declared that he would not depart thence until the priest
had finished the mass, and that he would not leave his heavenly
duty for earthly business; and he kept his resolution. This faith of
the christian king prevailed much with God, as will be more fully
displayed hereafter. So the Christians resolved, that king Aethered
with his own troops should engage the two pagan kings ; but his
brother Alfred was to be informed that he was, with his troops, to
try the fortune of war against all the pagan earls. Each side having
thus settled its arrangements, and the king being still at his prayers,
and the Pagans all equipped, having come in good time to the
battle-field : Alfred being then the second in command, finding
that he could no longer make head against the enemy, except he
retired from the contest, or charged the enemy before his brother's
arrival, at length manfully, and according to old custom, led the
christian forces against the enemy's army in manner before agreed
on, although the king had not yet arrived ; and relying on God's
counsel and trusting to his assistance, and closing up the ranks of
his division, immediately advanced the standards against the enemy.
At length, having concluded his devotions, king Aethered came up,
and invoking the assistance of the world's mighty Ruler, joined the
contest. But here we must inform those who do not know the
spot, that the combatants were on unequal terms, as far as the
ground was concerned ; for the Pagans had taken possession of an
acclivity, and the Christians had to move their forces up from
below. There was on the spot a rather low thorn-tree, around
which the hostile forces met together with great uproar, the former to
gain their wicked ends, but the latter in defence of their lives, their
dear ones, and their country. After the battle had been kept up
for some time with a great display of courage and ferocity on both
sides, God so ordered it that the Pagans were no longer able to
withstand the attacks of the Christians, and having lost the greater
portion of their army, began an ignominious retreat. Here fell one
of the two pagan kings and five of their earls, and several thousands
of their men were put to flight or slain, some in that place, and all

about the plain of Ashdown. So king Bagsegc was slain, and the old earl Sidroc, and earl Sidroc the younger, earl Osbern, earl Freana, and earl Harald : and the whole army of the Pagans kept up the flight until night, and even until the next day, when the fugitives reached the citadel.

Fourteen days after this, king Aethered and his brother Alfred, having again united their forces for the purpose of doing battle against the Pagans, arrived at Baseng : the armies met, and after a long struggle the Pagans gained the victory.

¹After the lapse of two months, king Aethered and his brother Alfred again fought against the Pagans (who had divided their army into two bodies) at Merton, and for some time got the better of them, all the enemy retreating ; but the latter returned to the charge, and after great slaughter on both sides, the Pagans gained the victory, and remained masters of the field of carnage.

After Easter in this year, to wit, on the 9th of the kalends of May ² [23d April], king Aethered, having reigned for five years under trying circumstances, yet with energy, honour, and great credit, went the way of all flesh, and was buried at Winburne, where he awaits the coming of our Lord and the first resurrection of the just. On his death the before-named Alfred, who up to that period, as long as his brothers lived, had been second in authority, by God's permission at once succeeded to the entire kingdom, amid the great good-will of all the inhabitants. And here we think it proper to insert a brief notice of his infancy and boyhood.

Both his father and mother loved him dearly, and better than all his brothers ; in fact, he was a great favourite with every one, and was brought up entirely in the king's court. As he grew up from childhood, he excelled all his brothers in beauty of shape and countenance, and in suavity of speech and disposition. But, alas ! owing to the negligence of his parents and nurses, he did not know how to read until he was twelve years old ; but day and night he eagerly listened to Saxon poems, and from the frequent recitation of them by others, easily committed them to memory. In all varieties of the huntsman's craft, his skill and success were unmatched, and it was the same with the rest of God's gifts.

It chanced that one day his mother, as she was showing to him and his brothers a volume of Saxon poetry which she had in her hand, said, " I will give this book to whichever of you shall first be able to learn it." Moved by this offer, or rather inspired and attracted by the beauty of the initial letter of the book, Alfred said to his mother, " Will you indeed give this book to such one of us as can first understand it and repeat it to you ? " She smiled, and said, " To him will I give it." Thereupon he took the book from her hand and went to his master, and he read it ; and when he had finished reading it, Alfred brought it back to his mother, and recited it to her. After this, by way of daily task, he learned some psalms and a number of prayers ; and to the end of his life, day and night he carried in his bosom, for the purpose of prayer, a volume in which

---

¹ This clause does not occur in Asser; compare, however, the Saxon Chronicle.
² This date does not occur in Asser.

they were all collected. But, alas! he was never able to acquire what he chiefly wished for, namely, the liberal science [of grammar], because at that time there were no grammarians in any part of the West-Saxon kingdom.

While in the first flower of his youth, he was desirous that his heart should stand firm in God's ordinances, but yet perceived that he was not free from the lusts of the flesh: so, lest he should incur God's displeasure by doing anything opposed to his will, he frequently rose privately at cock-crow and early morn, and went to pray in churches and before the reliques of saints; and there, long prostrate, he was wont to pray that Almighty God would in his mercy strengthen his mind in the love of his service, by means of some infirmity which he might be able to bear, but so nevertheless that he might not thereby be rendered unworthy and unfit for his worldly duties. He entreated this very often with great earnestness, and a short time afterwards he was, by God's permission, afflicted with the piles. This complaint increased so much in the course of many years, that even his life was despaired of; but it providentially happened that, being in Cornwall, where he had gone for the purpose of hunting, he turned aside to offer up his prayers in a certain church, where lie Saint Guerur and Saint Niot, and prostrating himself for a long time in silent prayer, he entreated of God's mercy that, in his unbounded love, He would exchange the pressure of his present troublesome disease for a somewhat less grievous infirmity; provided only that his person should not be outwardly affected thereby, lest he should become an object of contempt, and unfit for active service. Having concluded his prayer, he resumed his journey; and shortly afterwards he perceived that God had cured him of the disease, according to the tenor of his prayer, so that the complaint was thoroughly eradicated. But, alas! when that was removed, another still more grievous seized him on the day of his marriage, and from his twentieth to his forty-fifth year, and beyond, preyed upon him incessantly day and night. By Ealhsuith, his wife, (who has been mentioned before,) he had the following sons and daughters:— Aegelfled, his eldest child, then Eadward, then Aethelgeovu, then Alfthrith, then Aethelward. Aethelfled, when she became marriageable, was united to Aethered, ealdorman of the Mercians; Aethelgeofu made a vow of chastity, and embracing the rules of monastic life, and becoming a nun, she passed her life in the service of God; Aethelward, the youngest of all, was by the wise counsel and admirable foresight of the king well provided with literary instruction: and all the nobility, in nearly every part of the kingdom, and very many of the common people, were put under the strict care of masters, in order that they might be instructed in the liberal arts, before they became strong enough for the occupations of the world. Eadward and Alfthrith were entirely brought up in the king's court, and liberally educated; with their other pursuits, they diligently applied themselves to the Psalms and Saxon books, especially Saxon poems. In the midst of wars and the manifold disturbances of this life, the inroads of the Pagans, and the every day infirmities of his body, king Alfred, single-handed and diligently as far as his strength would allow, devoted himself to the government of his kingdom, hunting of all kinds, the superintendence of his goldsmiths and all his mechanics, the keepers of his falcons, hawks, and hounds, the construction (by means of machinery invented by himself) of buildings more wonderful and costly than any which his ancestors had erected, the reading of Saxon books, and especially the committing to memory of Saxon poems. He heard mass every day, also some psalms and prayers; kept the [canonical] hours day and night, and it was his constant custom to go by night, unknown to his attendants, into churches for the purpose of prayer. Never was there an almsgiver more bounteous, never was any one more affable or more pleasant; never any one more skilful in the investigation of unexplained subjects. Many of the nobility and commonalty of the Franks, Frieslanders, Gauls, Pagans, Britons, Scots, and Armoricans, came spontaneously to live under his rule; all of whom he treated in the same manner as he did his own people, governing, favouring, honouring, and advancing them to wealth and power, in accordance with their deserts. He was wonderfully kind to his bishops, all the clergy, his ealdormen and thanes, the officers of his court, and all his servants. He paid as much attention to the sons of those who were brought up in the royal family as to his own sons, and was continually inculcating on them virtuous habits, and amongst other things assisted personally in their education both by day and night.

Nearly a month after the commencement of his unwilling reign, (if we may use the expression,) he thought that he should not be able (unless supported by divine aid) to withstand alone the severe assaults of the Pagans; moreover, while his brothers were alive, and after he had sustained great losses, he with a small and very unequal force fought fiercely against the whole army of the Pagans at a hill called Wilton, situate on the south bank of the river Guilou, from which river the whole region takes its name. Now when both sides had kept up the fight in all directions, fiercely and perseveringly, for the greater part of the day, the Pagans began to see that their danger was imminent; and being unable any longer to sustain the attack of their enemies, they turned their backs and fled. But, oh misery! they took advantage of the overboldness of their pursuers, and again returned to the charge; and getting the victory remained masters of the field of carnage. Nor let any one be surprised that the Christians were only few in number at this battle; for the Saxons had been greatly thinned in the eight battles which they had fought in one year against the Pagans; in which eight battles one pagan king and nine earls were slain, with innumerable followers; not to mention the countless daily and nightly attacks on the Pagans which king Alfred and his generals and men, and also many of the king's thanes, had unceasingly kept up. Omitting those who were slain in the eight battles before mentioned, no one but God knows how many thousands of the pagan invaders were slain in those frequent irruptions. In this year the Saxons made peace with the Pagans on condition that the latter should depart from them; which condition they observed.[1]

A.D. 872.   [2]Alhun, bishop of the Hwiccas, having died, Were-frith, a man deeply read in the Scriptures, who had been brought up at the holy church of Worcester, was on the day of Pentecost,[3] being the 7th of the ides of June [7th June], ordained bishop by Aethelred, archbishop of Canterbury.   At the command of king Alfred he made the first translation from Latin into Saxon of the books of Dialogues of the blessed pope Gregory, and he executed his task with great accuracy and elegance.   The king invited Were-frith, and (in course of time) Pleigmund, a Mercian, archbishop of Canterbury, a venerable and erudite man, and also Aethelstan and Werulf, two very learned Mercian priests, to leave Mercia and come to him, and he advanced them to great honour and power, in order that they might assist him in his literary studies.   More-over he sent ambassadors to Gaul, and invited thence saint Grim-bald, priest and monk, a venerable man, a perfect singer, one well skilled in ecclesiastical discipline and in the sacred writings, and of most accomplished manners; also John, who was both priest and monk, and a man of very great intellectual acuteness; Asser, too, he called out of the monastery of St. David, in the western extre-mity of Britain.   By the wisdom and teaching of all these, the king's desire was so increased and fulfilled that in a short time he could understand any book.

The before-mentioned army of the Pagans went to London, and wintered there; and the Mercians made peace with them.[4]

A.D. 873.   That oft-mentioned army evacuated London and went into Northumbria, and wintered there in the district called Lindsey; and the Mercians again made peace with them.[5]

A.D. 874.   Quitting Lindsey, the aforesaid army marched into Mercia, and wintered at a place called Hreopedun [Repton]; it moreover compelled Burhred, king of the Mercians, to quit his kingdom against his will, in the twenty-second year of his reign, and go beyond sea and journey to Rome; he did not long survive his arrival there, but died in that city, and was honourably interred in the church of St. Mary, in the Saxon School, where in company with the just he waits for the coming of our Lord and the first resurrection.   After his expulsion the Danish pirates subdued the whole Mercian kingdom; it was in a miserable condition, and they made over the government of it to a stupid thane named Ceoluulf, on condition that he should resign it peaceably to them whenever they desired.   He gave hostages to them for the performance of the condition, and took an oath that he would in nowise act in opposi-tion to their will, but be obedient to them in all things.

A.D. 875.   The oft-named army quitted Hreopedun [Repton],

---

[1] " On the death of Cineferth, bishop of Chester, Tunberht succeeded."   A. addition.
[2] This first sentence does not occur in Asser.   [3] Therefore in A.D. 873.
[4] " Esne succeeded to the bishopric of Hereford, on the death of Aldberht." A. in a later hand.
[5] " On the death of Aldred, bishop of Chester, Ceolred succeeded."   Id.

and divided itself into two bodies. One of them went with Half-dene into the Northumbrian district, and wintered there near the river called Tine, and reduced all the Northumbrian district under its dominion, and oppressed the Picts and people of Strathclyde. The other division, with Guthrun, Oskitell, and Amund, three kings of the Pagans, came to a place called Grantebrycge [Cambridge], and there wintered. In this year king Alfred fought a naval battle against six of the Pagans' ships, and captured one of them, the rest escaping.

A.D. 876. The oft-mentioned army of the Pagans left Grantebrycg [Cambridge] by night, and entered the castle called Werham [Wareham]: there, between the two rivers Fraw and Terente [Frome and Trent], and in the region which in Saxon is called Dornseta [Dorset], is a nunnery posted in a most secure situation, except only on the western and landward side. With this army king Alfred made a treaty, which was to be lasting, and bound them to quit his dominions, and the army gave him unhesitatingly as many hostages as he chose to select; moreover they swore upon all the reliques in which next to God they most put their trust, and upon which they had always refused to swear to any other people, that they would depart from his kingdom as quickly as possible. Nevertheless, acting deceitfully as usual, and regarding neither their hostages, nor their oath, nor their plighted faith, they violated the treaty, and one night killed all the king's horsemen. Turning thence, the army came unexpectedly to another place, called in Saxon Eaxancestre [Exeter], and in Latin the city of Exe, situate on the eastern bank of that river, and near the southern sea which lies between Gaul and Britain. [1]King Alfred assembled an army and followed them, but could not overtake them, because they had just entered the city; but he extorted from them as hostages whomsoever and as many as he chose, and made a firm treaty with them, which they observed faithfully for a considerable time; and they wintered at that place. In the same year the pagan king Halfdene divided the Northumbrian region between himself and his followers, and took up his residence there with his army. [2]On the 15th of the kalends of December [17th Nov.], Rollo and his forces entered Normandy.

A.D. 877. [3]The pagan army which had been left with the fleet at Wereham came to Exeter; but before reaching that city, one hundred and twenty of their ships were sunk by a tempest. When autumn arrived, a portion of the Pagans remained at Exeter, and part marched into Mercia, and gave a portion of it to Ceoluulf, to whose charge it had been committed, as before mentioned, and divided the remainder among themselves.

A.D. 878. The oft-named army, leaving Exeter, marched to Chippenham, a royal town, situate in the left-hand part of Wiltshire, and wintered there, and by force of arms compelled many of the inhabitants of those parts to go beyond sea in consternation

---

[1] This sentence is not in Asser. See the Saxon Chronicle, A.D. 877.
[2] Not in Asser nor the Saxon Chronicle.
[3] See the Saxon Chronicle, A.D. 887. This sentence is not found in Asser.

and poverty, and brought under their dominion nearly all the inhabitants. At that time king Alfred, with a few of his nobles and some vassals, led a most disturbed and sorrowful life in the marshy woods of Somersetshire; for he had no means of subsistence, except what in frequent forays he took either secretly or openly from the Pagans, or those Christians who had submitted to the Pagans.

In the same year, the brother of Inguare and of Halfdene came with twenty-three ships from Demetia[1] [West Wales], (where he had wintered, and made great havoc among the Christians,) to Devonshire, and there, in front of the citadel of Cynuit, he and twelve hundred of his followers were, in the midst of their wickedness, miserably slain by the king's thanes, many of whom had shut up themselves and their families in that fort for the sake of security. But the Pagans, seeing that the fort was unprepared for a siege, and wholly undefended, except by walls constructed in our usual mode, did not attempt to take it by storm, (because the place is by its position naturally very secure on every side except the east,) but made preparations for besieging it; thinking that as there was no water near the fort, hunger and thirst, and the consciousness of being in a state of siege, would soon compel its defenders to surrender. But they were disappointed in their expectations; for before being reduced to such extremities, the Christians, nerved thereto by divine inspiration, and preferring either to die or to conquer, made an unexpected sally upon the Pagans very early in the morning, and at the very first onset overthrew their king and the greater part of his army, only a very few of them escaping to their ships.

After Easter in the same year, king Alfred with a small force constructed a fortress at a place called Aethelingaeig [Athelney], and from that fortress, in conjunction with his Somersetshire vassals, kept up a continued and indefatigable war against the Pagans. Again, in the seventh[2] week after Easter, he rode on to Egbriht's Stone, in the eastern part of the forest called Sealuudu [Selwood], the Latin denomination of which is, The great wood; and there he was met by all the people of Somersetshire, Wiltshire and Hampshire whom the fear of the Pagans had not driven beyond sea; who, when they saw the king, come to life again, as it were, after so many troubles, were deservedly elated, and encamped there for one night. Early on the following morning, the king broke up the camp, and came to a place called Ecglea, and encamped there for one night. Moving thence on the next day, he came to a place called Ethandun: there he fought a tremendous battle against the entire and close-serried pagan army, and after keeping it up for a long time with great spirit, at length, by God's help, he gained the victory, and overthrew the Pagans with great carnage. He pursued the fugitives as far as their fortress, and captured everything which he found outside, whether men, horses, or sheep; put the men to death immediately, and then boldly encamped with all his army before the gates of the pagan fortress. After he had

[1] See Camd. Brit. col. 621, ed. 1695.   [2] B. reads "in the fourth."

remained there a fortnight, hunger, cold and fear drove the Pagans to the lowest depths of despair, and they sued for peace, consenting that the king should take as many hostages of his own selection as he pleased, and should give them nothing in return; terms of peace such as they had never before made with any one. After hearing their proposition, the king's compassion was moved, and he took as hostages as many as, and whomsoever he pleased. After they were delivered over, the Pagans swore in addition that they would depart as quickly as possible from his kingdom; and moreover, their king Guthrum promised to embrace Christianity, and receive baptism at the hands of king Alfred. He and his men performed all that they promised; for seven weeks afterwards, Guthrum, the king of the Pagans, with thirty of the most chosen men of his army, came to king Alfred at a place called Aalr [Aller], near Aethelingaeig [Athelney] : the king stood godfather to him at the font of holy baptism, and gave him the name of Aethelstan : his chrism-loosing took place eight days afterwards at the royal town of Weadmor [Wedmore]. For twelve days after his baptism, he lodged with the king, who generously gave to him and all his attendants several superb houses.

A.D. 879. The aforesaid pagan army removed, according to promise, from Cippanham [Chippenham], and came to Cirencester, which is situate in the southern part of the Wiccian territory, and remained there for a year. In the same year a great army of the Pagans sailed over from the parts beyond sea, and came to the river Thames, and united with the before-mentioned army; they wintered, however, at a place called Fullanham [Fulham], by the side of the river Thames.

In this year,[1] also, an eclipse of the sun occurred between nones and vespers, but nearer nones. [2]Dunbert, bishop of Winchester, died, and was succeeded by Den{}eulf. If report may be credited, he was, up to an advanced age, not only illiterate, but a herdsman: king Alfred, while retiring from the violence of his enemies and a fugitive in a forest, chanced to meet him as he was feeding swine. Finding that he was a man of talent, the king caused him to be educated; and, when he was sufficiently advanced, made him bishop of Winchester, thinking that he was indicated by God for the office.

A.D. 880. The oft-mentioned pagan army evacuated Cirencester, and went to East Anglia, and parcelled out and began to settle in that district. In the same year the pagan army which had wintered at Fullanham [Fulham] quitted Britain, and sailing again beyond sea, arrived at the eastern part of France, and remained for a year at a place called Gendi, that is, Gent.

A.D. 881. The oft-mentioned army of the Pagans arrived in France, and the Franks fought against it. At the end of the battle, the Pagans, having obtained horses, became an army of cavalry.

A.D. 882. The aforesaid army of the Pagans drew their ships up the river called Mese [Meuse] into the heart of France, and

---

[1] This eclipse happened on the 14th March, 880.
[2] Not in Asser; but see William of Malmesbury, De Gestis Pontiff.

wintered there for a year. In the same year king Alfred fought a naval battle against the pagan fleet: he captured two of them, and slew all who were in them; and the commanders of two others, with all their comrades, being grievously wounded in the engagement, laid down their arms, and on bended knees and with humble supplications surrendered themselves to the king.

A.D. 883. The aforesaid army drew its ships up the river called Scaldad [Scheld], against the stream, to the monastery called Candath [Condé], and remained there for a year. [1]Asser, bishop of Scireburne [Sherborne], died, and was succeeded by Suithelm, who was the bearer of king Alfred's alms to St. Thomas in India, and returned thence in safety.

A.D. 884. Marinus was pope. He, for the love that he bore to, and at the request of, Alfred, king of the Anglo-Saxons, exonerated from all toll and tribute the School of the Saxons resident at Rome. He also sent over many presents to that king, and amongst others a large piece of the most holy cross on which our Lord Jesus Christ hung to obtain salvation for man. The aforesaid army of the Pagans entered the river Sunne [Somme], and sailing up as far as Amiens, remained there for a year.

A.D. 885. [2]The aforesaid army of the Pagans divided itself into two bodies, of which one went into Eastern France; but the other division, coming over to Britain, landed in Kent, and laid siege to the city which is called in Saxon Rochester, situate on the eastern bank of the river Medway. Opposite the gate of this city the Pagans, with great expedition, built up a strong castle; nevertheless, they were unable to take the city, because the citizens defended themselve manfully, until such time as king Alfred came up with a large army which he had collected for their assistance. On the sudden arrival of the king, the Pagans quitted their castle; and, abandoning all the horses which they had brought with them from France, and dismissing the greater proportion of their prisoners, fled in haste to their ships. The Saxons immediately took possession of the captives and horses which the Pagans had abandoned. So the Pagans, driven thereto by urgent necessity, returned that summer to France.

In the same year, Alfred, king of the Anglo-Saxons, steered his fleet filled with warriors from Kent towards East Anglia, with the intention of pillaging. When they arrived at the mouth of the river Stour, sixteen ships of the Pagans immediately came out to oppose them. The battle began, and after sharp fighting on both sides the Pagans were all slain, and all their ships and money were captured. As the royal fleet was returning in triumph the pagan inhabitants of East Anglia collected ships from all quarters, and putting out to sea came upon it at the mouth of the river: an engagement took place, and the Pagans gained the victory.

As Carloman, king of the Western Franks, was boar-hunting he met with a miserable end, being torn by the horrid tusk of a huge beast which he had singly attacked. His brother Louis, who was also king of the Franks, had died three years previously. They

---

[1] The death of Asser finds no place in the Saxon Chronicle.
[2] See Asser, A.D. 884.

were both sons of Louis, king of the Franks, who died in the year above mentioned when the eclipse of the sun took place. The latter was son of Charles, king of the Franks, whose daughter Judith became, with her father's consent, the queen of Aethelwulf, king of the West Saxons.

In this year, also, a great pagan army came down from Germany into the country of the Old Saxons. The Saxons and Frieslanders united their forces, and fought valiantly against them twice in one year; in which two battles the Christians, by God's merciful assistance, gained the victory.

Moreover, in this year, Charles [the Fat], king of the Germans, succeeded by universal consent to the kingdom of the West Franks and all the kingdoms which lie between the Tuscan sea and the bay which lies between Old Saxony and Gaul, the kingdom of Armorica excepted. This Charles was the son of king Louis, who was the brother of Charles, king of the Franks, who was the father of the before-mentioned Judith : the two brothers were sons of Louis, who was the son of Pepin.

In this year, moreover, an army of the Pagans who dwelt in East Anglia disgracefully broke the peace which they had concluded with king Alfred.

A.D. 886. The pagan army so often mentioned, leaving Eastern France, came again unto the country of the Western Franks; and entering the mouth of the river Seine, and sailing up a great way, came to the city of Paris and wintered there. They besieged the city for the whole of that year, but, through God's merciful interposition, they were unable to force its defences.

In the same year, Alfred, the king of the Anglo-Saxons, after all this burning of cities and slaughter of people, rebuilt the city of London in a splendid manner, and made it fit for habitation, and then placed it under the government of Aethered, ealdorman of the Mercians. All the Angles and Saxons who previously had been either dispersed in all quarters, or were free servants in the hands of the Pagans, came to this king, and voluntarily placed themselves under his dominion.

A.D. 887. The aforesaid army of the Pagans, finding that they could not otherwise succeed in their enterprise, left the city of Paris untaken, and for a considerable time rowed their fleet up the river Seine until they came to the mouth of the river Materne [Marne] : they then left the Seine, and entered the mouth of the Marne. They made a long and distant voyage up this river, and at last, after much exertion, they came to a place called Caziei [Chezy], which means, The royal town, and passed the whole of the winter there. In the following year they entered the mouth of the river Iona [Yonne], doing great damage to the neighbourhood; and there they remained for a year. In this year Charles, king of the Franks, went the way of all flesh; but, six weeks before his death, he had been driven from the kingdom by Arnulf, his brother's son. Immediately after his decease, five kings were chosen, and the kingdom was divided into five parts; but nevertheless, the chief seat of the kingdom fell to the possession of Arnulf, and that rightly and deservedly, if we except his sinful indignity to his uncle. The four other kings very properly promised fealty and obedience to Arnulf, for not one of those four had any hereditary right to the kingdom, as Arnulf alone had. So, on Charles's death, five kings were chosen; but the supreme dominion remained with Arnulf. The division of the kingdom was in this wise : Arnulf had the countries to the east of the river Rhine, Hrothulf [Rodolph] the interior part of the kingdom, Oda [Eudes] had the western [portion of the] kingdom, Beorngar [Berengar] and Witha [Guido] had Lombardy and the parts on that side of the mountains [Alps]. With such extensive and important kingdoms they nevertheless did not keep peace among themselves : for twice they fought general pitched battles, and mutually laid waste each other's kingdoms, and each in turn expelled the others from their dominions.

In this year Athelelm, ealdorman of the Wiltshire-men, carried the alms of king Alfred and the Saxons to Rome. In the same year, too, on the feast-day of St. Martin, bishop of Tours [11th Nov.], the oft-named Alfred, king of the Anglo-Saxons, by God's direction, began for the first time to read, and at the same time to explain the meaning [of what he read]. Though enjoying regal power, that king was pierced through with many afflictions. For, as we have mentioned, he was, from his twentieth to his forty-fifth year, and beyond it, continually suffering from the severe attacks of an inexplicable disorder : so that he did not pass a single hour in which he was not either suffering from it, or in melancholy fear of it. Besides this, he was constantly disturbed by the unremitting invasions of foreigners, kept up both by sea and by land, without any interval of peace. What shall I say of his frequent expeditions against the Pagans, of his wars, of his unceasing attention to affairs of state, of his reparations of towns and cities, and his building others in places where none formerly existed, of buildings glittering with gold and silver, exquisitely constructed under his own immediate directions, of the royal halls and chambers of wonderful wood and stone work which he ordered to be built, of the royal vills built of stone, removed from their ancient sites, and by his royal mandate elegantly rebuilt in more suitable positions ? True it is, that though he stood alone, yet, God being his helper, he did not suffer the helm of government to which he had once put his hand, to waver or become unsteady in passing through the billowy and manifold tempests of this present life. For, always, and with the greatest tact, he brought his bishops, ealdormen, the most noble and intimate of his thanes, and those who held command under him, to subserve his own will and the common weal of the whole kingdom ; gently instructing, or advising, or commanding them, and at last, after long endurance, severely punishing the disobedient; for he held vulgar stupidity and obstinacy in utter abomination. If, when the king commanded, his orders were, by reason of the people's indolence, either neglected, or, attended to only after long procrastination, were not ready sufficiently early to be of use to those who required them in time of need ; for instance, fortresses which he had ordered to be built, but which had not yet been begun, or from having been begun too late, had not been completed, and the enemy's forces had broke in by sea and by land ;—then the opponents of the royal decrees, touched with a too late repentance, were sorely troubled that they had not paid sufficient attention to the king's commands, vied in praising his wisdom, which they had denied before, and promised to strain every nerve to complete the works. This king, among his other good deeds, commanded two monasteries to be built, one for monks, at the place called Aethelingaeig [Athelney] ; whereof, monks of different orders being collected, he made John, by birth an Old Saxon, and both priest and monk, first abbot. He also caused a monastery for nuns to be erected, in a convenient situation near the eastern gate of Shaftesbury, and made his own daughter, Aethelgeofu, who had taken the vow of virginity, abbess thereof : and these two monasteries he richly endowed with landed possessions and all manner of treasures. Moreover, he promised that he would piously and faithfully dedicate to God one-half of all his lawful and ordinary annual income : and he applied himself, heart and soul, to do it. Lastly, God moving him thereunto, he ordered his ministers to divide into two equal portions the fiscal revenues of each year. When this had been done, he caused one-half to be again subdivided into three parts : one of which he divided annually between his noble thanes, who were always by turns engaged in his service, taking the administration of different offices. For the king's attendants were wisely divided into three sections, one of which remained for a month, night and day, in his service ; at the end of the month another section took its place, and the first returned home and remained there two months, attending to family affairs : when another month had ended, the third section arrived, and then the second returned home and remained there for two months; the third, their monthly term of service having expired, and the first section having again come round, likewise returned home and remained there for two months. In this mode was the king's administration conducted during the whole of his vicissitudinous life. Another third [he distributed] amongst the almost innumerable skilful builders whom he had collected and hired from different countries. The remaining third he joyfully and with admirable judgment apportioned between the foreigners who came to him from all countries, far and near, and asked for pecuniary assistance ; aye, and even those who did not ask it. The second of these two portions of all his fiscal revenues he ordered his ministers to divide into four exactly equal portions, to the intent that one portion should be discreetly expended on the poor people who should come to him, of whatever country they might chance to be ; another portion he gave to the two monasteries which had been built by his command, and to the servants of God therein ; a third to the school which he had made up, with great pains, of the children of the nobility and also the lower orders of his people. The fourth portion he distributed among the neighbouring monasteries of Saxony and Mercia, and also in some years, by turns and as he was able, among the churches of Britain, Cornwall, Gaul, Armorica, Northumbria, and Ireland. Having made these orderly arrangements, he vowed that he would strenuously devote to God half the powers of his mind and body, both by day and by night, so far as his infirmities, opportunity, and necessities would permit. So he began to devise some means whereby he might preserve his vow unbroken until death. At length, after sensible and careful consideration, he sent for a quantity of wax, and had it weighed against pennies: and when a weight of wax equivalent to seventy-two pennies had been measured off, he ordered his chaplains to make therewith six candles of equal size, each being twelve inches in length, and having the inches marked upon them. By this method those six candles kept burning day and night without intermission, for twenty-four hours, before the reliques of different saints, which always accompanied the king.

Moreover, as into other things, so into the administration of justice, the king was wont to make most careful inquiries. For he used to scrutinize with great sagacity the judgments which were given in his absence nearly all over the kingdom; considering of what character they were, whether just or unjust; and if he discovered any iniquity therein, he would mildly interrogate the judges, either by himself or by his confidants, why they gave such unrighteous judgments? whether it was by reason of ignorance or malevolence? if it was for the love, or fear, or hate of any person, or for the hope of pecuniary reward? If the judges asserted that they had so given judgment because they had been unable to arrive at a better conclusion, he discreetly and quietly rebuked their ignorance and foolishness, saying, " I marvel greatly at your insolence in having, by God's grace and mine, taken upon yourself the office and rank of men of wisdom, and yet neglected the study and practice of wisdom. Wherefore I command you, either at once to resign the exercise of the earthly power which you now hold, or to apply yourselves much more seriously than heretofore to the study of wisdom." Alarmed at these words, and as though they had suffered the greatest possible punishment, the ealdormen and governors strove to devote all their powers to the study of jurisprudence, so that almost all the ealdormen who had been illiterate from their infancy, and his governors and thanes, applied themselves in a wonderful manner to learn the study of learning, preferring to undergo the labour of such unwonted pupilage, rather than to lose their situations. If any one was not able to attain much proficiency in learning, by reason of old age or of the over-slowness of a hitherto unexerted intellect, he would make his son (if he had one), or some other relation, or in default thereof, one of his freemen or serfs, whom he had long previously employed to read to him, recite Saxon compositions to him, by day or by night, whenever he had leisure. Those old men sighed heavily, and heartily grieved, that in their youth they had not attended to such pursuits; thinking the youths of that present time fortunate in being able to study successfully the liberal arts, but considering themselves unfortunate in that they neither studied them while young, nor were able to acquire them in old age, though they most ardently desired to do so.[1]

---

[1] From the year 849 to this point, Florence has liberally used Asser; henceforward the Saxon Chronicle may be consulted with advantage.

A.D. 888.

A.D. 889.   A noble ealdorman, named Beocca, carried the alms of king Alfred and the West Saxons to Rome.   In the same year Aethelsuith, the king's sister, and queen of Burhred, king of the Mercians, died and was buried at Ticino [Pavia].   In this year too, and in the same month, died Aethelwold the ealdorman, and Aethelred archbishop of Canterbury; the latter was succeeded in the archbishopric by Pleigmund, a man of extensive literary acquirements.

A.D. 890.

A.D. 891.   Abbot Beornhelm carried the alms of king Alfred and of the West Saxons to Rome.   Guthrum, king of the Northmen, to whom, as we mentioned before, king Alfred stood godfather, and gave the name of Aethelstan, died this year.   He dwelt with his people in East Anglia, and first took up his abode in, and possession of that province, after the martyrdom of the holy king Edmund.   In the same year, the oft-mentioned pagan army left the Seine and went to a place called Santlaudan [St. Lo], situate between France and Armorica : the Britons fought against them, and gained the victory, some being slain with the edge of the sword, some put to flight, and some drowned in the river.

A.D. 892.   The aforesaid pagan army left Eastern, and went to Western France : but before their fleet could join them, the emperor Arnulf, with the East Franks, Old Saxons, and Bavarians, attacked the land army and put it to flight.   Three Scots, named Dusblan, Mahbethu, and Malmumin, desiring to lead a pilgrim's life for the service of God, took with them provisions for one week, fled secretly from Ireland, and, entering a canoe made of only two hides and a half, and although they were unfurnished with sails or other instruments of navigation, by wonderful chance they landed in Cornwall, after a voyage of seven days : they afterwards paid a visit to king Alfred.   In the same year died Swifneh, the best teacher among the Scots.   In this year, too, a star called a comet was seen about rogation week.[1]

A.D. 893.   The land and sea forces of the Pagans, quitting Eastern France, came to Boulogne, and thence, with their horses, crossed over to Kent in two hundred and fifty ships, landed at the mouth of the river Limene [Lyme], which runs out of the great forest of Andred.   From the mouth of that river they drew their ships four miles up into the forest, where they demolished a half-built fort, which was inhabited by a few villeins, and built for themselves a stronger one at a place called Apultreo [Appledore].   A short time afterwards the pagan king, Haesten, entered the mouth of the river Thames with eighty light barks, and built for himself a fortress in the royal vill called Middleton.

A.D. 894.   The Pagans who inhabited Northumbria swore to a lasting peace with king Alfred : so did those who dwelt in East Anglia, and in addition gave six hostages.   But they broke the treaty, and as often as the pagan army residing in Kent quitted their forts for the purpose of plundering, they too either joined

---

[1] " On the death of bishop Swithelm of Shirburn, Ethilwerd succeeded."   A. by a second scribe.

with the latter, or went plundering on their own account wherever they could. When king Alfred heard of it he took a portion of his army with him, leaving part at home, as was his custom, and, placing some as garrisons in forts and cities, marched with great expedition into Kent, and encamped between the two pagan armies, in a place of great natural strength, inasmuch as it was surrounded on all sides by streams, whose waves ran high, and whose banks were steep, and woods jutted out on all sides : in order that if the enemy took the field for the purpose of plundering or fighting, he might engage them without delay. But they, going about robbing in bands, sometimes on horse, and sometimes on foot, took every opportunity of plundering in those places where they ascertained there were none of the king's forces. But nearly every one, not only in the king's army, but also in the cities, let no opportunity slip of slaughtering them day and night, when they were off their guard, and thereby so disquieted them, that, quitting Kent, which they had again ravaged, they all in a body deserted the place where they had settled : for they had all gone out together for the purpose of plunder, when they first took up their abode in those districts. But this time they took a larger and richer booty, and determined to cross the river Thames with it, reach East Saxony, and join their fleet, which they had sent on before. They were, however, prevented by the king's army, and, a battle being fought near Feornham, in which they lost not only their booty, but also the horses which they had brought from beyond sea, they were all put to flight, and retreated to an island formed by the windings of the river Colne, having crossed the Thames at a place where there was no ford. There they were kept in a state of siege for such a long time, that the king's army began to lack provisions, and the appointed period came as well for its return home, as for the advance of the other army. That army therefore returned home, and king Alfred with his division made all haste to arrive at the spot ; but the Pagans, inasmuch as their king was grievously wounded, and they could not therefore carry him off with them, still kept their position. While king Alfred was yet on his march for the purpose of dislodging the enemy, behold, news came to him that the Pagans of Northumbria and East Anglia had collected two hundred and forty ships, and that some had sailed round to the south coast of England with a hundred ships, and others to the northern coast of [that part of] England with forty ships, and that the former were besieging Exeter, and the latter a certain fort in Devonshire, with a strong force. When he heard this, the king was moved, not to fear by reason of the audacity of the enemy, but to fury by reason of his subjects being besieged. He collected all his cavalry without delay, and rode to Exeter, leaving a small force behind to carry on the war against the enemy of whom he had previously been in pursuit. Then they marched to London, and [thence] in company with the citizens, and those who had come to their assistance from the western part of England, arrived at Beanflot [Benfleet] : for they heard that a large army which had been posted at Apultreo [Appledore] had assembled there, and that king Haesten and his army had arrived from Middleton and had constructed a fort there, but had then again made a descent for the object of plunder. This Haesten had, a short time previously, on the occasion of the peace which he made with king Alfred, given very many hostages, and at king Alfred's request, had allowed his two sons to be baptized; king Alfred standing godfather for one, and the most noble ealdorman Aethered for the other. But on his arrival at Beanflot [Benfleet], king Haesten hastily threw up fortifications, and anon laid waste the confines of the kingdom of his son's godfather, Aethered. So a severe battle was fought with the Pagans, and the Christians put them to flight at the first onset, demolished their works, took whatever they found there, carried their wives and children to London, sunk some of their ships, burned others, and transported some to London and Rochester. They took king Haesten's wife and two daughters before he returned to Beanflot [Benfleet], from his plundering expedition, and brought them to king Alfred. He did no injury to them, for, as we have before mentioned, one of the boys was his own, and the other was earl Aethered's godson; but, again making peace and receiving hostages, he not only restored to the suppliant father his wife and children, but presented him with a large sum of money. Afterwards the king went to Exeter, at the earnest entreaty of his said subjects there; and then, the Pagans, terrified at his arrival, retired to their ships, and returning to their old place of abode, began plundering in the neighbourhood of the city called in the English tongue Cissaceastre [Chichester], situate in the province of the South Saxons. But being put to flight by the citizens, the greater number of them were either killed or wounded, and very many of their ships were captured. In the meantime, the pagan army which was routed by the Christians at Benfleet, as before mentioned, came to a city of East Saxony, called in the English tongue Sceobyrig [Shoebury], and there built themselves a strong fort. Being joined by numerous Pagans from Northumbria and East Anglia, they began plundering, first, on the banks of the Thames, and then on the banks of the Severn. The noble ealdormen, Aethered, Athelm, and Athelnoth, and others of the king's thanes, to whom he had entrusted the defence of different forts, towns, and cities, not only eastward of Pedreda [the river Parret], but also westward of Selwood, and not only on the north, but also on the south of the Thames, not being able to endure any longer this terrible annoyance, collected a great army against the enemy, and were joined by auxiliaries from the Welsh who dwelt west of the Severn. Uniting in one body, they marched in pursuit of the enemy, and came up with him at Buttingtun, on the banks of the Severn, and presently besieged from both sides of the river the fortress into which he retreated. After the lapse of some weeks, some of the Pagans died of starvation, and some, having been reduced to eat their horses, broke out of the fort, and engaged with the besiegers on the eastern bank of the river. After slaughtering many thousands of the Pagans, and putting all the rest to flight, the Christians remained masters of the field of carnage. In this battle the most noble Ordeah and many of the king's thanes were slain. On the approach of winter the fugitive Pagans, after having retired to East Saxony, and reached their forts and ships, again collected a great army from East Anglia and Northumbria. Leaving their wives, their wealth, and their ships in East Anglia, and quitting their fortresses, they made a forced march, and entered the City of Legions [Chester], (which was at that time deserted,)[1] called in Saxon Legeceastre, before the lieutenants of the army of king Alfred and Aethered, who were in pursuit, could overtake them. However, they cut off and slew some of them, rescued the flocks of cattle and sheep which they had taken while pillaging, besieged the city for two days, burnt some of the corn-fields, and turned their horses into the others. These events occurred within the interval of one year after they [the Pagans] came from Gaul to the mouth of the river Limene.

A.D. 895. The oft-mentioned pagan army, having nothing whereon to subsist (for the Christians had deprived them of everything), invaded the territory of the North Britons, and laying it waste far and wide, carried off immense booty. Not daring to retrace their steps through Mercia, for fear of the Mercians, they marched first through Northumbria, and then through the country of the Middle Angles; and having rejoined their wives and ships in East Anglia, betook themselves to a little island in the sea, called Meresig [Mersey], off the eastern coast of East Saxony. In the same year they drew their ships up the river Thames, and after a while up the river Ligea [Lea], and began to build themselves a fort hard by that river, twenty miles from London.

A.D. 896. In the summer a great number of the citizens of London, assisted by many people from neighbouring places, endeavoured to demolish the fort which the Pagans had built: but the latter stoutly resisted the attack, and the Christians were put to flight, four of king Alfred's thanes being killed. In the autumn that king encamped not far from the city, in order to prevent the Pagans from forcibly carrying off the people's crops. One day, as he was riding along the banks, he looked out for a spot where he could block up the bed of the river, and so prevent the Danes from bringing out their ships: and without delay he caused impediments to be erected on both sides. When the Pagans heard this, they again left their wives in East Anglia, and abandoning their ships, fled swiftly, on foot, to a place called Quatbricg; and building a fort, passed the winter there. The Londoners transported some of the ships to London, and broke up others.

A.D. 897. In the summer, a portion of the pagan army which had wintered at Quatbricg went to East Anglia, and another portion to Northumbria; some of them remained in those places, but others procured ships and went over to the river Seine. Oh! with what incessant troubles, with what grievous trials, in what dreadful and lamentable ways was all England harassed, not only by the Danes who held possession of different parts of her, but also by

---

[1] The passage within parentheses does not occur in any copy of the Saxon Chronicle.

these children of Satan. Nevertheless, for the space of three years she suffered much more, from a murrain among the cattle, and a mortality among the nobility, many of whom, chiefly the king's thanes, died during that period. Among these were Suithulf, bishop of Rochester; Ealheard, bishop of Dorchester; Ceolmund, the Kentish ealdorman; Beorhtulf, the East-Saxon ealdorman; Eadulf, the king's thane in South Saxony; Beornulf, wic-reeve of Winchester; Ecgulf, the king's horse-thane, and very many others; but those above named were of the highest dignity. In the same year the army of the Pagans who inhabited East Anglia and Northumbria grievously annoyed the West Saxons, pillaged stealthily along the sea-coast, chiefly in long, swift ships, which they had constructed several years before. To oppose them, king Alfred ordered ships to be built, of twice the length and twice as deep, which were swifter and did not heel so much, so that by their weight they might destroy the enemy's ships. These were put to sea, with orders from the king to take as many prisoners as they could, and to kill such of the enemy as they could not take alive. So in that year twenty ships full of Danish pirates were taken, some of whom were slain, and the rest were brought to the king alive, and hung on gibbets.[1]

A.D. 898, 899.

A.D. 900. Healhstan, bishop of London, died, and was succeeded by Theodred. Eardulf, bishop of Lindisfarne, died, and was succeeded by the pious Cuthard.

A.D. 901. Renowned, warlike, and victorious,—a careful provider for the necessities of widows, wards, orphans, and the poor,—the most skilful of Saxon poets,—adored by his subjects, and affable and most liberal to all,—a man of prudence, fortitude, justice, and temperance,—most patient under the infirmity which troubled him,—most discreet and persevering in enforcing the judgments [of his courts of law],—most watchful and devout in the service of God,—Alfred, king of the Anglo-Saxons, son of the most pious king Aethelwulf, died on Wednesday, the 5th of the [2]kalends of November [28th Oct.], in the fourth indiction, having reigned twenty-nine years and six months; he was buried at the New Monastery in Winchester, and waits the robe of a blessed immortality and the glory of the resurrection with the just. He was succeeded by his son Eadward, surnamed the Elder, inferior to his father in the cultivation of literature, but his equal in dignity and power, and his superior in glory. For, as will be shown hereafter, he extended the limits of his kingdom much beyond what his father had done; moreover, he built many cities and towns, and rebuilt some which had been destroyed: he wrested from the hands of the Danes all East Saxony, East Anglia, Northumbria, and several Mercian provinces, which they had long possessed: after the death of his sister Aegelfled he obtained possession of, and retained, the

[1] "On the death of Æthelward, bishop of Shirburn, the see was vacant for seven years, in consequence of the pressure of the enemy." This addition in A. by another scribe, is copied from Malmesbury.
[2] See the Saxon Chronicle, which assigns a different date.

whole of Mercia : all the kings of the Scots, Cumbrians, Strathclyde
Britons, and West Britons submitted to him : many were the kings
and earls whom he conquered in battle and slew. By a woman of
noble birth, named Egwina, he had Aethelstan, his first-born son ;
by his queen Eadgiva he had three sons, namely, Eadwin, Eadmund,
and Eadred, a daughter named Eadburg, a virgin of the greatest
piety, and three other daughters. Of the latter, Otto, the emperor
of the Romans, married one ; another was married to Charles, king
of the Western Franks, whose aunt by the father's side, a daughter
of the emperor Charles, was married to Aethelwulf, king of the
West Saxons ; Sihtric, king of the Northumbrians, married the
third daughter. The etheling Aethelwald, cousin-german of this
king Eadward, took forcible possession of one of the king's towns,
called Tuueoxbeam,[1] without the permission of the king or his
magnates ; he also took another, called Winburn,[2] (where, as we
have before mentioned, St. Cuthburg, sister of king Ini, built a
monastery for nuns,) and fortified it with gates and bars. On
hearing this, king Eadward assembled an army, and encamped near
Winburn, at a place called in the English tongue Baddanbyrig.[3]
The king immediately commanded the etheling to evacuate the
place without delay. He refused, saying that he would live or die
there. But his boast was vain : for, affrighted at the numbers of
the king's army, he fled away by night, and went to Northumbria,
where he requested the Danes to allow him to join them, not so
much in the capacity of a leader as of a comrade : they, very shortly
afterwards, made him their king. The king complained much of
the indignity of such a desertion, and sent men to pursue him with
all speed : but finding it impossible to take him, he seized the nun
whom he had married against her will and without the permission
of the bishops, and ordered her to be taken back to her monastery
at Winburn.

A.D. 902.
A.D. 903. The stout ealdorman, Aethulf, brother of queen Ealhsuith, the mother of king Eadward, and Virgil, a venerable Scotch
abbot, died. The priest Grimbold also, a man of great holiness,
and one of the masters of king Alfred, entered on the joys of the
heavenly kingdom.
A.D. 904. The men of Kent fought a battle against a host of
Danish pirates, at a place called Holme ; [4]and they got the victory.
The etheling Aethelwold returned to England from the parts beyond
sea, with a numerous fleet, some of which he had purchased, and
the rest whereof he had got together from East Anglia.
A.D. 905. [5]An eclipse of the moon occurred. The etheling
Aethelwold invited the Danes who dwelt in East Anglia, by a
promise of a large share in the spoil, to accompany him in a plundering expedition into the Mercian territory. They agreed ; and

[1] Twynam, or Christchurch, in Hampshire.
[2] Wimborne, in Dorsetshire.   [3] Badbury, in Dorsetshire.
[4] This clause of the sentence does not occur in the Saxon Chronicle.
[5] The Saxon Chronicle, and more correctly, assigns this eclipse to the previous
year.

shortly afterwards, in company of king Eohric and king Aethelwold, burst into the Mercian territory, and, thirsting for prey, destroyed everything with fire and sword, and at last came to Creccanford [Cricklade], where, having crossed the Thames and marched through the wood which is called in Saxon Bradene, they attacked all the surrounding vills, destroying everything they could find. And now, enriched with immense booty, they prepared, in high spirits, to return home : but in vain; for the invincible king Eadward marched after them with an army which he had hastily collected, laid waste their territory, situate between the boundary of the possessions of the holy king Eadmund and the river Ouse, and then, being about to return from his expedition, ordered all the army to retire also. But the Kentish men scorned to obey, and remained there. The king sent seven messengers commanding them to retire; but they, nought fearing his hostility, boldly persisted in their resolution. Hearing this, the Danes quickly collected their forces into one body, came down upon them suddenly, and fought a severe battle, in which many fell on both sides. On the Kentish side there fell ealdorman Sigulf and his son Sigbriht, ealdorman Sigelm, Eadwold, one of the king's thanes, the abbot Kenulf, and many others. The Danes lost their king Eohric, the etheling Aethelwold, whom they had chosen for their king, and very many more than the English : nevertheless, they remained masters of the field of carnage. Queen Ealhsuith, mother of king Eadward, a devout handmaid of Christ, and foundress of a monastery of nuns at Winchester, departed this life.

A.D. 906. A star called a comet appeared. The pagan army from East Anglia and Northumbria, finding by experience that king Eadward was invincible, concluded a treaty of peace with him, at a place called in the English tongue Ittingaford.[1]

A.D. 907.

A.D. 908. [2]The city which is called in the British tongue Karlegion, and Legeceastre in the Saxon, was rebuilt, by the direction of ealdorman Aethered and Aegelfled.

A.D. 909. Denulf, bishop of Winchester, died.

A.D. 910. Denulf being dead, St. Frithestan succeeded him in the bishopric. [3]The bones of St. Oswald, king and martyr, were translated from Barthoneig [Bardney] to Mercia. The invincible Eadward, on the occasion of the Danes breaking the peace which they had concluded with him, sent an army of West Saxons and Mercians into Northumbria : when they arrived there, they ravaged the country incessantly for nearly forty days, slew many of the Danes, and took back with them many captives and immense booty, compelling their kings (whether they wished it or not) to renew with king Eadward the peace which they had broken.

A.D. 911. [4]A great battle was fought between the English and the Danes at Teottanhele, in the province of Stafford, and the English were victorious. In the same year the victorious king Eadward collected a hundred ships, and, selecting soldiers, ordered them on

---

[1] " Kyneferth, bishop of Lichfield, being dead, Tunbriht succeeded." A. in a second hand.   [2] See the Saxon Chronicle, A.D. 907.
[3] See the Saxon Chronicle, A.D. 909.   [4] See the Saxon Chronicle, A.D. 910.

board, with instructions to meet him in Kent, whither he intended
to go by land.   In the meantime the army of the Danes who dwelt
in Northumbria, having again broken the peace which they had
concluded with him, and rejected all the civil rights which he and
his nobles had offered to them, with rash boldness invaded the
Mercian territory ; for they thought that their great strength lay in
their ships, and that they could go wherever they pleased without
being obliged to hazard an engagement.   When the king heard this,
he sent an army of West Saxons and Mercians to drive them back.
This army met with them on their return from the scene of their
devastations, at a place called in the English tongue Wodnesfeld,
and slew their two kings, Eowils and Halfdene, brothers of king
Hinguar, two earls named Ohter and Scurfa,[1] nine of their chief
nobles, and several thousand men besides ; and putting all the rest
to flight, they recaptured all the spoil.   Aegelfled, the lady of the
Mercians, built the city of Bremesbyrig.

A.D. 912.   After a well-spent life, Aethered, a most honourable
man, ealdorman and patrician, lord and subregulus of the Mercians, died : after whose death, his wife Aegelfled,[2] daughter of king
Alfred, kept possession for some time, and with a strong hand, of
the kingdom of the Mercians, with the exception of London and
Oxford, which her brother king Eadward retained for himself.

A.D. 913.   [3]Aegelfled, the lady of the Mercians, came on the
2d of the nones of May [6th May], with an army, to a place called
Sceargete, and built a fortress there ; and afterwards built another
at a place called Bricge [Bridgenorth], on the western side of the
river Severn.   About the feast of St. Martin [11th Nov.] a city
was built by king Eadward's order to the north of Hertford,
between the rivers Memera, Ficcea, and Lyge [Lea].

A.D. 914.   After Easter [17th April], a pagan army from Northampton and Leogereceastre [Leicester], went plundering in the
province of Oxford, and slew very many people in the king's vill
of Hokenertune, and in many other vills.   Shortly after that one
returned home, they equipped another composed of cavalry, and
sent it towards Ligetun [Leighton ?] in the province of Hertford.
But the natives assembled in force to resist them, and after slaying
many of them and putting the rest to flight, captured some horses
and the greater part of their arms, and re-captured the booty which
they had taken.   Leaving a portion of the army to build a city on
the south side of the river Lige [Lea], king Eadward marched,
after the rogations [23d May], with the greater part of it into
East Saxony, and encamped at Mealdune : he remained there
until a city was built at Witham and fortified ; and a great number
of the people there, who were in subjection to the pagans, submitted themselves and all their property to him.   In the beginning
of the summer Aegelfled, the lady of the Mercians, went with the

---

[1] B. reads "Scrufa."
[2] The events concerning this lady appear to have been known to Florence in
some copy of the Saxon Chronicle, which represented them in a more authentic
state than any which has descended to our time.
[3] See Saxon Chronicle, A.D. 912.

Mercians to Tomeweorthigina [Tamworth], and by God's help restored that city. Thence she went towards Stafford, and built a fort on the north side of the river Sowe. The winter of this year was very long and severe.[1]

A.D. 915. Wereferth, bishop of the Hwiccas, a man of great learning and piety, died, and was succeeded by Aethelhun, [2] abbot of Beorclea [Berkeley]. At [3] the beginning of summer Aegelfled, the lady of the Mercians, built the city called Eadesbyrig, and at the end of the autumn another called Werewic [Warwick]. The [4] pagan pirates, who nearly nineteen years before had quitted Britain and gone into Gaul, returned to England from the province called Lydwiccum [Armorica or Brittany], with two earls named Ohter and Rhoald, and sailing round by West Saxony and Cornwall, at length entered the mouth of the river Severn. They immediately invaded the territory of the northern Britons, and utterly destroyed everything at the river's side which they could lay hands on. They captured Cymelgeac,[5] bishop of the Britons, at a plain called Yrcenefeld, and carried him in great triumph to their ships: [however] king Eadward ransomed him not long afterwards for forty pounds of silver. Shortly afterwards, the whole army landed, and marched towards the aforesaid plain for the purpose of pillage; but the men of Hereford, and Gloucester, and very many from the neighbouring cities, went out suddenly to meet them, and fought a battle with them. Rhoald, one of the enemy's chiefs, and brother of the other chief, Ohter, and a great portion of the army were slain: the rest were put to flight, and were driven by the Christians into an enclosed field, where they were so long and closely beset that they gave hostages as a security for their departure as quickly as possible from king Eadward's territories. So the king posted different portions of his army in suitable places on the south side of the river Severn, from Cornwall to the mouth of the river Avon, in order to prevent the pirates from laying waste any portion of those provinces. But, leaving their ships on the strand, they plundered stealthily by night to the east of Weced [Watchet], and again at a place called Portlocon [Portlock-bay]; but on each occasion all were slain by the king's army, except such as fled like cowards to their ships. Overpowered by this defeat, they retired to an island called Reoric [Flat-holme], where they remained until a number of them died of starvation: so, driven by necessity, they sailed first to Deomede,[6] and afterward, in the autumn, to Ireland. After these events, the unconquered king Eadward went with an army to Buckingham, and there remained for thirty days, and caused fortresses to be built on each side of the river Ouse, by reason whereof Turketil one of the Danish chiefs, and all those of the higher class from Bedford, and many from Northampton, found

---

[1] " On the promotion of Athelm, bishop of Wells, to the archiepiscopal see of Canterbury, Wulfhelm succeeded."   A. addition.

[2] These three words are supplied from A.; they do not occur in B. or in Howard's editions.

[3] See Saxon Chronicle, A.D. 914.   [4] Id. A.D. 918.

[5] He was bishop of Llandaff.   [6] Demetia, or South Wales.

themselves obliged to surrender to the king. Cuthard, bishop of Lindisfarne, died, and was succeeded by Tilred.

A.D. 916. Before the feast-day of St. Martin [11th Nov.] the unconquered king Eadward went to Bedford, which town and its inhabitants submitted to him; and, remaining there for thirty days, ordered a town to be built on the southern bank of the river Ouse. After our Lord's Nativity [25th Dec.], Aegelfled, the lady of the Mercians, built two cities, namely Cyricbyrig [Cherbury] and Weadbyrig: she also built a third called Runcofan [Runcorn]; but that was before the Nativity.

A.D. 917. Before the feast of the Nativity of St. John the Baptist [24th June], the unconquered king Eadward went to Meldun [Maldon], and rebuilt the city there; and did not leave until he had strengthened it with a garrison. In this year the above-named earl Turketil was permitted and assisted by king Eadward to go over to Gaul with all his men. The venerable abbot Ecgbriht was unrighteously slain on the 6th of the kalends of July.[1] Three nights afterwards Aegelfled, the lady of the Mercians, sent an army into the territory of the Britons to take the castle of Bricenanmere [Brecknock], who having captured the castle, carried away captive, into Mercia, the wife of the British king, and thirty-four men besides. Rollo, first duke of Normandy, died, and was succeeded by his son William.

A.D. 918. By king Eadward's command the city called Towcester was built before Easter [5th April], and another was built after Easter, and another about the rogations, at Wigingamere [Wigmore]. After the feast of the Nativity of St. John the Baptist [24th June] the Pagans of Northampton and Leogerecestre [Leicester] broke the peace, came to Towcester, and attacking it the whole day, endeavoured to take it by storm; but, the inhabitants resisting with all their might, and the people of the neighbourhood hastening to their assistance, they were all put to flight. They afterwards made frequent nocturnal attacks in the province of Buckingham on those who were unprepared for resistance, carrying away captive not only men but cattle, and slew many people between Birnwood and Aylesbury. About that time an army of the pagan inhabitants of East Anglia and Huntingdon left the strong fort which they had built at Huntingdon, and built a still stronger one at Temesford [Tempsford], thinking forsooth that they should be able to regain by battle the territory which they had lost. Thence they marched out to attack Bedford. But as soon as their arrival was known, the city guard went out to battle against them: an engagement took place, and the enemy was routed and put to flight, and very many of them were slain. After a short interval the Pagans again assembled from East Anglia, East Saxony, and Mercia, and came to the town called Winganmere [Wigmore], and passed the whole day in attacking it: but those within defended it stoutly, and the enemy retired; nevertheless as they retired they carried off much booty. After this, in the summer time, a multitude collected on all sides from the

---

[1] The Saxon Chronicle reads, on the 16th of the kalends of July [17th June].

neighbouring cities and districts under king Eadward's dominion, went to Tempsford, besieged, assaulted, took, burned, and rased it, and slew the pagan king, the earl Toglea, and earl Mannan his son, and also his brother, and all who offered any resistance; the remainder they took prisoners, and destroyed everything they could find. From that time the Danish power gradually decreased, and the English power increased from day to day. Just before the kalends of August [7th Aug.], Aegelfled, lady of the Mercians, took Derby by storm, and obtained possession of the province: four of its best thanes were slain while fighting bravely at the city gate. After this, in the autumn, a great multitude from Kent, Surrey, East Saxony, and the neighbouring cities and districts, united, and marched in a body to Colchester, and, laying siege to it, continued the assault until they took it. They slew all the inhabitants except a few who escaped, and pillaged everything they found inside. The Danes dwelling in East Anglia were very incensed thereat, and, burning to revenge their injuries, marched to Maldon, with pirates, whose assistance they had hired, and besieged and assaulted it, until such time as the people of the neighbouring places came to the aid of the English. When the Danes heard that aid had arrived, they raised the siege. The English, seeing this, pursued and attacked them fiercely, slew several thousands of the pirates and of the others, and put the rest to flight. Shortly afterwards, the invincible king Eadward led a West-Saxon army to Passaham, and remained until the city of Towcester was surrounded with a stone wall. In consequence, the Danish earl Thurferth, seeing that he could no longer make head against the energetic movements of the king, made his submission to the king, as did also the Danish and English citizens and natives of Northampton. After this the king returned home, and immediately sent another army to Huntingdon, to repair and renovate the city, and place a garrison therein. All which being achieved, such of the people of that province as had survived the cruelties of the Danes, thankful at having escaped from their hands, sought the peace and protection of the king, and tendered their submission to him. After a few days, the king, having assembled a West-Saxon army, marched to Colchester, put its walls in a perfect state of repair, and placed in it a stipendiary garrison. In the meantime, many of the English of East Anglia and East Saxony, who for nearly thirty years had been under the iron sway of the Pagans, joyfully placed themselves under the king's protection. The Danish inhabitants of East Anglia also presented themselves to him, and swore that neither by sea nor by land would they do anything to the king's prejudice. A Danish army from Cambridge came also, and made choice of him for their lord and master: moreover, at his request, they took oaths to the same effect.[1]

A.D. 919. At the beginning of this year, Aegelfled, the lady of the Mercians, by God's help, peaceably got possession of Leogereceastre [Leicester], and received the submission of nearly all the Danish army which was stationed there. Moreover, the Danes

[1] " On the death of Wustan, bishop of Sherburn, Aethelbald succeeded." A. addit.

stationed at York, some with promises, and the rest with oaths, engaged that they would in all things act according to her pleasure and by her direction. After the rogations [31st May], the most invincible king Eadward the elder marched with an army to Stanford, and fortified a strong tower on the south bank of the river Welund ; and he received the submission of not only the Danes who were in possession of a fort on the northern bank of the said river, but also of all who belonged to it. During these transactions, that is to say, on the 19th of the kalends of June,[1] the king's sister, Aegelfled, lady of the Mercians, died; in the eighth year from the year when she commenced her firm but moderate undivided sway over the Mercians : she was a very virtuous woman, and renowned for her prudence and justice : she left an only daughter, named Aelfwinna, by the sub-regulus Aethered, heir to her kingdom. Her body was taken to Gloucester, and honourably buried in St. Peter's church. The king, on hearing of her death, hastened to Tomwrthigene [Tamworth], and reduced it to submit to him. Thence he moved his army, and went to Snotingaham [Nottingham], ordered the city, which had been captured, to be repaired, and stationed both English and Danes therein. In course of time he received the submission first of all the Mercians and the Danish inhabitants of Mercia, and then of three British kings named Howell, Clyttwic, and Juthwal, together with all their subjects.[2]

A.D. 920. In the autumn the most invincible king Eadward went to Thelwall, built a city there, and left some of the bravest of his army as a garrison. Moreover he sent an army of Mercians into Northumbria to repair the city of Mameceaster [Manchester], and stationed valiant soldiers therein. He afterwards entirely deprived his niece Aelfwinna of her Mercian kingdom, and ordered her to be taken into West Saxony.

A.D. 921. [3]Just before the feast of the Nativity of St. John the Baptist [24th June], the most invincible king Eadward the elder went with an army to Nottingham and built a city on the southern bank of the river Trent, facing the city on the opposite bank, and ordered a strong bridge connecting both cities to be built. Thence he went with the army to Beadecanwealla [Bakewell], built a town not far off, and stationed powerful soldiers therein. At that time [Constantine] the king of the Scots and all his subjects, Reignald king of the Danes, with the English and Danes who dwelt in Northumbria, and the king of the Strathclyde Britons and all his subjects, adopted king Eadward the elder for their chief and lord, and made a lasting peace with him.

A.D. 922. On the 17th of the kalends of November [16th Oct.], Aethelward the etheling, brother of king Eadward, died, and was carried to Winchester and buried there. Aethelhun bishop of the Hwiccas died, and was succeeded by Wilferth.

A.D. 923.[4]

[1] Compare the Saxon Chronicle as to this date.
[2] "On the death of Adhelstan, bishop of Wilton, Odo succeeded." A. in a second hand.　　　[3] See the Saxon Chron. A.D. 924.
[4] "On the death of Bernech, bishop of Selsey, Kinred succeeded." Addit. in A.

A.D. 924.   After accomplishing many signal achievements, Eadward the elder, that most invincible king of the English, who had ruled with the greatest glory over all the inhabitants of Britain, whether English, Scots, Cumbrians, Danes, or Welsh, departed this life at a king's vill named Fearndun, in the twenty-fourth year of his reign and the fifteenth indiction, leaving the helm of state to his son Aethelstan. His body was carried to Winchester, and buried, as was usual with kings, in the new monastery. His son Alfward shortly afterwards died at Oxford, and was buried in the same place with his father. Aethelstan was proclaimed king at Kingston, which signifies the king's town, and was crowned with due ceremony by Athelm, archbishop of Canterbury.   In his time the energetic Dunstan was born in the West-Saxon territory.

A.D. 925.   The energetic and glorious English king Aethelstan gave his sister, with great state and magnificence, in marriage to Sihtric, king of the Northumbrians, who was of Danish descent.

A.D. 926.   Fiery rays in the northern sky were seen throughout all England.   Shortly afterwards Sihtric, king of the Northumbrians, died; and king Aethelstan expelled Guthferth, his son and successor, from his kingdom, and added it to his own dominions. Moreover, he routed in battle and put to flight all the kings throughout Albion; namely, Huwal, king of the West Britons, then Constantine, king of the Scots, and Wer, king of the Wenti [people of Monmouthshire].   He also expelled Aldred, the son of Eadulf, from the royal town which is called in the English tongue Bebbanbirig [Bamborough].   Seeing that they could no longer withstand his power, they all sued for peace; and meeting at a place called Eamot, on the 4th of the ides of July [12th July], made a solemn treaty with him, ratifying it with an oath.

A.D. 927.

A.D. 928.   Tilred, bishop of Lindisfarne, died, and was succeeded by Wigred.[1]

A.D. 929.   Wilferth, bishop of the Hwiccas, died, and was succeeded by Kinewold.

A.D. 930.

A.D. 931.   Eadulf, bishop of Devonshire, died, and was buried at Cridiantune [Crediton].

A.D. 932.   Frithestan, bishop of Winchester, a man of the most exalted piety, continued to reside at Winchester, after the holy man Birnstan had been ordained his successor in the bishopric. He was a saintly man; every day he sang mass for the repose of the dead, and at night went round the cemeteries, singing psalms for their souls' weal.   Once, after having been thus engaged, and when by way of conclusion he had said, "May they rest in peace," he heard as it were a mighty host answer from out of the graves, "Amen."

A.D. 933.   Saint Frithestan died.

A.D. 934.   Aethelstan, the brave king of the English, went to Scotland with a powerful fleet and a large army of cavalry, and laid waste the greater part thereof, in revenge for Constantine, king of the Scots, having broken the peace which he had concluded with

[1] " On the death of Tunbriht, bishop of Lichfield, Aelle succeeded."   A. add.

him. King Constantine was thereby forced to surrender his son as a hostage, and give suitable presents, to him [Aethelstan] : peace being restored, the king returned to West Saxony. In this year St. Birstan, bishop of Winchester, died.

A.D. 935. The pious monk Alfeag, surnamed the Bald, a relation of St. Dunstan, was appointed to the bishopric of Winchester.

A.D. 936.

A.D. 937. Otto, the 90th [emperor] of the Romans, reigned thirty-six years and ten months. Aethelstan, king of the English, gave to him one of his sisters in marriage.

A.D. 938. Anlaf, the pagan king of the Irish and of many islands besides, at the instigation of his father-in-law, Constantine, king of the Scots, entered the mouth of the river Humber with a powerful fleet. King Aethelstan and his brother, Eadmund the etheling, met him with their army at a place called Brunanburgh ; and after a battle which lasted from daybreak until evening, slew five reguli and seven earls, whom the enemy had brought with them as auxiliaries, shedding more blood than had ever before in England been shed in battle, and returned home in great triumph, having driven the kings Anlaf and Constantine back to their ships: the latter were terribly cast down by the destruction of their army, and returned to their country with a very few followers.

A.D. 939.

A.D. 940. On Wednesday, the 6th of the kalends of November [27th Oct.], in the fourteenth indiction, and the sixteenth year of his reign, Aethelstan, the brave and glorious king of the English, departed this life, at Gloucester, and was carried to the city of Maidulf [Malmesbury], and buried there with due honour. His brother Eadmund, then in his eighteenth year, succeeded him in the kingdom.

A.D. 941. The Northumbrians, preferring rebellion to the fealty which they owed to Eadmund, the glorious king of the English, chose Anlaf, king of the Northmen, to be their king. In the same year died Alfred, bishop of Sherborne.

A.D. 942. Eadmund, the glorious king of the English, completely wrested five cities, namely, Lincoln, Nottingham, Derby, Leicester, and Stamford, from the hands of the Danes, and brought all Mercia under his dominion. He became mighty and glorious, by the counsels of God's servant, Dunstan ; whom, after dignifying with several honourable offices, he promoted to the abbacy of the monastery of Glastonbury, where he had been brought up. On the 16th of the kalends of January [17th Dec.], William, duke of Normandy, the son of Rollo, was slain : he was succeeded by his son Richard.

A.D. 943. On the occasion of Aelfgiva, the saintly queen of the glorious king Eadmund, giving birth to her son Eadgar, the holy abbot Dunstan heard voices on high, giving praise and saying, " In the time of the child who is now born, and of our beloved Dunstan, the English church shall have peace." This year the said king stood godfather to king Anlaf (whom we have before mentioned) at the font of holy regeneration, and made him a kingly present : a short time afterwards he presented Reignold, king of the Northumbrians, to be confirmed by the bishop, and adopted him for a son.[1]

A.D. 944. Eadmund, the glorious king of the English, expelled from Northumbria two kings, namely, Anlaf, son of king Sihtric, and Reignold, son of Guthferth ; and brought that province under his own sway. Wigred, bishop of Lindisfarne, died, and was succeeded by Uhtred ; on the death of the latter, Sexhelm was ordained to supply his place ; but he, too, dying a few months afterwards, Aldred was consecrated in his stead.

A.D. 945. Eadmund, the glorious king of the English, laid waste Cumberland, and gave it to Malculm, king of the Scots, on condition of his being faithful to him, by sea and by land.

A.D. 946. On the feast day of St. Augustine, the teacher of the English, being Tuesday, the 7th of the kalends of June [26th May], in the fourth indiction, Eadmund, the glorious king of the English, after a reign of five years and seven months, was killed at a royal vill called Pucelecirce [Pucklechurch], by Leof, an atrocious robber, while attempting to prevent the murder of his steward by the said Leof : his body was carried to Glastonbury, and buried by the abbot St. Dunstan. Thereupon Edred, his brother and next heir, succeeded to the kingdom, in due course ; and on Sunday, the 7th of the kalends of September [16th August], was crowned king, at Kingston, by St. Odo, archbishop of Canterbury. He [Edred] brought all Northumbria under his dominion, in the same manner as his brother had previously done, and received an oath of fidelity from the Scots.

A.D. 947, 948.[2]

A.D. 949. Wulfstan,[2] archbishop of York, and all the nobles of Northumbria, swore fealty to Edred, the glorious king of the English, at a vill called Taddenes-scylf : but they did not long abide by their oath ; for they elected for their king a certain Dane of royal descent, named Irc.

A.D. 950. In return for the defection of the Northumbrians, Edred, the famous king of the English, overran the whole of Northumbria. In the course of this devastation the monastery of Ripon, formerly built by the holy bishop Wilfrid, was destroyed by fire. But as the king was on his return home, an army issued from the city of York, and made great havoc among the rear of his army, at a place called Casterford. The king was exceedingly indignant at this, and meditated returning and utterly laying waste all that district. The Northumbrians, alarmed at the news, deposed Irc, whom they had chosen for king, made amends to the king, with personal obeisance, for the indignity, and with presents for the damage which he had sustained, and appeased his anger with a large sum of money.

---

[1] " On the death of Aethelbald, bishop of Sherburn, Aelfred succeeded." A. in another hand.

[2] " On the death of Kenred, bishop of Selsey, Guthred succeeded." A. in another hand. In this year B. has inserted some passages respecting St. Ethelwold, and the foundation of the monastery of Abingdon, which, following the example of Petrie, are here omitted.   [3] See Saxon Chronicle, A.D. 947.

A.D. 951. St. Aelfeag, bishop of Winchester, surnamed the Bald, (the same who gave St. Dunstan monk's and priest's orders,) departed this life : he was succeeded in the bishopric by Alfsin.

A.D. 952. Edred, the renowned king of the English, placed Wulstan, archbishop of York, in close custody at Juthanbirig [Jedburgh?], on account of accusations of different kinds, which were constantly being brought against him. Moreover, he ordered many of the citizens of Thetford to be executed, in revenge for their having murdered abbot Aldhelm.

A.D. 953. Aethelgar, bishop of Crediton, departed in Christ, in the twenty-first year of his office, and was buried at Crediton. By the advice of the holy abbot Dunstan, the venerable Alfwold succeeded to the bishopric.

A.D. 954. Wulstan, archbishop of York, was released from prison, and restored to his episcopal functions at Dorchester.

A.D. 955. In the tenth year of his reign, Edred, the glorious king of the English, fell sick, and his life was despaired of ; so he sent swift messengers commanding the attendance of the blessed abbot Dunstan, his father confessor. The latter accordingly set out in all haste for the palace. As he was half way on his journey, he heard a voice from on high say distinctly, " Now king Edred rests in peace." Thereupon his horse, unable to endure the awfulness of the angel's voice, fell dead ; but the rider was unhurt. The king's corpse was carried to Winchester, and was honourably interred by the said abbot Dunstan, in the Old Monastery. His nephew, Eadwi the etheling, son of king Eadmund and his saintly queen, Alfgiva, succeeded him in the empire, and in the same year was crowned king at Kingston, by Odo, archbishop of Canterbury.

In this year died Louis [the Fourth], king of the West Franks, son of king Charles by a daughter of Eadward the elder, king of the English. Liutolf also, son of the emperor Otto, by another daughter of the same king Eadward, died, [1]and was buried in the choir of St. Alban's monastery, at Mentz.

A.D. 956. The holy abbot Dunstan, being banished by legal sentence by Eadwi, king of the English, crossed over the sea, and, being honourably received by Arnulf,[2] a man of royal descent, remained during his exile at a monastery called Blandinium [at Ghent].

On the 7th of the kalends of January [26th Dec.], Wulstan, archbishop of York, died, and was buried at Oundle. He was succeeded by the venerable Oskitell.

A.D. 957. Eadwi, king of the English, was deserted in disgust by the Mercians and Northumbrians, because of his evil management of the government with which he had been entrusted ; and they chose his brother, Eadgar the etheling, to be king over them : so the government was split in two, and the river Thames was the boundary of the two kingdoms. Shortly afterwards Eadgar, king of the Mercians, recalled the holy abbot Dunstan with honour and glory.

Not long after this, Coinwald, bishop of Worcester, a man of great humility and [devotion to the] monastic profession, died ; the holy abbot Dunstan was elected to succeed him in the bishopric,

[1] The conclusion of this year is from Marianus.   [2] Count of Flanders.

and was consecrated by Odo, archbishop of Canterbury. In the following year Edgar, king of the Mercians, committed to his charge the see of London, which had become vacant by the death of its pious bishop [Brihthelm].

A.D. 958. Alfsi, bishop of Dorchester, died ; and was succeeded by Brihthelm, a man of piety, modesty, humility, and affability. The holy Odo, archbishop of Canterbury, separated Eadwi, king of the West Saxons, and Alfgiva, either because she was reported to be his kinswoman, or because he preferred her to his own wife. In the same year this archbishop, a man of great talent and of praiseworthy virtues, gifted moreover with the spirit of prophecy, departed this life, and was borne by angels to paradise. He was succeeded by Alfsin, bishop of Winchester; and Brihthelm[1] was ordained bishop of Winchester in Alfsin's stead.

A.D. 959. As Alfsin, archbishop of Canterbury, was journeying to Rome to obtain the pall, he was overtaken on the Alps by frost and snow, and perished. Eadwi, king of the West Saxons, died, having reigned four years, and was buried in the new monastery at Winchester. His brother Eadgar, king of the Mercians, then in his sixteenth year, was elected by all the English people to succeed him, in the 510th year from the coming of the Angles into Britain, and the 363d year from the arrival in England of St.Augustine and his companions; and thus united the two kingdoms.

Brihthelm, bishop of Dorchester, was elected to the archiepiscopal see of Canterbury, but being incompetent for that high office, he left Canterbury at the king's command, and returned to the church which he had lately quitted. Thereupon, St. Dunstan was (after deliberation) appointed primate and patriarch of the chief metropolis of England. Wrought upon by the prudent counsels of him and of other wise men, Eadgar, king of the English, punished the wicked in every quarter, reduced the rebels to submission by his severity, showed favour to the just and humble, repaired and enriched God's ruined churches, removed all vanities from the monasteries of the clerks, collected great numbers of monks and nuns, to the glory of the Almighty Creator, and supplied more than forty monasteries. All these he honoured as his brethren, and loved as his very dear children, personally exhorting the pastors whom he placed over them to admonish them that they should live according to the rule and without reproach, and so be well pleasing in all things to Christ and the saints. He was discreet, mild, humble, kind, liberal, merciful, powerful in arms, warlike, and defended the rights of his kingdom by his army as became a king; he taught the people to reverence the nobles, and the nobles to obey the laws of the empire ; he enacted good laws and enjoyed a most peaceful reign : he neither had occasion to undertake an offensive or defensive war ; but by God's assistance and his own prudence, fortitude, justice, and moderation, he preserved during his life the limits of his kingdom : and as he was fierce as an angry lion against his enemies, not only did the princes and kings of the islands fear him, but some of the kings of other countries were

---

[1] A. here adds that he was the fifth bishop of Wells.

fear-stricken and terrified at the report of his wisdom and energy, while his munificence gained for him the love, honour, and great applause of others. The emperor Otto the First, who had married his aunt, sent splendid presents to him, and made a treaty of lasting peace with him.

A.D. 960. In the third indiction, St. Dunstan went to the city of Romulus, and received the pall from pope John [the Twelfth]; and afterwards, by peaceful stages, returned to his own country. After the lapse of a few months he went to the king's palace, and knocking [so to speak] at the portals of the king's devotion, he humbly requested and entreated him to advance to the dignity of bishop of Worcester St. Oswald, a religious, meek, and humble monk, nephew of his predecessor Odo, and one whom he had ascertained to be truly abounding in the fear of the Lord, and in the holy practice of virtue. King Eadgar granted the holy Dunstan's request, and St. Oswald was authorized by him in the bishopric.[1]

A.D. 961, 962.

A.D. 963. The venerable abbot St. Aethelwold,[2] who had been brought up by St. Dunstan, succeeded to the bishopric of Winchester; and in the same year he filled the old monastery with monks, the clerks being expelled by the king's orders. He was the king's chief counsellor, and took the chief part in persuading him to expel clerks from the monasteries, and cause monks and nuns to be placed therein.[3]

A.D. 964. Eadgar, the pacific king of the English, married Alftryth, daughter of Ordgar, ealdorman of Devonshire, after the death of her husband Aethelwold, the glorious ealdorman of the East Angles; and had by her two sons, Eadmund and Aethelred. He had also previously by Egelfleda the Fair, surnamed Ened,[4] a son called Eadward, afterwards king and martyr; and by St. Wulfrith a daughter named Eadgith, one of God's most pious virgins. In this year the king placed monks in the new monastery [at Winchester] and at Middleton, and made Aethelgar abbot over the former, and Kineward abbot over the latter.

A.D. 965, 966.

A.D. 967. The pacific Eadgar, king of the English, placed nuns in the monastery of Rumsey, which his grandfather Eadward the elder, king of the English, had built, and made the holy Mearwinna abbess over them.

A.D. 968. The pacific Eadgar, king of the English, made the pious Sidemann abbot over the monks assembled at Exeter. Aldred, bishop of Lindisfarne, died, and was succeeded by Alfsi.

A.D. 969. Edgar, the pacific king of the English, commanded St. Dunstan, archbishop of Canterbury, the blessed St. Oswald,

---

[1] " On the death of Guthard, bishop of Selsey, Alfred succeeded." A. addit.
[2] B. here adds, " of the church of Abingdon."
[3] " Osgar, a monk of the same church, is appointed abbot of Abingdon, in the stead of Aethelwold; but because he had left the church of Abingdon undedicated before he had received his own bishopric, when he was consecrated, he and St. Dunstan, and certain other bishops, dedicated it to the honour of Mary the Mother of God, on the fifth of the kalends of January [28th Dec.]." B. addition.
[4] That is, " The Swan."

bishop of Worcester, and St. Aethelwold, bishop of Winchester, to expel the clerks and place monks in the larger monasteries of Mercia. Thereupon St. Oswald accomplished what he desired, and expelled such of the clerks of the church of Worcester as refused to become monks: but on their compliance this year, as he relates, he made monks of them, and appointed Winsin, a monk of Ramesey, a very religious man, to be their dean.

A.D. 970. On Friday the ides of July [15th July], in the thirteenth indiction, the reliques of the holy and venerable bishop Swithun, after having been buried one hundred and ten years, were removed from the tomb by the venerable bishop St. Aethelwold, and most honourably re-interred in the church of the apostles Peter and Paul [at Winchester], by Aelfstan, abbot of Glastonbury, and Aethelgar, abbot of the New Monastery. In the same year Osulf, bishop of Wiltshire, died, and was buried at Wilton: the venerable abbot Alfstan[1] was ordained in his stead.[2]

A.D. 971. Eadmund the etheling, son of king Eadgar, died, and was buried with due honour in the monastery of Rumsey. In the same year Alfeag, ealdorman of Southampton, died, and was buried at Glastonbury. Shortly afterwards, Ordgar, ealdorman of Devonshire, father-in-law of king Eadgar, died, and was buried at Exeter.

A.D. 972. Eadgar, the pacific king of the English, ordered the church of the New Monastery, which had been begun by his father, king Eadmund, but perfected by himself, to be solemnly dedicated. In this year Alfwold, bishop of Devonshire, died, in the nineteenth year of his bishopric, and was buried at Crediton.[3] Oskitell, archbishop of York, died, and his kinsman, St. Oswald, bishop of Worcester, was elected to succeed him in the archbishopric.

A.D. 973. [4]Stephen was pope, being the one hundred and thirty-fourth. From him St. Oswald received the pall. On the day of Pentecost, being the 5th of the ides of May [11th May], in the first indiction, Eadgar, the pacific king of the English, being then in the thirtieth year of his age, received the benediction of the holy bishops Dunstan and Oswald, and all the other English bishops, in the city of Acamann [Bath], and was crowned and anointed king with great honour and glory. Thence, after a short time, he sailed round the north part of Britain with a large fleet, and landed at Chester.[5] Eight petty kings, namely, Kynath, king of the Scots, Malcolm, king of the Cumbrians, Maccus, king of several isles, and five others, named Dufnall, Siferth, Huwall, Jacob, and Juchill, met him there as he had appointed, and swore that they would be faithful to him, and assist him by land and by sea. On a certain day they attended him into a boat, and when he had placed them at the oars, he himself took the helm and skilfully steered it down the river Dee, and thus, followed by the whole company of earls and nobles, in this order went from the palace to the

[1] "Alfgar," A.
[2] "On the death of Aelfred, bishop of Selsey, Eadelm succeeded." A. in another hand.
[3] "He was succeeded by Sideman." A. addit.
[4] This first sentence is from Marianus.   [5] " ad Legionum civitatem.'

monastery of St. John the Baptist. After having prayed there, he returned with the same pomp to the palace. As he was entering it, he is reported to have said to his nobles, that then his successors might boast themselves to be kings of the English, when, attended by so many kings, they should enjoy the pomp of such honours. Brihthelm, bishop of Somerset, died, and was buried at Wells: he was succeeded by Kineward, abbot of Middleton.

A.D. 974. In this year there was a tremendous earthquake all over England. [1] Eberger, archbishop of Cologne, gave to the Scots for ever the monastery of St. Martin in Cologne: Minborin, a Scot, was the first abbot thereof.

A.D. 975. The pacific king Eadgar, sole ruler of England, the flower and glory of our former kings, not less renowned among the English, than Romulus among the Romans, Cyrus among the Persians, Alexander among the Macedonians, Arsaces among the Parthians, or Charles the Great among the Franks, after having finished in royal style all that he took in hand, departed this life on Thursday, the 8th of the ides of July [8th July], in the third indiction, being in the thirty-second year of his age, the nineteenth of his reign over Mercia and Northumbria, and the sixteenth of his reign over all England, leaving his son Eadward heir to his kingdom and qualities. His body was carried to Glastonbury, and buried there according to kingly custom. He collected, during his life, a fleet of 3,600 stout ships; after Easter, in every year, he used to make 1,200 of them assemble on the east, 1,200 on the west, and 1,200 on the north shore of the island; he would then sail to the western with the eastern fleet, and sending that back would sail to the northern with the western fleet, and dismissing it in turn, would sail with the northern fleet back to the western: thus every summer he used to sail round the whole island; performing this brave feat by way of defence against foreigners, and for the purpose of inuring himself and his subjects to war. In the winter and the spring he used to make a progress through every province in England, and diligently inquire into the mode of the administration of justice, and the observance of the laws by the nobles, so that the poor might not suffer oppression at the hands of the powerful. By the former practice he excited [national] courage, by the latter the love of justice; and by each he consulted the interests of the kingdom and commonweal. Hence, all his enemies' fear, and all his subjects' love for him increased. At his death the whole kingdom sustained a shock, and after the glad time of peace, which existed all his life, troubles began to come in on every side. For, dazzled by numerous presents, Alfere, chief of the Mercians, and very many nobles of the kingdom, expelled the abbots and monks from the monasteries in which the pacific king Eadgar had placed them, and introduced clerks and their wives. But this piece of madness was opposed by some conscientious men, to wit, Athelwin, ealdorman of the East Angles, a friend of God, and his brother Alfwold, and the pious ealdorman, Brihtnoth; who, meeting together, declared that they could not permit the monks, who were

[1] The remainder of the year is from Marianus.

the depositaries of all the religion of the kingdom, to be expelled therefrom. They then assembled a great army, and bravely defended the monasteries of the East Angles. In the meantime the nobles of the kingdom were very much at variance in the matter of electing a king : for some chose the king's son, Eadward, and some chose his brother Aethelred. On this account the archbishops Dunstan and Oswald, with a great number of bishops, abbots, and ealdormen, met in a body, and chose Eadward, according as his father had desired; and after his election crowned and anointed him king. Kyneward, bishop of Somerset [Wells], died. A comet star was seen in the autumn.

A.D. 976. There was a great famine in England. In the same year the magnificent earl Oslac was unjustly expelled from England.[1]

A.D. 977. A great synod was held at a vill called Kyrtling, in East Anglia. At another synod, which was afterwards held at Kalne, a king's vill, all the elders of England who were there assembled, with the exception of St. Dunstan, fell through the [floor of an] upper chamber ; some of them were killed, and some barely escaped with their lives. A third synod was held at Ambresbyrig. Sidemann, bishop of Devonshire [Crediton], died.[2]

A.D. 978. Eadward, king of the English, was wickedly slain at Corvesgeate [Corfe], by his own servants, acting under the commands of his step-mother, queen Alftryth, and was buried at Wareham, without any royal pomp. His brother, Aethelred, the noble etheling, [a youth] of fascinating manners, handsome countenance, and graceful appearance, was, after Easter, in the sixth indiction, to wit, on Sunday, the 18th of the kalends of May [14th April], crowned king at Kingston, by the holy archbishops Dunstan and Oswald, and ten bishops. Alfwold, bishop of Dorchester, died, and was buried at Sherborne. At midnight, there was seen throughout all England a cloud, which was sometimes of a blood-colour, and sometimes fiery ; it afterwards broke out into rays of different colours, and disappeared about day-break.

A.D. 979. Alfer, ealdorman of the Mercians, came with a multitude of people to Werham, and ordered the sacred corpse of the precious king and martyr Eadward to be disinterred : when it was unwrapped it was discovered to be fresh and free from all signs of death or corruption ; so they washed it, and put new grave-clothes on it. They carried it to Shaftesbury and entombed it with due honours.

A.D. 980. On the 6th of the nones of May [2d May], Aethelgar the venerable abbot of the New Monastery was made bishop of Selsey.[3] In the same year Southampton was laid waste by the

---

[1] In A. another hand has added the following note :—" On the death of Algar, bishop of Wilton, Alfstan, a monk of St. Aethelwold, at Abingdon, succeeded; for whom Siric was substituted."

[2] " His body was conveyed to Abingdon, and honourably buried there in the aisle of St. Paul the apostle." B. addit. Another hand adds, in A., that he was succeeded by Alfric.

[3] An addition in A. by another hand states that this was on the death of Eadelm.

Danish pirates, and nearly all the citizens were either slain or carried away captives. Shortly afterwards the same horde laid waste the isle of Thanet. In this year too the city and province of Chester were laid waste by Norwegian pirates.

A.D. 981. The pirates, who in the preceding year had laid waste Southampton, now pillaged St. Petroc, the confessor's monastery [at Padstow] in Cornwall: they afterwards made frequent piratical descents on the shores of Devonshire and Cornwall. Aelfstan, bishop of Wiltshire, died, and was buried at Abingdon:[1] Wulgar succeeded him in the bishopric. Wulstan, dean of Glastonbury, a man of exalted piety, died.

A.D. 982. Three ships, full of pirates, landed at Dorsetshire, and laid waste Portland. London was destroyed by fire. Aethelmar, ealdorman of Hampshire, and Eadwin, ealdorman of the South Saxons, died; the latter was buried at Abingdon, and the former in the new monastery at Winchester. Hereluve, abbess of Shaftesbury, and Wulfuin, abbess of Werham, departed this life. [2]In the same year, Otto the Second, emperor of the Romans, went to Greece, and there fell in with an army of the Saracens, who were on their way to plunder the Christians: he engaged with them, and after great slaughter on both sides, gained the victory. As he was returning home, Otto, the son of his brother Liutolf, who was the son of the emperor Otto the First by a daughter of Eadward the elder, king of the English, died.

A.D. 983. Alfer, ealdorman of the Mercians, a relation of Eadgar, king of the English, died, and was succeeded in his dignity by his son Alfric.

A.D. 984. On the kalends of August [1st Aug.], in the second indiction, St. Aethelwold, bishop of Winchester, departed this life. He was succeeded by Alfeag, abbot of Bath, who had assumed the religious habit in the monastery of Deorhyrste.[3]

A.D. 985. [4]The venerable monk Eadwin was made abbot of the monastery of Abingdon.

A.D. 986. Aethelred, king of the English, on account of some quarrel, laid siege to the city of Rochester; but seeing that it would be difficult to reduce it, retired in wrath, and laid waste the lands of [the church of] St. Andrew the apostle. Alfric, ealdorman of the Mercians, son of the ealdorman Alfer, was driven out of England. [5]Abbot Minborin, a Scot, died on Sunday the 18th day of July, in the monastery of St. Martin, at Cologne. Kilian succeeded him.

A.D. 987. In this year two diseases unknown to the English in former ages, to wit, a fever among men, and a murrain among

---

[1] " honourably, as he himself had desired," B. addit.

[2] The remainder of the year is from Marianus.

[3] B. adds, "for at this time Osgar, abbot of Abingdon, had deceased."

[4] Instead of this and the following year, B. enters under the years 984 and 985 the following passage:—" A certain powerful person named Aelfric was then the mayor of the royal household, who had a brother named Edwin, a monk. Aelfric procured, by the payment of a sum of money to the king, that this brother of his should be appointed abbot of Abingdon, and so it was managed."

[5] The conclusion of the year is from Marianus.

beasts, called in the English tongue " scitta," which in Latin may be said to signify a flux of the bowels, grievously troubled all England, and raged in every part of it beyond expression, causing great mortality among the inhabitants and the wholesale destruction of cattle.

A.D. 988.   Wecedport [Watchet] was pillaged by the Danish pirates, who also slew a thane of Devonshire named Goda, Stren-wold, a very brave soldier, and several others.   However, the loss was greatest on the side of the Danes, and the English remained masters of the field of carnage.   On [1]Saturday the 14th of the kalends of June [19th May], in the first indiction, the blessed archbishop Dunstan departed this life, and went to his abode in the heavenly city.   Aethelgar, bishop of Selsey, succeeded him in the archbishopric, and held it for one year and three months.

A.D. 989.

A.D. 990.   [2]Siric was consecrated archbishop of Canterbury. Eadwin, abbot of Abingdon, died, and was succeeded by Wulgar. Alfsy, bishop of Lindisfarne, died, and was succeeded by Aldhun.

A.D. 991.   In this year the Danes, under the command of Justin and Guthmund, the son of Stercan,[3] laid waste Ipswich. Byrthnoth, the bold ealdorman of the West Saxons, shortly after-wards fought a battle against them near Maldon ; but, after great slaughter on both sides, the ealdorman fell, so the Danish fortune prevailed.   Moreover in this year, first of all, and that by the advice of Siric, archbishop of Canterbury, and the ealdormen Aethelward and Alfric, a tribute of ten thousand pounds was paid to the Danes, as the price of their cessation from the frequent plunderings, burnings, and slaughters, which they used to make on the sea coast, and their concluding a lasting peace.   On Tuesday the 6th of the ides of November [8th Nov.], St. Oswald the arch-bishop, aided by divine assistance, and cheered by the co-operation of Aescwi, bishop of Lincoln [Dorchester], consecrated the mona-stery of Ramsey, which he and Aethelwin, ealdorman of the East Angles, the friend of God, had built.

A.D. 992.   On Monday the 2d of the kalends of March [29th Feb.], in the fifth indiction, St. Oswald the archbishop departed this life, and entered on the joys of the heavenly kingdom : he rests at Worcester in St. Mary's Church, which he built from the foundations.   He was succeeded by the venerable Aldulph, abbot of Medehamstead, to whose abbacy Kenulph succeeded.   Shortly after the departure of St. Oswald, died the renowned ealdorman [of East Anglia] Aethelwin, the friend of God : although younger than his brothers Aethelwold, Alfwold, and Agelsin, he excelled them in meekness, piety, goodness, and justice ; and, as being a man of exalted virtue and purity, was, we may believe, received

---

[1] MS. A., in another hand, reads, " to whom succeeded Athelgar, first ap-pointed abbot to Newminster by the blessed Ethelwold, of Winchester, after-wards bishop of the South Saxons, whose see was then at Selsey, in which place he was succeeded by Ordbriht."
[2] " Siric, bishop of Wilton, succeeded Aethelgar, archbishop of Canterbury; he expelled the monks, and introduced clerks into Canterbury." A. in another hand.
[3] Steitan, B.

among the dwellers in Paradise. His body was carried with great pomp to Ramsey, and was buried by St. Alfeag, bishop of Winchester. By the advice and command of Aethelred, king of the English, and of his nobles, the strongest ships from every part of England were assembled at London. The king manned them with chosen soldiers, and put them under the command of ealdorman Alfric, whom we have mentioned before, ealdorman Thored, Aelfgar, bishop of Wiltshire, and Aescwi, bishop [of Dorchester], with orders to catch the Danish army, if they could, in some port, and enclose them there. But the ealdorman Aelfric secretly sent a messenger to the enemy, advising them to be on their guard, and take care that they were not unexpectedly surrounded by the king's army. The ealdorman himself, (a singular example of wickedness,) on the very night before the English had determined to fight a pitched battle with the Danes, secretly went over with all his men to the Danish fleet, and shortly afterwards made a shameful retreat along with them. The king's fleet finding this out pursued the fugitives with all haste ; one ship only was taken, and was pillaged after all on board had been massacred ; the rest were accidentally encountered in their flight by only the Londoners and East Saxons, when, an engagement taking place, many thousand Danes were slain. Moreover they captured the ealdorman Alfric's ship, with the soldiers and arms therein, just after he had fled from it, and they got the victory.

A.D. 993. In this year the aforesaid army of the Danes broke into Bamborough, and carried away all that they found therein. Thence they directed their course to the mouth of the river Humber, and took much spoil in Lindsey and Northumbria, burning many vills and slaying a great number of people. The natives assembled and went up against them in great haste ; but just as they were about to give battle, their generals Frana, Frithogist, and Godwin, being Danes by the father's side, betrayed their men and were the first to flee. The same year king Aethelred ordered Algar, son of the said ealdorman Alfric, to be deprived of eye-sight.

A.D. 994. On the day of St. Mary's nativity [8th Sept.], Anlaf, king of the Norwegians, and Suuein, king of the Danes, arrived at London, with ninety-four ships, and presently endeavoured to break in and burn it : but by the aid of God and his mother Mary, they were repelled by the citizens, with no small loss to their army. Maddened with rage and sorrow, they retired thence the same day, and first on the sea-coast of East Saxony and Kent, and then in South Saxony and the province of Hampshire, burnt the vills, laid waste the fields, destroyed as many as possible of both sexes by fire and sword, and carried off great spoil. Finally, they obtained horses by force, and madly scouring numerous provinces, spared neither women nor children of tender age, but slew all with brutal ferocity. Then king Aethelred, by the advice of his nobles, sent messengers to them, promising that if they would entirely desist from their barbarities, he would pay to them a tribute and a regular stipend. They agreed to the king's terms, and returned to their ships, and so assembled their whole army at Southampton, and wintered there. The whole of the stipend was paid by West Saxony, but the tribute, which amounted to sixteen thousand pounds, was made up by all England.

In the meanwhile, Alfeag, bishop of Winchester, and the noble ealdorman Aethelward, went to king Anlaf by order of king Aethelred, and, hostages being given, conducted him in state to Andover, a royal vill, where the king was staying: the king received him graciously, caused him to be confirmed by the bishop, adopted him for his son, and made him a splendid present. He, on his part, promised to king Aethelred that he would never more come with an army to England, and then returned to his fleet: at the beginning of summer he sailed for his own country, and faithfully observed his promise.

A.D. 995. A comet was seen. [1]Siric, archbishop of Canterbury, died, and Alfric, bishop of Wiltshire, succeeded him. Lindisfarne-Ii is the name of an island commonly called Halig-Ealand [Holy Island], and is situate in the sea. Every day the going down of the tide leaves a dry road across for such as wish to go there. Cuthbert, and his predecessors and successors, for a long time had their episcopal see in this island. But when Hinguar and Hubba ravaged England [A.D. 875], Eardulf, who was then bishop of Lindisfarne, and those who belonged to his church, took the uncorrupted corpse of St. Cuthbert, and quitted the island on account of the cruelties of the barbarians, and for some years, with the body of St. Cuthbert, shifted his residence from place to place, until the episcopal see was fixed at a place called Kunege-ceastre [Chester-le-street], which happened in the time of Alfred, king of the English. After the lapse of many years, in the reign of Aethelred, king of the English, the sacred corpse was brought to Durham, as had been foreshown by an oracle from heaven, and the episcopal see was fixed there. For this reason, the holy Beda places the church of Lindisfarne where the episcopal see originally was; for in Beda's time Durham was not known. However, in the year 995 from the Incarnation of Christ, the episcopal see was transferred to Durham.

A.D. 996. Alfric, archbishop of Canterbury, was consecrated.

A.D. 997. The Danish army, which had remained in England, sailed round West Saxony, entered the mouth of the river Severn, and ravaged sometimes North Wales, sometimes Cornwall, and then Watchet in Devonshire, burning many vills, and slaying a multitude of men. Thence returning to Penwithsteort [Land's-End], and arriving at the mouth of the river Tamar, which divides Devonshire and Cornwall, and meeting with no opposition, they landed, and kept on burning as far as Lideford, and renewed their massacres. In addition, they burned the monastery of Ordulf, ealdorman of Devonshire, called Tavistock: they then returned to their ships, laden with immense booty, and wintered there.[2]

---

[1] " On the death of Siric, archbishop of Canterbury, he was succeeded by Alfric, bishop of Wilton, who had been a monk of Glastonbury; who, on his part, was succeeded at Wilton by Brihtwold." A. in another hand.

[2] " Sigar, bishop of Wells, being dead, Alwin succeeded." A. addit.

A.D. 998. The aforesaid army of Pagans landed at the mouth of the river called Frome, and laid waste the greater part of Dorsetshire. It thence made frequent expeditions to the Isle of Wight, and back again to Dorsetshire, hunting after plunder as usual ; and as often as it lay at the Isle of Wight, it got provisions from South Saxony and Hampshire. Many times was an army collected to oppose this terrible nuisance ; but as often as they were about to join battle, the English, either victims to treachery or some mischance, turned their backs, and left the victory in the hands of the enemies.[1]

A.D. 999. The oft-mentioned army of Pagans entered the mouth of the river Thames, and went up the Medway to Rochester, and in a few days laid siege to it. The men of Kent assembled to drive them back, and fought a sharp battle with them ; but, after great slaughter on both sides, the Danes remained masters of the field of carnage. They then took horse, and laid waste nearly all the western portion of Kent. On hearing this, Aethelred, king of the English, by the advice of his nobles, collected a fleet and a land army. But while the fleet was being got ready, the generals of the army day by day made some excuse for delaying the expedition, and in consequence were a great burden on the people. The end of it was that neither the fleet nor the land army performed any action of general benefit, but oppressed the people, wasted a great deal of money, and exasperated the enemy.

A.D. 1000. [2]This year the aforesaid army of Danes went to Normandy. King Aethelred laid waste nearly the whole of the Cumbrian territory. He gave orders to his fleet to sail round North Wales, and meet him at an appointed place : it was prevented from so doing by the violence of the wind, but, nevertheless, laid waste the island of Mona.

A.D. 1001. The body of St. Ivo, the archbishop, was discovered. The aforesaid army of Pagans returned from Normandy to England, and entered the mouth of the river Exe, and presently set out to storm the city of Exeter ; but while endeavouring to make a breach in the wall, it was driven back by the citizens, who defended their city with valour. Exasperated beyond measure at this, the said army roamed through Devonshire, as usual burning the towns, laying waste the fields, and slaughtering the inhabitants. So the men of Devonshire and Somersetshire joined in a body, and fought a battle with them at a place called Penho ; but the English, not having many soldiers among them, were unable to withstand the multitude of the Danes, and took to flight ; so the Danes made great havoc among them, and got the victory. After that, having supplied themselves with horses, they scoured nearly all Devonshire, doing more mischief than ever, and having obtained immense booty, went back to their ships. Thence they directed their course

---

[1] "Aelfric, bishop of Devonshire, being deceased, Alfwold succeeded, and to him Alwold the Second." A. in another hand.

[2] From this point Petrie has preserved in his text of Florence all the passages which that writer has introduced into his own work from Marianus Scotus; and in this respect his edition has been followed.

to the Isle of Wight, and plundered as usual without opposition, sometimes there, sometimes in Hampshire, and sometimes in Dorsetshire, attacking the inhabitants and burning the towns, to such an extent, that the fleet dared not assail them by sea, nor the army by land ; whereat the king was not a little sad, and the people were downcast beyond expression.

A.D. 1002. Aethelred, king of the English, having consulted with the magnates of his kingdom, thought it prudent to make a treaty with the Danes, and to give them a stipend and pay a tribute by way of appeasing them, and inducing them to cease from their evil doings. Leofsi the ealdorman was sent to them on this matter; and on his arrival urged them to accept the stipend and tribute. They were well pleased at his mission, accepted the terms, and fixed the amount of tribute for which they were to keep peace. Shortly afterwards, twenty-four thousand pounds were paid to them. In the interval, the said ealdorman Leofsi slew Eafic, the king's high-reeve, a man of noble birth ; at which the king was very wroth, and drove him out of the country. In the same year, king Aethelred married Emma, called in Saxon Alfgiva, the daughter of Richard the First, duke of the Normans. On Wednesday the 17th of the kalends of May [15th April], in the fifteenth indiction, and the twenty-fifth year of Aethelred, king of the English, Aldulf, arch-bishop of York, in company with his bishops, abbats, priests, monks, and religious men, disentombed the bones of the arch-bishop St. Oswald, and deposited them with great pomp in a chest prepared for the purpose: he, too, shortly afterwards, to wit, on the 2d of the nones of May [6th of May], died, and was buried in the church of St. Mary at Worcester ; abbot Wulstan succeeded him. Moreover, in this year king Aethelred ordered all the Danes who were in England, both great and small, of either sex, to be slain, inasmuch as they had endeavoured to deprive him and his nobles of their lives and kingdom, and to get possession of the whole realm of England.

[1] Henry, the 93d [emperor] of the Romans, reigned twenty-two years. He was elected by the people on Sunday the 7th of the ides of June [7th June], and on the same day was consecrated and crowned king by Willigis, archbishop of Mentz, before the altar of St. Martin.

A.D. 1003. [2] Octavian was pope, being the 138th. In this year Suuein, king of the Danes, broke into the city of Exeter through the stupidity, carelessness, and surrender of Hugo, a Norman earl,[3] whom queen Emma had set in command over Devonshire; and he plundered it, broke down the wall from the eastern to the western gate, and having gotten great booty went back to his ships. After this, as he was ravaging Wiltshire, a strong army out of Hamp-shire and Wiltshire assembled, and went up boldly and perseveringly to fight against the enemy. But when the armies had approached so near as to be in sight of each other, the before-mentioned

---

[1] To the end of the year is from Marianus.
[2] This first sentence is also from Marianus.
[3] The Saxon Chronicle calls him " ceorl."

ealdorman Alfric, who then was in command of the English, immediately began his old practices—feigned illness, and began to vomit, saying that he was grievously ill, and therefore could not engage the enemy. The army, seeing his inactivity and cowardice, very sorrowfully turned aside from the enemy without fighting; as it is said in the old proverb, " If the leader trembles in the fight, all the other combatants are thereby made more fearful." Suuein, seeing the irresolution of the English, led his army to the city of Wilton, and pillaged and burned it. In like manner he burned Saerbyrie [Old Sarum], and then returned to his ships. [1] Kilian, a Scot, and abbot of St. Martin in Scotland, died on the 19th of the kalends of January [14th Dec.]. Helias, a Scot, succeeded him.

A.D. 1004. Suuein, king of the Danes, came with his fleet to Norwich, and pillaged and burned it. Then Ulfketell, ealdorman of the East Angles, a man of great bravery, inasmuch as he had come up on a sudden and had no time to collect an army, took counsel with the magnates of East Anglia, and made peace with him. But three weeks afterwards he [Sweyn] broke the treaty, and, landing his forces secretly, attacked Thetford, and pillaged it ; remained there for one night, and early the next morning burned it. The ealdorman Ulfketell, when he heard this, ordered some of the natives to break up the enemies' ships : but they either dared not do this or else neglected his orders. He, however, in the meantime, secretly and with all celerity assembled his army, and went up boldly against the enemy. As they were marching back to their ships he met them with a very inferior force, and fought a very severe battle with them: the slaughter was great on both sides, and the chief men of the East Anglians fell; the Danes were barely able to make their escape, but if the East Anglians had been in full force they would never have got back to their ships. They themselves confessed that they had never in England sustained such a stubborn and fierce attack as that made on them by ealdorman Ulfkettel.

A.D. 1005. In this year there was a great and terrible famine in England ; in consequence, Suuein, king of the Danes, went back to Denmark ; but only to return after a short time.[2]

A.D. 1006. Alfric, archbishop of Canterbury, died,[3] and was succeeded by Alfeag, bishop of Winchester, [4] Kenulf being appointed to the bishopric of the latter. King Aethelred deprived his especial favourite Wulfgeat, son of Leoueca, of his possessions and dignities ; [this he did] because of his unjust decrees and haughty deeds. The crafty and perfidious Edric Streona, plotting mischief against the noble ealdorman Alfhelm, prepared a great feast for him at Shrewsbury : and on his arrival pursuant to the invitation, Edric welcomed him like an intimate friend. On the third or fourth day of the entertainment, having laid an ambush,

---

[1] From Marianus to the end of the year.
[2] " On the death of Alwin, bishop of Wells, Living succeeded, who was also called Athelstan." A. addit.
[3] "and was buried at Abingdon, of which he had been a monk ; but during the reign of king Cnut he was translated to his own see." B. addit.
[4] A. adds that he was abbot of Burgh [Peterborough].

he took him into a wood to hunt. There, when all were occupied in the chase, the hangman of Shrewsbury, called Godwin Porthund (which signifies, The town's hound), whom Edric had long before steeled to commit the crime by great gifts and many promises, suddenly leapt out of ambush, and vilely slew the ealdorman Alfhelm. A short time afterwards, his sons Wulfheag and Ufeget were by king Aethelred's orders deprived of sight at Cocham, where he was then staying. Kenulf, bishop of Winchester, died, and was succeeded by Aethelwold.

In the succeeding month of July, an immense fleet of the Danes came over to England, landed at the port of Sandwich, destroyed everything that lay in their way with fire and sword, and took large booty, sometimes in Kent and sometimes in South Saxony. Wherefore king Aethelred assembled an army from Mercia and West Saxony, and resolved to fight stoutly against them : they, however, were by no means desirous of meeting him in the field, but went perpetually plundering from place to place, and then by-and-by went back as usual to their ships : in this way they harassed the English army during the whole autumn. As the latter returned (for the winter was now at hand) they crossed over to the Isle of Wight with great booty, and remained there until the feast of the Nativity of our Lord [25th Dec.] ; when, as the king was staying in Shropshire, they went through Hampshire into Berkshire, and burned Reading, Walinford, Cholsey, and many other places. Thence they moved on, and crossing Ashdown came to Cuuic-elmeslawe [Cuckamsley-hill]. Returning thence by another road, they came upon the people who dwelt near the Kennet drawn up there in battle array, and immediately attacked them and put them to flight : they then returned to their ships with the spoil which they had taken.

A.D. 1007. [1]The twenty-sixth cycle of nineteen years began on the fifth indiction. In this year Aethelred, king of the English, with the assent of his nobles, sent messengers to the Danes, bidding them say, that he would supply them with provisions and pay a tribute if they would refrain from pillage and keep peace with him. They agreed to his terms; and thenceforth all England supplied them with provisions: and 36,000 pounds were paid to them by way of tribute. In the same year the king made the aforesaid Edric, son of Aegelric, ealdorman of the Mercians; he was a man of humble birth, but his tongue procured him both riches and high station; he was of a ready wit, of persuasive eloquence, and surpassed all his contemporaries in malice, perfidy, pride, and cruelty. His brothers were Brihtric, Alfric, Goda, Agelwin, Agelward, and Agelmer, the father of Wulnoth, who was the father of Godwin, ealdorman of the West Saxons.

A.D. 1008. [2]The solar cycle began, four bissextile years falling together. Aethelred, king of the English, commanded ships to be built all over England, making every 310 hides supply one ship, and every nine furnish a coat of mail and a helmet. When all

---

[1] This first sentence is from Marianus.
[2] This sentence also is derived from Marianus.

the ships were ready, he manned them with picked soldiers and victualled them; and then, with a view to protect the boundaries of the kingdom against foreign invasions, assembled them at the port of Sandwich.   At that time or a little before, Brihtric, one of the brothers of the traitorous ealdorman Edric Streona, (a wavering, ambitious, and haughty man,) brought to the king a false accusation against Wulnoth, a South-Saxon thane, who, in order to avoid being made prisoner, presently fled, and having got possession of twenty ships, frequently pillaged the sea coast.   But when it was told to the king's fleet that any one who chose could easily capture him, Brihtric took eighty ships, and went after him; but, after a quiet voyage of some duration, a most violent storm arose and separated the ships, shattered them, and cast them on the beach: and shortly afterwards Wulnoth burned them.   On the arrival of this news, the king, with his ealdormen and nobles, returned home; but the fleet by his orders went to London; and so this great effort on the part of the people was thrown away.

A.D. 1009. [1] Leo was pope, being the hundred and thirty-ninth. Turkill, a Danish earl, came over to England with his fleet; afterwards, in the month of August, another countless fleet of Danes, under the command of Hemming and Eiglaf, came over to the Isle of Thanet, and without delay joined the other fleet.   Thence both fleets went to Sandwich, where the troops landed, marched in battle array to the city of Canterbury, and began to attack it.   The citizens of Canterbury, with the inhabitants of East Kent, soon sued for peace, and obtained it, giving three thousand pounds as a consideration.   The Danes went back to their ships, and directed their course to the Isle of Wight; whence (as usual) they made frequent descents for pillage on the sea coasts of South Saxony and the province of Southampton, and burned numerous vills.   In consequence, king Aethelred collected an army from all parts of England, and stationed it along the sea coast to oppose their descents.   But for all this, they did not desist from plundering at every point.   But once, when they had gone pillaging further inland than usual, and were returning laden with booty, the king posted himself with many thousand men on the road along which they were returning to their ships; and, as he had the whole army with him, made up his mind to conquer or die.   But the perfidious ealdorman Edric Streona (he was the king's son-in-law, having married his daughter Eadgith) used all his endeavours, by wiles and crafty speeches, to prevent a battle, and to allow the enemy to depart on that occasion.   He persuaded, and gained his point: like a traitor to his country, he rescued the Danes from the hands of the English, and suffered them to escape.   So the Danes turned aside, and with great joy regained their ships.   After the feast-day of St. Martin [11th Nov.], they sailed to Kent, and fixing their winter quarters in the river Thames, obtained provisions by plundering East Saxony and the other provinces on either side of the river.   They often attacked the city of London, and endeavoured

---

[1] Marianus furnishes this first sentence.

to take it by storm; but the citizens drove them back with great
loss.[1]

A.D. 1010. [2]Bishop Bruno suffered martyrdom. The aforesaid
Danish army quitted their ships in the month of January, marched
to Oxford through the wood called Chiltern, and plundered it and
burned it; then they returned, pillaging both sides of the river
Thames.   Information being given to them that an army was
assembled at London for the purpose of giving them battle, that
portion of their army which was going along the northern bank
crossed over at a place called Stane, and their united forces, laden
with spoil, marched through Surrey back to their ships; these they
refitted during Lent, while they were staying in Kent.   After
Easter [9th April] they sailed to East Anglia, and, landing near
Ipswich, marched to a place called Ringmere, where they knew
the ealdorman Ulfketell was posted with his army, and on the 3d
of the nones of May [5th May], fought a severe battle with him.
While the fight was raging, the East Anglians fled; one Turkitel, a
Danish thane, surnamed Myrenheafod, that is, Mare's-head, being
the first to fly.   The Cambridge men fought manfully, and kept
their ground for a long while, but were at last overcome and compelled to retire.   In this battle fell Aethelstan, the king's son-in-
law, a noble thane named Oswi and his son, Wulfric, the son of
Leofwin, Eadwi, brother of the afore-mentioned Alfric, many
other noble thanes, and common people innumerable.   The Danes
being [thus] masters of the field of carnage, got possession of East
Anglia; and having provided themselves with horses, for three
months without ceasing scoured the whole province, pillaging,
burning the vills, and slaughtering men and cattle; in the fens too
everything shared the same fate.   They afterwards plundered and
burned Thetford and Cambridge.   After this they went back to
the river Thames, the infantry going by ship, and the cavalry on
horseback.   After the lapse of a few days they again went out to
plunder, and marching straight to Oxfordshire, first laid waste that
province, and then Buckinghamshire, Bedfordshire, and Hertfordshire, burning the vills and putting man and beast to death: they
then returned with great booty to their ships.   After this, about
the feast-day of St. Andrew the apostle [30th Nov.], they burned
Northampton and as much of its environs as they pleased; going
thence, they crossed the river Thames, went into West Saxony,
burned Caningamersce, and the greater part of Wiltshire, and,
with great spoil as usual, returned to their ships about the feast of
our Lord's Nativity [25th Dec.].

A.D. 1011. [3]Willigis, archbishop of Mentz, died, on Friday
the 7th of the kalends of March [23d Feb.]: he was succeeded by
Erkanbald, abbot of Fulda.   East Anglia, East Saxony, Middle
Saxony, Hertfordshire, Buckinghamshire, Oxfordshire, Bedford-
shire, Cambridgeshire, half of Huntingdonshire, and a great part of
Northamptonshire, and—on the south side of the Thames—Kent,

---

[1] " On the death of Osbriht, bishop of Selsey, Almar succeeded." A. addit.
[2] The first sentence is from Marianus.
[3] This sentence also is from the same authority.

Surrey, South Saxony, Southamptonshire, Wiltshire, and Berkshire, being, by the aforesaid Danish army, utterly wasted with fire and sword, Aethelred, king of the English, and the nobles of his kingdom, sent messengers to them suing for peace; promising pay and tribute if they would desist from their ravages. Having given audience to the messengers, they agreed to the terms offered; but, as the event showed, not without fraud and simulation : for although provisions were supplied to them in abundance, and a tribute fixed by themselves was paid, yet they continued in bands to scour the country in every direction, laying waste the vills, plundering some of the unfortunate inhabitants, and killing others. At length, between the feast-day of the Nativity of St. Mary [8th Sept.] and the feast-day of St. Michael [29th Sept.], they dug a trench round Canterbury, and laid siege to it. On the twentieth day of the siege the city was set on fire by the treacherous contrivance of the archdeacon Almear, whose life St. Alfeg had formerly saved; and so the army entered and the city was taken : some [of the citizens] were slain by the sword, some were burned in the flames, many were hurled from the walls, and some were hung up by their private parts, and so died. Matrons were dragged by their hair through the streets of the city, and then flung into the fire. Infants torn from their mother's breasts were caught on the points of spears, or ground to pieces by chariots driven over them. Meanwhile, the archbishop Alfeg was taken prisoner, put in fetters, imprisoned, and tortured in various ways. Almar, abbot of St. Augustine's monastery, was allowed to depart; Godwin, bishop of Rochester, was taken prisoner, and so were Leofruna, abbess of St. Mildrith's monastery [in Thanet], Alfred, the king's reeve, the monks and canons also, and countless people of both sexes. There Christ's church was pillaged and burned, and all the monks and laity, both men, women, and children, were decimated; nine out of every ten being slain, and the tenth kept alive. This decimation extended to the total amount of four monks and eight hundred laymen. After this slaughter of the people, devastation, and conflagration of the city, the archbishop Alfeag was brought out in fetters, driven along, wounded grievously, and led to the fleet; then he was thrust back into prison and there badly treated for the space of seven months. In the meanwhile the wrath of God broke out against that murderous people, and slew two thousand of them by means of excruciating disorders of the bowels. The rest, being attacked in a similar manner, were admonished by the faithful to make satisfaction to the archbishop; but they refused so to do. The mortality went on increasing, carrying them off by tens, twenties, and upwards.

    A.D. 1012. The traitorous ealdorman, Edric Streona, and all the chief men of every degree in England, assembled at London before Easter, and remained there until the tribute of forty-eight thousand pounds, which had been promised to the Danes, was paid. Meanwhile, on the holy Saturday, when our Lord rested in the tomb [12th April], the Danes proposed to archbishop Alfeag that he should purchase his life and liberty for three thousand pounds.

On his refusal they put off killing him to another Saturday. When that day arrived they wrought themselves up to great fury against him; and inasmuch as they were exceedingly drunk with wine, and he had forbidden any person to pay anything towards his ransom, they took him out of prison and dragged him before their council. Presently they started from their seats, and, putting aside their axes, flung him down and battered him with stones, bones, and oxen's heads. At length, a fellow named Thrum, whom he had confirmed the day previously, moved with impious pity, split his head with an axe: thereupon, being the 13th of the kalends of May [19th April], he slept in the Lord, and his conquering spirit went triumphantly to heaven. On the following day his corpse was carried to London, received with great reverence by the citizens, and buried in St. Paul's church, by Eadnoth, bishop of Lincoln [Dorchester], and Alfhun, bishop of London. After these things, the tribute being paid, and the peace confirmed with oaths, the Danish fleet, which before kept together, dispersed far and wide; but forty-five of their ships remained with the king, and swore fealty to him, and engaged on their fealty to defend England against foreigners, on condition that he would supply them with food and raiment.

A.D. 1013. Living was appointed to the archbishopric of Canterbury.

In the month of July, Sweyn, king of the Danes, came with a strong fleet to the port of Sandwich, and after remaining there for a few days, departed; and sailing round East Anglia, entered the mouth of the river Humber; thence he went up the river Trent as far as Gainsborough, and encamped there. Earl Uhtred and the Northumbrians, and the inhabitants of Lindesey, immediately submitted to him; then the people of the Five Burghs, and afterwards all who dwelt north of Watling-street, that is, the street which the sons of king Weatla made right across England, from the eastern to the western sea; and having agreed upon a peace with him, and given hostages, swore fealty to him : [then] he commanded them to supply his army with horses and provisions. Having completed these arrangements, and entrusted the army and hostages to his son Canute, he made a selection from those who had submitted to him, and made an expedition against the South Mercians; and, passing Watling-street, gave orders to his men to lay waste the fields, burn the vills, pillage the churches, slay all the men who fell into their hands, keep the women to appease their lust, and do as much mischief as ever they could. Then he came to Oxford (his men all the while obeying his orders and rioting with beastly ferocity), and got possession of it sooner than he expected; and, taking hostages, he hastened on to Winchester. On his arrival at Winchester, the citizens (terrified at his excessive cruelty) quickly made peace with him, and gave him as many hostages of his own selection as he chose to demand. Having taken the hostages, he moved his army towards London, but many of his men were drowned in the river Thames, because they would not [take the trouble to] seek for a bridge or a ford. On reaching London, he tried in various ways to take it, either by stratagem or by force. But Aethelred, king of the English, and the citizens, assisted by the often-mentioned Danish earl, Turkill, who was then in the city with him, bravely defended the city walls, and drove him off. Thus repulsed he departed, pillaging and destroying, as usual, everything in his path, and went first to Wallingford, and afterwards to Bath, where he sate down to refresh his army. Then there came to him Athelmar, ealdorman of Devonshire, accompanied by the western thanes, who made peace with him, giving hostages. Having accomplished all things according to his wishes, he returned to his fleet, and was called and esteemed king by all the English people, if indeed he can be called a king who acted in most things like a tyrant. Moreover, the citizens of London sent hostages and made peace with him ; for they feared that he was so enraged against them that he would deprive them of all their property, and either cause their eyes to be put out, or have their hands or feet amputated. When king Aethelred saw this, he sent queen Emma into Normandy, to her brother, Richard the Second, earl of Normandy, together with his sons, Eadward and Alfred, their tutor Alfhun, bishop of London, and Alfsin, abbot of Medhamstead. He himself, however, remained for a short time with the Danish fleet, which then lay in the river Thames, at a place called Grenewic [Greenwich] ; and afterward sailed over to the Isle of Wight, and celebrated Christmas there. After Christmas he sailed to Normandy, and was honourably received by earl Richard. Meanwhile the tyrant Sweyn commanded that his fleet should be abundantly supplied with provisions, and ordered that payment of an almost insupportable tribute should be made. Earl Turkill issued the same orders with respect to the fleet which was lying at Greenwich : in addition, each of them went plundering whenever he chose, and committed great enormities.

A.D. 1014. The tyrant Sweyn, after having committed innumerable and cruel atrocities, both in England and in other countries, filled up the measure of his damnation by demanding a large tribute from the town where rests the uncorrupted corpse of the precious martyr, Eadmund,—a thing which no one had dared to do since the town was given to the church of that saint. He threw out frequent threats that if it was not speedily paid he would certainly burn the town and the townsmen, rase to the ground the church of the said martyr, and torture the clerks in various modes. Moreover, he frequently dared to depreciate the martyr in many ways, and with profane and sacrilegious mouth to bawl out that he was a person of no sanctity. But because he would not curb his malice, divine vengeance did not suffer his blasphemy to last any longer. As he was reiterating his threats, towards evening, in a general muster which he was one day holding at Gainsborough, and surrounded by very dense files of Danes, he alone saw St. Eadmund coming armed against him. He was terrified at the sight, and began to cry in a very loud voice, " Help, my comrades, help ! lo ! St. Eadmund is coming to kill me." As he was speaking, the saint ran him through fiercely with a spear, and he fell from the stallion whereon he was sitting, and remaining in great agony until twilight, he died miserably,

on the 3d of the nones of February [3d Feb.].   On his death the
Danish fleet chose his son Canute to be their king.   But the elders
of all England unanimously sent messengers in great haste to Aethelred, king of the English, saying they neither did nor would love any
one better than their natural lord, if he would govern them better
and treat them with greater kindness than formerly.   On hearing
this message, he sent his son Edward to them, accompanied with
messengers, and greeted in a kindly way all his people, both great
and small, and promised that if they would unanimously and without
treachery receive him for king, he would be a gentle and loving lord
to them, would consult their wishes and abide by their counsels in
everything, and would benevolently pardon all their outrageous and
disgraceful speeches against him, and all their opposition to him.
To this they all sent back a kind answer.   Then both sides agreed,
verbally and by treaty, to a comprehensive peace.   In addition, the
chief men engaged that they would never more admit the Danish
king into England.   After this the English sent to Normandy, and
the king was very soon, to wit, in Lent, brought over, and was
received with universal honour.

Meanwhile Canute and the people of Lindesey agreed, that when
his army was provided with horses, they would make a joint plundering expedition ; but before the horses were ready, king Aethelred
arrived there with a strong army, and having expelled Canute and
his fleet, laid waste and burned the whole of Lindesey, and slew as
many of the inhabitants as he could.   Canute, however, consulted
his safety by a speedy flight ; and, directing his course to the south,
soon arrived at the port of Sandwich : there he brought out the
hostages which had been given to his father from all parts of England ; and after their hands and ears had been cut off, and their
nostrils slit up, allowed them to depart : he then went to Denmark,
but only to return the next year.   In addition to these calamities,
king Aethelred ordered a tribute of thirty thousand pounds to be
paid to the fleet which lay at Greenwich.   On the 3d of the
kalends of October [29th Sept.] the sea broke its bounds, and
overwhelmed many vills and innumerable people in England.

A.D. 1015.   In this year, as a great council was being held at
Oxford, the traitorous ealdorman Edric Streona craftily invited
Sigeferth and Morcar, sons of Earngrim, and the most considerable
and powerful thanes of the Seven Burghs, to come to his chamber,
and had them secretly killed there: king Aethelred took possession
of their property, and ordered Aldgith, the widow of Sigeferth,
to be taken to the city of Maidulf [Malmesbury]: during her captivity, Eadmund the etheling came there and married her against
his father's will: between the feast of the Assumption [15th Aug.]
and the feast of the Nativity of St. Mary [8th Sept.] he went to the
people of the Five Burghs, invaded the possessions of Sigeferth
and Morcar, and brought the inhabitants thereof under his own
dominion.   During the same period Canute, king of the Danes,
came with a great fleet to the port of Sandwich; and afterwards
sailing past Kent, entered the mouth of the river Frome, and
plundered greatly in Dorsetshire, Somersetshire, and Wiltshire.

Then, because king Aethelred lay sick at Cosham, his son Eadmund
the etheling, on one side, and Edric Streona, that ealdorman full
of treachery and guile, on the other, assembled a great army; but
on uniting their forces the ealdorman laid all manner of snares for
the etheling, and endeavoured to compass his death. On this plot
being discovered, they both separated and gave place to their
enemies. Shortly afterwards the ealdorman enticed away from the
king's fleet forty ships full of Danish soldiers, and, going to Canute,
entered into his service. The West Saxons did the same, giving
hostages; they afterwards also supplied the army with horses.[1]

A.D. 1016. Canut, king of the Danes, and the traitorous
ealdorman Edric Streona, crossed the river Thames with a large
body of cavalry at a place called Cricgelade [Cricklade], and
entered Mercia in hostile guise just before the feast of our Lord's
Epiphany [Jan. 6], and devastated and burned many vills in Warwickshire, and slew everybody they met. When this came to the
ears of the etheling Eadmund, surnamed Ironside, he mustered an
army in great haste; but when it was mustered the Mercians refused to attack the Danes and West Saxons unless in company with
Adelred and the citizens of London: so the expedition was laid
aside, and every one returned home. After the feast [of Epiphany],
the etheling Eadmund again raised a still larger army: when he
had mustered it he sent messengers to London requesting his
father to meet him as quickly as possible with all the men whom
he could command : the latter levied a large body of fighting men,
and hastened to meet him. But when the two armies had united,
it was hinted to the king that unless he was very careful some of
his auxiliaries would betray him. On that account he shortly
afterwards dismissed the army and returned to London: but the
etheling went into Northumbria. Wherefore some persons con-
jectured that he was going to raise a still larger army against Canute:
but as Canute and Edric on the one hand laid waste provinces, even
so did he and Uhtred, earl of the Northumbrians, on the other.
They first laid waste Staffordshire, then Shropshire, and Leicester-
shire, for refusing to go out to fight against the Danish army.
Meanwhile Canute and Edric Streona laid waste Buckinghamshire,
Bedfordshire, Huntingdonshire, Northamptonshire, Lincolnshire,
and Nottinghamshire, and afterwards Northumbria. As soon as
the etheling Eadmund heard this, he left off the work of devastation, and hastened to his father in London. But Uhtred the earl
returned home, and, driven by necessity, he and all the Northumbrians went over to Canute, and gave hostages to him; nevertheless,
with Canute's connivance, if not by his command, he and Turkettel,
son of Neavana, were put to death by Thurebrand, a noble Dane.
Canute then made Egric an earl in Uhtred's place, and, marching
rapidly to the south by a different road, he and all his army regained the fleet before the festival of Easter.

About this time, namely on Monday the 9th of the kalends of
May [23d April], in the fourteenth indiction, Aethelred, king of

---

[1] "On the death of Aethelwald, bishop of Winchester, Aelsi, called also Elfwin,
succeeded." A.

the English, died at London after a life of great disquiet and manifold tribulations, all which St. Dunstan on his coronation-day, after placing the crown on his head, prophetically announced as about to come upon him: "Because," said he, "thou hast obtained the kingdom by the death of thy brother, whom thy mother has slain, therefore, hear now the word of the Lord; thus saith the Lord, 'The sword shall not depart from thy house, but shall rage against thee all the days of thy life, slaying thy seed, until thy kingdom be given to another kingdom whose manners and language the nation whom thou governest knoweth not.' And thy sin, and the sin of thy mother, and the sins of the men who have wickedly shed blood by her direction, shall be expiated only by long-continued punishment." His body was honourably buried in the church of St. Paul the apostle. After his death, the bishops, abbots, ealdormen, and all the nobles of England assembled, and unanimously chose Canute to be their lord and king; and having come to him at Southampton, and renounced and repudiated all the descendants of king Aethelred, made peace with and swore fealty to him; and he, in his turn, swore that both in Divine and secular affairs he would be a faithful master to them. But the citizens of London and some of the nobles who were then at London, unanimously chose Eadmund the etheling to be king. Exalted to the kingly throne, he boldly and without delay marched into West Saxony, and being gladly welcomed by the whole population, he quickly reduced it under his dominion; and a great number of the English people, hearing of this, hastened to make spontaneous submission to him.

Meanwhile, about rogation week [7th May], Canute went to London with all his fleet. On their arrival they dug a great trench on the south side of the river Thames, and drew their ships [along it] to the west of the bridge; they afterwards dug a deep and broad trench round the city and closely besieged it, thereby preventing all ingress and egress, and made frequent assaults on it; but the citizens made a vigorous resistance, and drove them to a distance from the walls. So, abandoning the siege for a time, and leaving a portion of the army to guard the ships, they marched into West Saxony with such speed that king Eadmund Ironside had no time to muster his army. Nevertheless, with the troops which in this short time he had got together, he boldly marched into Dorsetshire against them, trusting in God for help, and attacking them at a place called Peonn [Pen], near Gillingham, routed them and put them to flight. After midsummer, having again assembled a larger army than before, he boldly resolved to attack Canute, and fell in with him at a place called Scearstan,[1] in Hwiccia. There he arranged the positions and division of his forces, placed all the best men in the foremost ranks, supporting them and the remainder of the army, and, addressing each by name, exhorted and entreated them to remember that they were about to fight for their country, their children, their wives, and their homes, and by an excellent address stirred up the courage of his troops: then he ordered the trumpets

[1] Probably Sherston in Wiltshire.

to sound and the army to advance by degrees.   The enemy's army
did the like.   When they came to a spot where they could join
battle, the hostile standards met with tremendous uproar; they
fought with sword and spear, and with the greatest obstinacy.
Meanwhile king Eadmund Ironside exerted himself to the utmost
in the foremost ranks, provided for every emergency, fought hard
in person, often struck down an enemy, and fulfilled at one and the
same time the duties of a brave soldier and an able general.   But,
inasmuch as that most traitorous ealdorman Edric Streona, and
Almar the beloved, and Algar the son of Meawe, who ought to
have assisted him, had, with the men of Southamptonshire and
Wiltshire, and a countless host, joined the Danes—his army was
overworked.   However on the first day of the battle, which was
Monday, the contest was so severe and bloody that at sunset both
armies were unable to continue the fight for very weariness, and
separated as it were with one accord.   But on the next day the
king would have exterminated the Danes, had it not been for the
trick of that faithless ealdorman Edric Streona.   For as the battle
was raging, and he perceived that the English were gaining advantage, he cut off the head of a man named Osmear, whose face and
hair were very like king Eadmund's, and, holding it up, cried out
that it was useless for the English to fight, saying, "Oh! ye men
of Dorsetshire, Devonshire and Wiltshire, flee quickly; ye have
lost your leader: Lo! here I hold the head of your lord and king
Eadmund: flee with all speed."   When the English heard these
words they were terror-struck, more by the atrocity of the thing
than by the credit which they gave to their informer.   Some
waverers were nearly induced thereby to flee; but as soon as it was
known that the king was alive they took courage, pressed the Danes
harder than ever, slew many of them, and kept fighting with all
their might until dusk, when the armies separated just as they did
the previous day.   But when the night was far advanced, Canute
ordered his men to leave the camp silently, and, setting out for
London, regained his ships, and shortly afterwards he renewed the
siege of London.   When the morning came, and king Eadmund
Ironside discovered that the Danes had fled, he returned to West
Saxony for the purpose of raising a larger army.   His brother-in-
law, the traitorous ealdorman Edric, seeing how energetic he was,
betook himself to him as his lawful lord, and having renewed his
peace with him, swore that he would continue faithful to him.   So
the king, with the army which he had assembled for the third time,
delivered the Londoners from their state of siege, and drove back
the Danes to their ships.   Two days afterwards he crossed the
Thames at a place called Brentford, fought a third battle against
the Danes and gained the victory, putting them to flight.   Many of
the English were drowned on that occasion while crossing the river
in a careless manner.   Thence the king hastened into West Saxony
for the purpose of collecting a larger army.   The Danes, however,
went back to London, laid siege to it, and assaulted it on every
side; but through God's mercy were wholly unsuccessful.   Wherefore they departed thence with their fleet, entered the river Arewe,

landed and went into Mercia to pillage, slaying all whom they met, burning the vills and plundering as usual, and afterwards returned to their ships : the infantry were taken in ships to the river Medway, but the cavalry kept the whole country in alarm by their incessant ravages.

Meanwhile king Eadmund Ironside, for the fourth time, collected a large army out of all parts of England, and fording the river Thames at the same spot as before, quickly arrived in Kent, and fought a battle with the Danes near Ottaford [Otford]. They were unable to withstand his attack, but turned their backs and fled with their horses to Sheppey. However he slew all whom he overtook, and if the traitorous ealdorman, Edric Streona, had not by his wiles and insinuations prevented the king from pursuing his enemies, by detaining him at Eagelesford [Ailesford], his victory would that day have been complete. When the king had gone back into West Saxony, Canute led his forces into East Saxony, and again went into Mercia to pillage, ordering his army to commit greater enormities than before. They were not backward in obeying his orders ; and after having beheaded all who fell into their hands, burnt numerous vills and laid waste the fields, returned laden with spoil to their ships. Eadmund Ironside, king of the English, pursued them with the army which he had collected from all parts of England, and came up with them on their march at a hill called Assandun [Ashdown], which means The ass's hill. There he quickly formed his line of battle, supporting it with bodies of reserve three deep. He then went round to each troop, commanding and adjuring them to be mindful of their former valour and victories, and to defend themselves and his kingdom from the rapacity of the Danes ; and [reminded them] that they were going to engage the men whom they had conquered before. Meanwhile Canute very slowly brought his men down to a level ground ; but king Eadmund, on the contrary, moved his forces as he had arranged them with great rapidity, and suddenly gave the word to attack the Danes. The armies fought obstinately, and many fell on both sides. But the traitorous ealdorman, Edric Streona, seeing that the Danish line was giving way, and that the English were getting the victory, kept the promise which he had previously made to Canute, and fled with the Magesetas [men of Herefordshire], and that division of the army which he commanded ; thus craftily circumventing his lord king Eadmund and the English army, and by his craft throwing the victory into the hands of the Danes. There were slain in this battle Alfric the ealdorman, Godwin the ealdorman, Ulfketel, ealdorman of the East Angles, Aethelward the ealdorman, son of God's friend Athelwin, ealdorman of the East Angles, and almost all the English nobility, who never sustained greater loss in battle than on that day. Moreover Eadnoth, bishop of Lincoln [Dorchester], formerly abbot of Ramsey, was slain, as was likewise abbot Wulsi, both of whom had come to offer up prayers to God for the soldiers while they were fighting. A few days after this, king Eadmund Ironside still wished to renew the battle with Canute, but the traitorous ealdorman Edric and some others pre-

vented him from so doing, and advised him to make peace with
Canute and divide the kingdom. At length he yielded, although
unwillingly, to their suggestions ; and messengers having passed to
and fro, and hostages having been exchanged, the two kings met at
a place called Deorhyrst. Eadmund and his attendants took up
their station on the western bank of the Severn, and Canute with
his attendants on the eastern bank. Then each king went in a
fishing-boat to an island called Olanege, situate in the middle of
the river Severn. There they agreed and swore to be at peace, and
in friendship, and brotherhood, and the kingdom was divided.
West Saxony, East Anglia, East Saxony, and London, were allotted
to Canute, but the supremacy of the kingdom was to remain with
Eadmund. Afterwards, having exchanged presents of arms and
robes, and fixed the tribute to be paid to the fleet, they separated.
The Danes, however, retired to their ships with the plunder which
they had taken ; and the citizens of London paying a sum of
money, made peace with them, and allowed them to pass the
winter there.

After these things, about the feast-day of St. Andrew the apostle
[30th Nov.], in the fifteenth indiction, king Eadmund Ironside
died at London, and was buried at Glastonbury by the side of his
grandfather, king Edgar the Pacific. After his death, king Canute
commanded all the bishops and ealdormen, and the chief men
and magnates of England, to assemble at London. When they
came into his presence, he, as though in ignorance, cunningly
asked those who were witnesses when he and Eadmund made a
treaty of friendship and divided the kingdom, what conversation
passed between him and Eadmund with regard to the sons and
brothers of the latter ; and whether it was agreed that if Eadmund
died in his lifetime, his brothers and sons were to succeed to the
West-Saxon kingdom after their father's death. They immediately
answered that they knew for certain that king Eadmund had not
reserved any portion of his dominions for his brothers, neither
during his lifetime nor after his death : and they added that they
knew that king Eadmund wished Canute to be protector and
guardian of his sons, until they were of a fit age to reign. But,
(as God knows,) they bore false witness and lied deceitfully, thinking
that he would show them favour and give them large presents in
consideration of their lies : but some of these false witnesses were
shortly afterwards slain by the said king. Then king Canute, after
putting the aforesaid questions, tried to get the aforesaid magnates
to swear fealty to him. So they swore that they would choose him
for their king, and humbly obey him, and raise taxes for the payment of his army; and receiving the king's bare hand by way of
pledge, and the oaths of the Danish chiefs, they passed by entirely
the brothers and sons of king Eadmund, and denied their right to
become kings. Eadwi, a renowned and most estimable brother of
king Eadmund, was one of the ethelings, and him they then most
unwarrantably exiled. When king Canute heard of the flatteries
of these men, and the insult which they had offered to Eadwi, he
was glad, and entering into his chamber, summoned the traitorous

ealdorman Edric, and asked him if he could so entrap Eadwi as to put his life in danger. He answered and said, that he knew a certain man named Aethelward who could betray him to death easier than he himself could, and that the king could speak with him and offer him a good reward. Having ascertained the man's name, the king summoned him and said cunningly—"Thus and thus has Edric the ealdorman spoken to me, saying that you can manage to procure the death of Eadwi the etheling. Follow now our counsels, and you shall enjoy all the honours and dignities of your fathers; and ask his head of me, and I will hold you dearer than mine own brother." So he said that he would seek him out, and slay him if possible. But his promise was only by way of pretence; for he did not wish to slay him, being descended from one of the noblest families in England.[1]

A.D. 1017. [2]Benedict was pope, being the 140th. In this year king Canute began to reign over all England, and divided it into four parts, reserving West Saxony for himself, and committing East Anglia to earl Turkill, Mercia to Edric the ealdorman, and Northumbria to earl Irc.

The native nobles and people on the one side, and he on the other, entered into a treaty, swore to remain firm friends, and laid aside and extinguished their old animosities. Subsequently king Canute, acting on the advice of the traitorous ealdorman Edric, outlawed Eadwi the etheling, brother of king Eadmund, and Eadwi, who was called king of the Churls. The last-named Eadwi was afterwards reconciled to the king; but Eadwi the etheling fell a victim to the treachery of those whom he had up to that time thought to be his best friends, and was in the same year, at the instance and command of king Canute, unjustly slain. Moreover, Edric advised him to slay the little ethelings, Eadward and Eadmund, the sons of king Eadmund. But thinking that his reputation would suffer if they were made away with in England, he sent them to the king of the Swedes to be put to death; who, although he was in league with him, would not comply with his request, but sent them to Salomon, king of the Hungarians, in order that they might be educated and their lives preserved. One of them, namely Eadmund, in course of time died there: but Eadward married Agatha, a daughter of the brother of the emperor, Henry [II.], by whom he had Margaret, queen of the Scots, Cristina, a nun, and Eadgar the etheling. In the month of July king Canute married Alfgiva, the widow of king Aethelred; and on the feast of our Lord's Nativity [25th Dec.], being at London, he ordered the traitorous ealdorman, Edric, to be slain in the palace, (fearing that he himself would at length suffer from his perfidy in the same manner as Aethelred and Eadmund, Edric's former lords, had frequently suffered,) and commanded his body to be thrown down from the walls and left unburied. Along with him were slain a [3]Norman earl, son of earl

---

[1] "Leofsi, the reverend abbot of Thorney, succeeded to the episcopal see of Worcester." A. marg.   [2] This first clause is from Marianus.
[3] This passage may be translated thus:—"Along with him were slain earl Norman, the son of earl Leofwin," &c.

Leofwin, and brother of earl Leofric, and Aethelward, son of Agelmar the ealdorman, and Brihtric, son of Alpheg, a Devonshire thane, although they had committed no crimes. The king made Leofric an ealdorman in the place of his brother, the Norman, and afterwards took him very high into favour.[1]

A.D. 1018. This year London contributed ten thousand five hundred, and the rest of England seventy-two thousand pounds, for the pay of the Danish army; forty ships of their fleet remained with king Canute, and the rest returned to Denmark. The English and the Danes agreed at Oxford to live under king Eadgar's law.

A.D. 1019. In this year Canute, king of the English and the Danes, went to Denmark, and remained there during the winter.[2]

A.D. 1020. [3]On the feast-day of the nativity of Saints Philip and James [1st May], pope Benedict sang mass in public in the monastery of Fulda, before the emperor Henry, and Richard, abbot of Fulda. King Canute returned to England, and held a great council at Cirencester on Easter-day [17th April], and outlawed Aethelward the ealdorman. Living, archbishop of Canterbury, died, and was succeeded by Aethelnoth, surnamed The Good, son of the noble Aegelmar. In the same year the church which king Canute and earl Turkill had built at the hill called Assandun [Ashdown], was consecrated with great pomp and magnificence in their presence by Wulstan, archbishop of York, and several other bishops. Aldhun, bishop of Lindisfarne, dying, that church was bereaved of pastoral care for nearly three years. At a chapter held to discuss concerning the election of a bishop, a certain religious presbyter named Eadmund stood up, and said jokingly, "Why do you not choose me for bishop?" Those present did not regard his joke as if it were simply a jest, but elected him, and after a three days' fast consulted St. Cuthbert's wishes on that point. While the presbyter stood at the saint's head singing mass, lo! in the middle of the canon, a voice was heard coming as it were from that father's tomb, and thrice naming Eadmund as bishop.

A.D. 1021. [4]On the 16th of the kalends of September [17th Aug.], Erkenbald, archbishop of Mentz, died, and was succeeded by Aribo. Just before the feast-day of St. Martin [11th Nov.], Canute, king of the English and Danes, banished from England

---

[1] "Wulgar, the abbot of Abingdon, that good shepherd, died in the twenty-eighth year after God's providence had placed him over that church. By the vigilant care of this abbot, and by God's protecting mercy, the monastery of Abingdon continued free from the ravages of the Danes, amidst the troubles which pervaded all the rest of England; while, in the meantime, the incursions of the enemies overthrew on the right hand and on the left all that came in their way; or if they acted more mercifully, the inhabitants could redeem themselves only by the payment of a large ransom. He was succeeded in the government of the monastery by Adelwin, whom king Canute, out of regard to his holy life, made the depository of his secrets, and endeavoured by his advice to withdraw himself from what was evil, and to follow what was good. Hence the king loved the monastery of Abingdon, and loaded it with gifts. For, among other presents, he caused a casket of silver and gold to be made, in which should be placed the relics of St. Vincent, deacon and martyr." B. addition.

[2] "On the death of Aelmar, bishop of Selsey, Aethelric succeeded." A. addition.

[3] This first sentence is from Marianus.

[4] The first sentence is from Marianus.

the oft-named earl Turkill, and his wife Edgitha. Algar, bishop of the East Angles, died, and Aldwin succeeded him.

A.D. 1022.   Aethelnoth, archbishop of Canterbury, went to Rome: pope Benedict [VIII] received him with great honour, and gave him the pall.

A.D. 1023.   [1]One day in spring, at the ninth hour, there was an eclipse of the sun.   The body of St. Alpheag, the martyr, was translated from London to Canterbury.   On Tuesday, the 5th of the kalends of June [28th May], Wulstan, archbishop of York, died at York; but his corpse was taken to Ely and buried there. He was succeeded by Alfric Puttoc, provost of Winchester.

A.D. 1024.   [2]Pope Benedict died.   John became pope, being the 141st.   On the 2d of the ides of July [14th July], the pious Henry died, and he was buried at Babo's Mount [Bamberg].

A.D. 1025.   Cuonrad [II.] was the 94th emperor of the Romans, and he reigned fifteen years.   The monk Eadmund was appointed to the bishopric of Lindisfarne.

A.D. 1026.   The twenty-seventh cycle of nineteen years began in the ninth indiction.   Alfric, archbishop of York, went to Rome, and received the pall from pope John [XIX].   Richard, the second duke of Normandy, died; and was succeeded by Richard the third, who died the same year: he was succeeded by his brother Rotbert.

A.D. 1027.   News came to Canute, king of the English and Danes, that the Norwegians held Olaf their king in contempt, on account of his simplicity and meekness, his justice and piety; so he sent much gold and silver to certain of them, and importuned them to renounce and depose Olaf, and submit themselves to him [Canute], and suffer him to reign over them.   They greedily accepted his presents, and ordered word to be sent back that they were ready to receive him whenever he chose to come.

A.D. 1028.   Canute, king of the English and Danes, went over with fifty great ships, and drove king Olaf out of Norway, and subdued it to himself.   [3]In this year was born Marianus the Hibernian, a renowned Scot, by whose study and diligence this excellent Chronicle was compiled from divers books.

A.D. 1029.   Canute, king of the English, Danes, and Norwegians, returned to England; and after the feast of St. Martin [11th Nov.], he banished Hacun, a Danish earl, who had married the noble lady Gunhilda, daughter of his sister by Wyrtgeorn, king of the Winidi, sending him away under pretence of an embassy: for he feared that the said earl would either kill him or deprive him of the kingdom.

A.D. 1030.   The aforesaid earl Hacun died at sea; but some say that he was slain in the island of Orkney.   St. Olaf, king and martyr, son of Harold, king of the Norwegians, was wickedly slain in Norway by the natives.

A.D. 1031.   Canute, king of the English, Danes, and Norwegians, went from Denmark with great state to Rome, and made large

[1] From Marianus.
[2] The whole of this year and the first clause of the following are from Marianus.
[3] Also from the same authority.

offerings of gold, and silver, and other valuables, to St. Peter, prince of apostles; and obtained from pope John [XIX.] the exemption of the School of the English from all toll and tribute. On his journey there and back he gave great alms to the poor, and abolished at great pecuniary cost many border barriers, where taxes used to be extorted from pilgrims. Moreover he vowed to God, before the sepulchre of the apostles, that he would amend his life and conversation; and he sent thence to England a memorable letter by the hands of Living, his companion on the journey, a very prudent man, who was then abbot of Tavistock, but afterwards, in the same year, succeeded Eadnoth in the bishopric of Crediton, and others of his ambassadors; whilst he returned from Rome the way he went, visiting Denmark before England. I think it right to subjoin the text of this letter.

" *Canute, king of all England, Denmark, Norway, and part of Sweden, to Aethelnoth, metropolitan, and Alfric, archbishop of York, and to all bishops and nobles, and to the whole nation of the English, high and low, greeting.* I notify to you that I have lately been to Rome, to pray for the forgiveness of my sins, for the safety of my dominions, and of the people under my government. I had long since vowed such a journey to God; but hitherto hindered by the affairs of my kingdom, and other causes preventing, I was unable to accomplish it sooner. I now return thanks most humbly to my Almighty God for suffering me in my lifetime to approach the holy apostles Peter and Paul, and all the holy saints within and without the city of Rome, wherever I could discover them; and there present to worship and adore according to my desire. I have been the more diligent in the performance of this, because I have learnt from the wise that St. Peter the apostle has received from God great power in binding and in loosing; that he carries the key of the kingdom of heaven; and consequently I have judged it matter of special importance to seek his influence with God. Be it known to you that, at the solemnity of Easter, a great assembly of nobles was present with pope John and the emperor Cuonrad, that is to say, all the princes of the nations from Mount Garganus to the neighbouring sea. All these received me with honour, and presented me with magnificent gifts. But more especially was I honoured by the emperor with various gifts and offerings, in gold and silver vessels, and palls, and costly garments. Moreover, I spoke with the emperor himself, and the sovereign pope, and the nobles who were there, concerning the wants of all my people, English as well as Danes—observing that there ought to be granted to them more equitable regulations and greater security on their passage to Rome; that they should not be impeded by so many barriers on the road, nor harassed with unjust exactions. The emperor assented to my request, as did Rodolph the king, who has the chief dominion over those barriers; and all the princes confirmed by an edict that my subjects, traders as well as those who went for a religious purpose, should peaceably go and return from Rome without any molestation from warders of barriers or tax-gatherers. Again I complained before the pope, and expressed my high displeasure that my archbishops were oppressed by the immense sum of money which is demanded from them, when seeking according to custom the apostolical residence to receive the pall ; and it was determined that it should be so no longer. Moreover, all things which I requested for the advantage of my kingdom from the sovereign pope, and the emperor, and king Rodolph, and the other princes through whose territories our road to Rome is situated, they have freely granted and confirmed by oath, under the attestation of four archbishops, twenty bishops, and an innumerable multitude of dukes and nobles who were present : wherefore I give most hearty thanks to God Almighty for having successfully completed all that I had wished in the manner I had designed, and fully satisfied my intentions.

Be it known, then, that since I have vowed to God Himself hence-forward to reform my life in all things, and justly and piously to govern the kingdoms and the people subject to me, and to maintain equal justice in all things ; and have determined, through God's assistance, to rectify anything hitherto unjustly done, either through the intemperance of my youth, or through negligence; therefore I call to witness and command my counsellors, to whom I have entrusted the counsels of the kingdom, that they by no means, either through fear of myself, or favour to any powerful person, suffer henceforth any injustice, or cause such to obtain in all my kingdom. Moreover, I command all sheriffs or governors throughout my whole kingdom, as they tender my affection or their own safety, not to commit injustice towards any man, rich or poor, but to allow all, noble and ignoble, alike to enjoy impartial law, from which they are never to deviate, either on account of royal favour, the person of any powerful man, or for the sake of amassing money for myself, for I have no need to accumulate money by unjust exaction.

Be it known to you, therefore, that returning by the same way that I went, I am now going to Denmark, through the advice of all the Danes, to make peace and firm treaty with those nations who were desirous, had it been possible, to deprive me both of life and of sovereignty : this, however, they were not able to perform ; God, who by his kindness preserves me in my kingdom and in my honour, and destroys the power of all my adversaries, bringing their strength to nought. Moreover, when I have established peace with the surrounding nations, and put all our sovereignty here in the east in tranquil order, so that there shall be no fear of war or enmity on any side, I intend coming to England as early in the summer as I shall be able to get my fleet prepared. I have sent this epistle before me, in order that my people might rejoice at my prosperity ; because, as yourselves know, I have never spared, nor will I spare, either myself or my pains for the needful service of my whole people. I now, therefore, command and adjure all my bishops and governors throughout my kingdom, by the fidelity you owe to God and me, that you take care that, before I come to England, all dues to God owing by ancient custom be discharged : that is to say, plough-alms, the tenth of animals born in the current year, and the pence owing to Rome for St. Peter, whether from cities or villages ; and in the middle of August, the tenth of the produce of the earth; and on the festival of St. Martin [11th Nov.], the first fruits of seeds to the church of the parish where each one resides, which is called in English ' ciricsceatt.' If these and such like things be not paid ere I come to England, all who shall have offended will incur the penalty of a royal mulct, to be exacted without remission according to law. Farewell."

Aribo, archbishop of Mentz, died on the 6th of April, and was succeeded by St. Bardo, who received the staff on the holy day of Pentecost [30th May], and held it for twenty years.

A.D. 1032. In this year the church of St. Eadmund, king and martyr, was dedicated.

A.D. 1033. Leofsi, bishop of the Hwiccas, a man of great piety and humility, died on Tuesday, the 19th day of August, at the episcopal vill of Kemesey, and, as we may hope, went to the heavenly kingdom : his body was honourably buried in the church of St. Mary at Worcester. Brihteag, abbot of Pershore, son of the sister of Wulstan, archbishop of York, succeeded him in the see.

A.D. 1034. Aethric, bishop of Lincoln [Dorchester], died, and was buried in the monastery of Ramsey: Eadnoth succeeded him. Malcolm, king of the Scots, died.

A.D. 1035. Before his death, Canute, king of the English, made Sweyn king over the Norwegians. This Sweyn was said to be the son of Canute and Alfgiva of Northamptonshire, who was a daughter of Alfhelm the ealdorman, and of the noble lady Wulfruna ; some, however, asserted that he was not the son of the king and the said Alfgiva ; but that the said Alfgiva desired to have a son by the king, and being unable, ordered the new-born child of a certain presbyter to be brought to her, and fully persuaded the king that she had borne him a son. He made Hardecanute, his son by queen Alfgiva, king over the Danes. Afterwards, in the same year, to wit, on Wednesday, the 12th day of November, Canute died at Shaftesbury, but he was buried in the old monastery at Winchester with due pomp. After his burial, queen Alfgiva took up her residence there. Now, Harold said that he was the son of king Canute and Alfgiva of Northamptonshire, although in truth he was not; for some say that he was the son of a cobbler, and that Alfgiva had acted in the same manner in regard to him as she had done with regard to Sweyn ; but because the thing is doubtful, we do not know that we can state anything certain respecting the parentage of either. Harold then, taking on himself the royal dignity, sent his guards with all speed to Winchester, and tyrannically deprived queen Alfgiva of the greater part and the best of the wealth and treasures which king Canute had given to her, and sent her away in poverty in the place where she had just begun to reside ; and with the consent of very many of the elders of England, began to reign as though he was the rightful heir, but not with such great sway as Canute, because Hardecanute, who was the truer heir, was then expected. Hence, after a short time, the kingdom was divided by lot, Harold taking the northern and Hardecanute the southern portion. Rotbert, duke of Normandy,

died, and was succeeded by William the Bastard, his infant son.
Brun, bishop of Wurtzburg, died.

A.D. 1036.   The solar cycle began, four bissextile years coming
together.   Piligrin, archbishop of Cologne, instigated by the
speeches of certain envious monks of the monastery of St. Pantaleon, who hated Helias, abbot of the Scots, and also their abbot,
on account of his severity, and the other Scots whom he had
with him,—this archbishop, I say, threatened the said Helias
that on his return from the king's court he would not leave a
Scot, not even him, remaining there.   Then Helias and the
rest of the Scots answered, " If Christ is truly a pilgrim in us,
archbishop Piligrin will not return alive to Cologne."   And
this the Lord brought to pass, and so Helias presided over two
monasteries.

The innocent ethelings, Alfred and Eadward, sons of Aethelred,
formerly king of the English, quitted Normandy, where they had
remained a long time with their uncle Richard, and with many
Norman knights in their company, crossed over in a few ships to
England for the purpose of holding a conference with their mother,
who was then staying at Winchester.   At this some of the great
men were very indignant, being, although improperly so, much
more attached to Harold than to him ; earl Godwin, it is said,
more than any of them.   As Alfred was hastening to London to
confer with Harold, as he had commanded, Godwin seized him
and put him in close confinement, dispersed some of his companions, put some in chains, and then deprived them of sight ;
some he scalped and tortured, cut off their hands and feet, and then
made them pay fines; many too he ordered to be sold, and slew five
hundred more of them at Guildford by various and cruel deaths.
But we believe that the souls of those whose bodies were so cruelly
and without a cause slain in the fields, are now rejoicing with the
saints in paradise.   On hearing of this, queen Alfgiva sent back
in all haste to Normandy her son Eadward who remained with
her.   Then by the orders of Godwin and some others, Alfred the
etheling was taken heavily chained to the Isle of Ely.   But as soon
as the ship touched the land, his eyes were plucked out on board in
a most barbarous manner, and in this state he was taken to the
monastery, and handed over to the custody of the monks.   There
he shortly afterwards died, and his body was buried with due
honours in the south porch at the western end of the church ; but
his spirit is enjoying the delights of paradise.

A.D. 1037.   Harold, king of the Mercians and Northumbrians,
was by the chiefs and the whole people chosen king to reign over
all England ; but Hardecanute was wholly passed by, because he
wasted his time in Denmark, and delayed coming to England when
requested so to do.   At the commencement of the winter, his
mother, Alfgiva, formerly queen of the English, was driven from
England without pity.   She immediately went over to Flanders in
a ship which had been made ready, and was there honourably
received by the noble count Baldwin, who, as became his degree,
took pleasure in supplying her with all things needful as long as she

required them. A little before this, in the same year, the very
pious Avic, dean of Eversham, died.

Piligrin, the archbishop, died on Thursday, the 25th day of
August. Herimann was his successor for twenty years. On
Thursday, the 10th of November, in the fifth indiction, St. Bardo,
the archbishop, dedicated, in the presence of the emperor Conrad,
St. Martin's monastery, in the archbishopric of Mentz, in honour
of St. Martin, bishop and confessor.

A.D. 1038. Aethelnoth, archbishop of Canterbury, departed
this life on the 29th of October. Seven days afterwards, Aethelric, bishop of South Saxony, died; for he had prayed to God
that he might not survive his beloved father Aethelnoth. Grimketel succeeded him in the bishopric, and Eadsi, the king's
chaplain, succeeded Aethelnoth in the archbishopric. In the same
year died Alfric, bishop of the East Angles. On Wednesday, the
20th of December, Brihteag, bishop of the Hwiccas, died; and
king Harold gave his bishopric to Living, bishop of Crediton.
Stigand, the king's chaplain, was made bishop in Alfric's place,
but was afterwards ejected, and Grimketel was chosen in his stead,
and thus had the two dioceses of the South Saxons and the East
Angles. But Stigand was again appointed, and Grimketel ejected:
and Stigand kept the bishopric of the South Saxons for himself, and
procured the bishopric of the East Angles for his brother Agelmar;
and not satisfied with this, he mounted the episcopal thrones of
Winchester and Canterbury. He earnestly entreated, and very
nearly obtained, that he might be ordained separate bishop of the
South Saxons. Agelmar was succeeded by Arfastus, bishop of
Helmham, who, lest he should seem to have achieved nothing, for
the Normans are most greedy of notoriety with posterity, transferred the bishopric from Helmham to Thetford.

A.D. 1039. The emperor Conrad died on Wednesday, the 12th
of January, and was buried at Spires. Richard, abbot of Fulda,
died on the 20th of July. Sigeward succeeded him. In this year
there was a very hard winter.

Brihtmar, bishop of Litchfield, died; and was succeeded by
Wulsi. The Welsh slew Eadwin, the brother of earl Leofric,
Turkill and Alfgeat, two of the king's thanes, and many of their
men. Hardecanute, king of the Danes, went to his mother Alfgiva,
in Flanders.

Henry, the 95th emperor of the Romans, son of the emperor
Conrad, [began to reign, and he] reigned twenty-seven years.

A.D. 1040. Harold, king of the English, died at London, and
was buried at Westminster. After his interment, the nobles of
almost every part of England sent ambassadors to Hardecanute,
who was then at Bruges with his mother; and thinking that they
were doing what was right, requested him to come to England and
undertake the government of the kingdom: so he got ready sixty
ships, and filling them with Danish soldiers, came over to England
before midsummer, and was received with universal joy, and soon
afterwards raised to the throne; but during his reign he did nothing
worthy of his kingly power. For as soon as he began his reign,

recollecting the injuries which both he and his mother had suffered at the hands of his predecessor king Harold, who was reputed to be his brother, he sent to London Alfric, archbishop of York, earl Godwin, Stir, his major-domo, Edric, his treasurer, and Thrond, his executioner, and others of high station, with orders to dig up the body of the said Harold and throw it into a sewer; and afterwards to take it out and fling it into the river Thames. A short time afterwards it was picked up by a fisherman, and, being immediately taken to the Danes, was honourably buried by them in their cemetery at London. After these things he ordered that all England should pay eight marks to every rower in his fleet, and twelve marks to every helmsman; this was so heavy a tax that scarcely any one could pay it. So he became thoroughly hated by all those who had previously been most anxious for his coming. Moreover he was highly incensed against earl Godwin and Living, bishop of Worcester, for the death of his brother Alfred; Alfric, archbishop of York, and certain others having charged it on them. Wherefore he took the bishopric of Worcester from Living, and gave it to Alfric; but in the following year he took it from Alfric, and kindly restored it to Living, who had appeased him. But Godwin, in order to purchase the king's friendship, gave to him an exquisitely wrought galley, with a gilded prow, well fitted with all warlike stores, and manned with eighty chosen soldiers, splendidly armed. Every one had on each arm a golden bracelet, weighing sixteen ounces, and wore a triple coat of mail and a helmet partly gilt, and a sword with gilded hilt, having a Danish battle-axe adorned with silver and gold hanging from his left shoulder; whilst in his left hand he held a shield, the nails and boss whereof were also gilded, and in the right hand a lance, in the English tongue called " ategar." And besides this, in company with nearly all the chief men and thanes in England, he made oath to the king that it was not by his counsel or desire that the king's brother had been deprived of his eyes, but that he had only obeyed the commands of king Harold his master.

A.D. 1041.   This year Hardecanute, king of the English, sent his house-carls over all the kingdom to collect the tribute which he had imposed. But the citizens of Worcester and the Worcestershire men rose in rebellion, and on Monday, the 4th of May, slew two of them, named Feader and Turstan, who had hidden themselves under the roof of one of the towers of the monastery of that city. This enraged the king, and to avenge their deaths he sent Thurum, earl of the Middle Angles, Leofric, earl of the Mercians, Godwin, earl of the West Saxons, Siward, earl of the Northumbrians, Roni, earl of the Magesetas [men of Herefordshire], and all the other English earls, and almost all his house-carls, to Worcester, where Alfric was still bishop, with orders to slay all the inhabitants if they could, to plunder and burn the city, and lay waste the country round about. On the 12th of November they began to lay waste the city and province, and continued [the work of destruction] for four days; but very few of the citizens or provincials were taken prisoners or slain, because having received advice of their coming, the people fled in all directions. A great number of the citizens fled to a little island called Beverege, in the middle of the river Severn, which they fortified, and defended themselves against the enemy so long and stoutly, that they obtained terms of peace and were permitted to return quietly home. But on the fifth day the enemy burned the city, and they all returned home with great booty, and then the king's anger was appeased. Shortly afterwards Eadward, son of Aethelred, formerly king of the English, came over to England from Normandy, where he had been an exile for many years, and being honourably received by his brother, king Hardecanute, took up his abode at court.

A.D. 1042. Hardecanute, king of the English, while standing at the wedding-feast, given at a place called Lamhithe, by Osgod Clapa, a great lord, on the occasion of the joyful marriage of his daughter Githa with Tovi, surnamed Pruda, a Danish nobleman, and drinking full of health and mirth with the bride and the guests, suddenly fell down in the act of drinking, and remained speechless until the 8th day of June, when he died. He was carried to Winchester, and buried by the side of his father, king Canute. His brother Eadward was proclaimed king at London, chiefly by the exertions of earl Godwin and Living, bishop of Worcester. He was the son of Aethelred, whose father was Eadgar, whose father was Eadmund, whose father was Eadward the elder, whose father was Alfred.

Abbot Helias, a Scot, died on the 12th of April; being a prudent and pious man, he was made ruler over the monastery of St. Pantaleon, in addition to his own of St. Martin. He burned in the monastery of St. Pantaleon a very splendid mass-book, which a French monk had, without permission, written in the vulgar tongue, in order that no one else should dare to do such a thing without leave. The holy Maiolus, a Scot, succeeded him.

A.D. 1043. On the first day of Easter, being the 3d of April, Eadward was crowned king at Winchester, by Edsi, archbishop of Canterbury, Alfric, archbishop of York, and nearly all the bishops of England. In the same year, fourteen days before the feast-day of St. Andrew the apostle [16th Nov.], the king went suddenly and unexpectedly from the city of Gloucester to Winchester, accompanied by earls Leofric, Godwin, and Siward, and by their advice took from his mother all the gold, silver, jewels, precious stones, and other valuables which she possessed; because she had treated him with parsimony and severity, as well before he became king as after. Nevertheless, he ordered her to live there quietly, and had her well supplied with necessaries.

Animchad the Scot, monk and hermit, died at Fulda; and lights were seen, and psalmody was heard, above his tomb. Marianus, the author of this chronicle, dwelt as a hermit at his feet for ten years, and sang mass over his sepulchre. He gives the following account of the aforesaid Animchad. "Being in Ireland," says he, "in an island called Keltra, he entertained some brethren who one day came there, his superior, named Kortram, having given permission. After the meal was ended some went their way, but those who remained, after warming themselves at the fire, sat down and asked him for something to drink. He declined to do so without permission; but they pressed him very hard, and at length he consented; but before giving it he sent some of the beverage to his superior, as a blessing. On the morrow, when his superior asked him his reason for sending the draught, he related all the circumstances : for this slight fault the superior ordered him to quit Ireland. He obeyed submissively; and, going to Fulda, lived as a holy hermit, and died as I have before mentioned. Tigernach, my superior, related these things to me, on the occasion of my committing some slight fault in his presence. I myself, when a hermit in Fulda, heard a most pious monk of that monastery, named William, entreat the aforesaid Animchad, who was then in his tomb, to give him his benediction; and he afterwards assured me that the same night he really saw Animchad standing in his sepulchre, shining with exceeding splendour, and giving his benediction with outstretched hand : and I also passed the whole of that night in the midst of a delicious odour."   These are the words of Marianus.

A.D. 1044. Benedict was pope, being the 142d. He bought the papacy; so the emperor Henry went to Rome, and appointed Clement to be pope in his stead: for, according to St. Peter's own words [Acts viii. 20], he who buys and he who sells the grace of the Spirit, are to be cursed, in company with Simon Magus. Aelfward, bishop of London, who was abbot of the monastery of Evesham both before and after he was bishop, being unable, by reason of his infirmities, to fulfil properly the duties of his bishopric, was desirous of returning to Evesham : but the brethren of that place would by no means allow it. So he took away the greater part of the books and ornaments which he had brought to that place, and, as it is said, some which other persons had brought; he then withdrew to the monastery of Ramsey, and took up his abode there, offering all that he had brought with him to St. Benedict; he died on Wednesday, the 25th of July in this year, and was buried there. At a general council which was held about that time in London, Wulmar, also called Manni, a religious monk of Evesham, was elected abbot of his monastery, and was ordained on Friday, the 10th of August. In the same year the noble lady Gunilda, daughter of king Wurtgeorn, by the sister of king Canute, and successively the widow of earls Hacun and Harold, was expelled from England, with her two sons, Hemming and Thurkill. She went over to Flanders, and resided for a short time at a place called Bruges; and by that route got into Denmark. Stigand, the king's chaplain, was made bishop of East Anglia.

A.D. 1045. The twenty-eighth cycle of nineteen years began in the thirteenth indiction. Brihtwold, bishop of Wilton, died; and was succeeded by the king's chaplain, Heremann, a native of Lorraine. In this year Eadward, king of the English, collected a very powerful fleet, at the port of Sandwich, to oppose Magnus, king of the Norwegians, who was meditating an invasion of England; but whose coming was stayed by Sweyn, king of the Danes, making war against him.

A.D. 1046. Clement was pope, being the 143d. Living, of the Hwiccas, bishop of Devonshire and of Cornwall, died, on Sunday the 23d day of March. After his death, the bishoprics of Crediton and Cornwall were given to Leofric, the king's chancellor, a Welshman : and Aldred, who had been first a monk at Winchester, and then abbot of Tavistock, was made bishop of the Hwiccas. Osgod Clapa was expelled from England. Magnus, king of the Norwegians, son of the saintly king Olaf, routed Sweyn, king of the Danes, and subdued Denmark to himself.

A.D. 1047. Pope Clement died, on the 9th day of October. Poppo, also called Damasus, was the 144th pope. So much snow fell in the west, that the woods were broken down by it : and in this year, too, the winter was very severe. Grimkitel, bishop of South Saxony, died, and was succeeded by Heca, the king's chaplain. Alfwin, bishop of Winchester, also died, and Stigand was appointed to the East-Anglian see in his place. Sweyn, king of the Danes, sent his ambassadors to Eadward, king of the English, requesting him to send his fleet against Magnus, king of the Norwegians. Then earl Godwin advised the king that he should send at least fifty ships, manned with soldiers ; but this meeting with the disapproval of earl Leofric and all the people, he declined to send any. Afterwards Magnus, king of the Norwegians, having got together a large and strong fleet, fought a battle with Sweyn, and after many thousands had fallen on both sides, expelled him from Denmark, and subsequently reigned there, and made the Danes pay heavy tribute to him : shortly afterwards he died.

A.D. 1048. Pope Poppo died. Sweyn recovered Denmark, and Harold Harvager, who was son of Siward, king of the Norwegians, and brother by the mother's side to St. Olaf, and uncle by the father's side to king Magnus, went over again to Norway ; and shortly afterwards sent ambassadors to king Eadward, making offers of peace and friendship, which were accepted. Sweyn, king of the Danes, also sent ambassadors to him, requesting him to despatch a fleet to his assistance. But although earl Godwin wished to send at least fifty ships, earl Leofric and all the people unanimously opposed him. On Sunday, the 1st of May, there was a great earthquake at Worcester, Wic, Derby, and many other places. There was a mortality among men and cattle in many parts of England : and a fire in the air, commonly called wild-fire, burned many vills and corn-fields in Derbyshire, and several other provinces. Eadmund, bishop of Lindisfarne, died at Gloucester, but was carried by his own people to Durham, and buried there. Edred succeeded him ; but being struck down by divine vengeance, Aegelric, a monk of Bury, was appointed in his stead.

A.D. 1049. Leo was pope, being the 145th. This was that Leo who invented a new hymn respecting pope Gregory. The emperor Henry assembled an innumerable army against Baldwin, count of Flanders, chiefly because he had burned and destroyed his beautiful palace at Neomagus [Nimeguen in Gueldres]. In this expedition were pope Leo, and very many nobles and powerful men from different countries. Moreover Sweyn, king of the Danes, was there, at the emperor's bidding, with his fleet, and swore fealty, for that occasion, to the emperor. He sent also to Eadward, king of the English, and requested him not to let Baldwin escape if he should retreat to sea. In consequence, the king went with a great fleet to the port of Sandwich, and remained there until the emperor had obtained from Baldwin all he desired. Meanwhile earl Sweyn, son of earl Godwin and of Githa, who had quitted England and gone over to Denmark, because he was not able to marry Eadgiva, abbess of the monastery of Leominster, whom he had corrupted, returned with eight ships, saying falsely that he would now remain with the king as a faithful subject. Earl Beorn, son of his uncle Ulf, the Danish earl, who was the son of Spracling, who was the son of Urse, and brother of Sweyn, king of the Danes, promised him to obtain from the king the restoration of his earldom. Count Baldwin having made peace with the emperor, earls Godwin and Beorn came, with the king's permission, to Pevensey, with forty-two ships; and keeping a few ships with him, he ordered the rest of the fleet to return home. When it was told him that Osgod Clapa was lying with twenty-nine ships at Ulpe, he recalled as many as possible of the ships which he had dismissed. But Osgod, taking with him his wife, whom he had left at Bruges, returned with six ships to Denmark. But some of them went to East Saxony, and returned, having taken great spoil about Eadulf's promontory : however, a great storm overtook them on their return, and sunk them all except two, which were taken at sea, and all on board were slain. While these things were going on, earl Sweyn came to Pevensey, and treacherously asked his cousin, earl Beorn, to go with him to the port of Sandwich, and make his peace with the king, as he had promised. Beorn, relying on his relationship, took only three companions with him, and set out with his cousin ; but the latter took him to Bosanham, where his ships were stationed, and taking him into one, ordered him to be strongly fettered, and carried him with him as far as the mouth of the river Dart. There, having slain him, and thrown him into a deep trench, and covered him with earth, they dismissed the six ships. The men of Hastings, shortly afterwards, captured two of them ; and, having slain all on board, took them to Sandwich and presented them to the king. Sweyn, however, fled to Flanders with two ships, and remained there until he was brought back by Aldred, bishop of Worcester, who set him at peace with the king.

In the month of August in the same year, some Irish pirates with thirty-six ships entered the mouth of the river Severn, and landed at a place called Wylesceaxan, and in unison with Griffin, king of the South Britons, plundered the neighbourhood and did considerable damage. Then the king and they joined their forces, and crossing the river called Weage, burned Dymedham, and put to death every one whom they found therein. They were quickly opposed by Aldred, bishop of Worcester, and a few of the natives of Gloucestershire and Herefordshire. But the Welsh who were with them, and who had promised to be faithful to them, sent a messenger privately to king Griffin, requesting him to attack the

English as quickly as possible. Griffin flew to their assistance with his own men and the Irish pirates, and rushing at day-break on the English, slew many of them, and put the rest to flight. Eadnoth, bishop of Dorchester, died, and Ulf, the king's chaplain, a Norman by birth, succeeded him. Oswi, abbot of Thorney, and Wulnoth, abbot of Westminster, died. Siward too died, who was co-bishop with Eadsi, archbishop of Canterbury, and he was buried at Abingdon. Moreover, in this year the holy pope Leo came to France, at the request of the very pious abbot, Herimar, having among his attendants the prefect and some of the nobles of Rome : and he dedicated, with great pomp, the monastery of St. Remi, the apostle of the Franks, at Rheims ; in which city he afterwards held a great synod of six days' duration, composed of archbishops, bishops, and abbots. To this synod Eadward, king of the English, sent Alfwin, abbot of Ramsey, and the abbot of St. Augustine's monastery.

A.D. 1050. Macbaethad, king of the Scots, gave largess at Rome. Eadsi, archbishop of Canterbury, died ; and Rotbert, bishop of London, a Norman by birth, succeeded him. Spearheafoc, abbot of Abingdon, was appointed to the bishopric of London : but before he was consecrated, he was expelled by king Edward. Heremann, bishop of Wilton, and Aldred, bishop of Worcester, went to Rome.

A.D. 1051. Alfric, archbishop of York, died at Southwell, and was buried at Medhamstead ; Kinsig, the king's chaplain, succeeded him. King Eadward released the English from their heavy tax in the thirty-eighth year after his father, Aethelred, had ordered it to be paid to the Danish soldiers. After these things, in the month of September, Eustace the elder, the earl of Boulogne, who had married Goda, a sister of king Eadward, came with a small fleet to Dover. His soldiers, while inquiring for lodging in a stupid and uncivil manner, slew one of the citizens. One of his fellow-citizens seeing this, avenged him by slaying one soldier. The earl and his men were very wroth at this, and slew many men and women with their weapons, and trampled down their babes and children under the horses' feet. But when they saw the citizens coming out to oppose them, they began to flee in a cowardly manner : seven of their number were slain, and the rest escaped with difficulty, and betook themselves to king Eadward, who was then staying at Gloucester. Indignant and excessively wroth that such transactions should occur in his jurisdiction, earl Godwin collected an innumerable army from his earldom, namely, from Kent, South Saxony, and West Saxony : his eldest son, Swayne, did the same in his, namely, in Oxfordshire, Gloucestershire, Herefordshire, Somersetshire, and Berkshire : and his other son, Harold, collected another from his earldom, namely, East Saxony, East Anglia, Huntingdonshire, and Cambridgeshire. Of this king Eadward was aware ; so sending messengers in haste to Leofric, earl of the Mercians, and Siward, earl of the Northumbrians, he entreated them, that, inasmuch as he stood in great danger, they would come quickly to him with all the men whom they could collect. At first they came with only a few men, but finding what the state of affairs was, they sent swift horsemen through their territories, and assembled a large army. Likewise, earl Ralph, son of Goda, daughter of king Eadward, assembled as many men as he was able from his territory. Meanwhile, Godwin and his sons and their respective armies came to Gloucestershire after the feast of St. Mary's Nativity, encamped at a place called Langetreo [Langtree], and sent ambassadors to the king at Gloucester, threatening war unless he gave up earl Eustace and his companions, and also the Normans and Bolognese who held a castle in Dovercliff. Thereat the king was for a time alarmed and in great distress, not knowing in the least what to do. But when he found that the army of earls Leofric, Siward, and Ralph was coming on, he stoutly replied that he would not in any way deliver up Eustace and the rest who were demanded. Hearing this, the ambassadors returned without having attained their object. On their departure the army entered Gloucester, so excited and unanimously anxious for the fight, that if the king would have permitted they would immediately have attacked earl Godwin's army. But seeing that there were some of the best men in all England in his army and in theirs, earl Leofric and some others thought that it was a great piece of foolishness that they should fight with their own countrymen; and advised that each side should give hostages, and that on a certain day the king and Godwin should have a meeting in London to arrange matters.

This suggestion was approved, messengers from either side went to and fro, and, hostages having been exchanged, the earl went into West Saxony; and the king assembled a larger army out of all Mercia and Northumbria, and took it with him to London. Godwin and his sons came to Southwark with a great host of West Saxons, but by reason of his army deserting him little by little, he dared not keep his appointment with the king, and fled in the night. In consequence, when the morning came, the king in council and the whole army with one accord banished him and his five sons. Straightway, he, and his wife Githa, and Tosti, with his wife Juthita, who was the daughter of Baldwin, count of Flanders, and two of his other sons, namely, Sweyn and Gurth, went to Thorney, where his ship lay ready for them. They speedily laded her with as much gold, silver and other valuables as she could carry, and embarking in great haste, went their way to Baldwin, count of Flanders. But his sons Harold and Leofwin, going to Bricgstow [Bristol], went on board a ship which their brother Sweyn had got ready for them, and sailed over to Ireland. The king repudiated his queen Edgitha on account of his wrath against her father, Godwin, and sent her very disrespectfully with only one female attendant on foot to Hwerewealla [Wherwell], and delivered her to the custody of the abbess there. After these things, earl William, the Norman, came to England with a host of North-men: king Eadward entertained him and his companions honourably, and sent them back to Normandy laden with presents. In the same year, William, the king's chaplain, succeeded to the bishopric of London, which had been formerly given to Spearheavoc. St. Bardo, archbishop of Mentz, died, on the 10th of June, and was succeeded by Liupold.

A.D. 1052. Marianus, the chronographer, retired from this life. Alfgiva Emma, wife of the kings Aethelred and Canute, died at Winchester on the sixth day of March, and was buried there. In the same year Griffin, king of the Welsh, laid waste great part of Herefordshire, the natives whereof, and many Normans from a castle, went up against him; but he got the victory, slaying many of them and carrying off great booty. This battle was fought on the thirteenth anniversary of the day when the Welsh slew in ambush Eadwin, the brother of earl Leofric. A short time after this, earl Harold and his brother Leofwin returned from Ireland, and entering the mouth of the river Severn, landed on the confines of Somersetshire and Dorsetshire, and plundered the vills and many fields in those parts. A great host from Devonshire and Somersetshire went up against them; but Harold got the victory over them, slaying more than thirty noble thanes and a great number of other men. Then he returned to his fleet with the booty, and shortly afterwards sailed round Penwithsteort [Lands-End]. Then king Eadward sent in haste to the port of Sandwich forty ships well found in provisions, and manned with picked soldiers, with orders to wait and watch for the arrival of earl Godwin; but nevertheless he returned with a small fleet, and wholly unobserved landed in Kent, and by means of his secret emissaries, first won over to his side the men of Kent, then the South Saxons, East Saxons, the men of Surrey, and the shipmen of Hastings, and all along the sea-coast, and numbers beside; who all with one voice declared that they were ready to live or die with him. The king's fleet which lay in the port of Sandwich hearing this, pursued him, but he took to flight and concealed himself wherever he could; so the fleet sailed back to Sandwich, and thence returned to London. When earl Godwin found this out, he crossed over to the Isle of Wight, and kept wandering up and down the sea-coast until his sons Harold and Leofwin joined him with their fleet; but after their junction they left off their plunderings and devastations, confining themselves to getting provisions for their army when they required it. After inveigling over to their assistance as many men as they could on the sea-coast and other places, and taking all the shipmen they met in every direction, they framed their course towards the port of Sandwich. Having arrived there, they notified the fact to king Eadward, who was then staying at London. Thereupon he quickly sent out his messengers to command all who had not deserted from him to make speed and come and help him. But they were very tardy in their movements and did not come in time. Meanwhile earl Godwin with his fleet, having sailed up the Thames against the tide, arrived at Southwark on the day of the exaltation of the holy Cross [14th Sept.], being a Monday, and waited there until the flood-tide came up: during which time he had meetings with the citizens of London (whom he had previously allured with promises of various kinds), in part by his emissaries and in part personally,

and brought over nearly all of them to his own views. So everything being arranged and set in order, on the tide coming up they
weighed anchor in haste, and meeting with no opposition at the
bridge, sailed up the river along the southern bank. The land
army also arrived, and putting itself in array along the bank of the
river, showed a close and imposing front. Then the fleet made for
the northern bank, as though for the purpose of enclosing the
king's fleet (for the king too had a fleet and a numerous land army);
but inasmuch as there were very few men of any bravery, whether
with the king or with Godwin, who were not Englishmen, nearly
all were very averse from fighting against their kinsmen and
countrymen. This circumstance enabled the wiser sort on both
sides to effect a peace between the king and the earl, and both
disbanded their armies. The next morning the king held a council
and fully restored Godwin, and his wife, and all his sons, except
Sweyn, to their former honours; for Sweyn, led by repentance for
having (as before mentioned) slain his cousin Beorn, was gone
from Flanders barefoot as far as Jerusalem, and in his return home-
ward died in Lycia of a disease contracted through extreme cold.
The king also took back again with honour queen Eadgitha, the
earl's daughter, and restored her to her former dignity. A firm
concord and peace being thus concluded, they [the king and the
earl] promised right law [*i.e.* justice] to all people, and banished all
those Normans who had introduced unjust laws, and given false
judgments, and committed many outrages upon the English; but
they allowed some of them to remain in England, namely Robert
the Deacon, and Richard Fitz-Scrob, his son-in-law, Alfred, the
king's horse-thane, Anfrid, surnamed Cocksfoot, and some others
who had been the king's greatest favourites, and always faithful to
him and all the people. But Rodbert, archbishop of Canterbury,
and William, bishop of London, and Ulf, bishop of Lincoln [Dor-
chester], with their Normans, barely managed to escape, and
crossed beyond sea. William, however, being a good-natured man,
was recalled in a short time, and again received into his bishopric.
Osbern, surnamed Pentecost, and his companion Hugh, surrendered their castles, and, by the licence of earl Leofric passing
through his earldom, went into Scotland, and were there kindly received by Macbeoth, king of the Scots. In the same year, during
the night of the feast-day of St. Thomas the apostle [21st Dec.],
the wind was so violent that it blew down many churches and
houses, shattered many trees, and tore others up by the roots.

A.D. 1053. Res, the brother of Griffin, king of the South
Welsh, was, on account of his frequent incursions, put to death by
order of king Eadward at a place called Bulendun; and on the vigil
of our Lord's Epiphany [5th Jan.] his head was brought to the king
at Gloucester. In the same year, on Easter Monday [12th April],
which was being celebrated at Winchester, the hand of death came
on earl Godwin as he was sitting at table with the king as usual;
for being suddenly seized with a violent distemper he fell speechless from his seat. When his sons earl Harold, Tosti, and Gyrth
saw it, they carried him into the king's chamber, in the hope that

he would shortly recover; but losing his strength, he died in great agony five days afterwards, and was buried in the Old Monastery. His son Harold succeeded to his earldom; and Harold's earldom was given to Algar, the son of earl Leofric. In the month of October died Wulsi, bishop of Lichfield, Godwin, abbot of Winchelcombe, and Agelward, abbot of Glastonbury. Leofwin, abbot of Coventry, succeeded Wulsi, and Aegelnoth, a monk of the same monastery, succeeded Agelward. But Aldred, bishop of Worcester, kept the abbacy of Winchelcombe in his own hands until such time as he appointed Godric, the son of Godman the king's chaplain, to be abbot thereof. Alfric, brother of earl Odda, died at Deorhirste on the 11th of the kalends of January [22d Dec.]; but he was buried at Pershore.

[1] Aedd, a clerk with a beard in Ireland, was a man of great renown and of exemplary piety; he had a large school of clerks, maidens, and laymen, and made the maidens receive the tonsure in the same manner as the clerks; on which account he was expelled from Ireland.

A.D. 1054. [2] Pope Leo died on the 16th of the kalends of May [16th April]. Siward, the valiant earl of the Northumbrians, by the king's command, marched into Scotland accompanied by an army of cavalry and a powerful fleet, and fought a battle with Macbeoth, king of the Scots; after slaying many thousands of the Scots and all the Normans whom we mentioned before, he put him to flight, and as the king had directed, elevated to the throne Malcolm, son of the king of the Cumbrians. However, his own son and many English and Danes fell in that battle.

In the same year, on the feast-day of St. Kenelm the martyr [17th July], Aldred, bishop of Worcester, appointed Godric to be abbot of Winchelcombe; he was then sent as ambassador to the emperor with great presents; and being received with great honour by him, and also by Herimann, archbishop of Cologne, he remained there for a whole year; and on the king's behalf he prompted the emperor to send ambassadors into Hungary to bring back Eadward the king's cousin, son of king Eadmund Ironside, and send to him into England.

A.D. 1055. [3] Victor was pope, being the 146th. Siward, earl of the Northumbrians, died at York, and was buried in the monastery of Galmanho which he had built: his earldom was given to Tosti, brother of earl Harold. Shortly afterwards king Eadward summoned a council at London, and outlawed earl Algar, son of earl Leofric, although he had committed no crime. Algar presently went over to Ireland, and returning with eighteen pirate ships, went to Griffin, king of the Welsh, and requested his assistance against king Eadward. Griffin immediately collected from every part of his kingdom a numerous army, and commanded Algar to meet him and his army at an appointed place with his own forces. Having met, they entered Hereford-

[1] The following passage is from Marianus.
[2] The first sentence is from Marianus.
[3] This first notice is also from Marianus.

shire, with intent to lay waste the English marches.   The cowardly
earl Radulph, son of king Eadward's sister [Goda], assembled an
army against them, and falling in with them on the 9th of the
kalends of November [24th Oct.], two miles from the city of Worcester, ordered the English, contrary to their custom, to fight on
horseback.   But just as they were about to join battle, the earl
with his Frenchmen and Normans set the example of flight: the
English seeing this, fled with their commander: and nearly the
whole body of the enemy pursued them, slew four or five hundred
of them, and wounded a great number.   The victory being thus
obtained, king Griffin and earl Algar entered Hereford, and
having slain seven canons who defended the doors of the principal
church, and burned the monastery which Aethelstan, that true
servant of God and worshipper of Christ, had built, together with
all its ornaments, and the reliques of St. Aethelbriht, king and
martyr, and other saints, and having slain several of the citizens
and taken captive many others, and moreover pillaged and burned
the city, they returned laden with spoil.   When the king was
informed of this, he ordered an army to be raised from all parts of
England; and having marshalled it at Gloucester, placed it under
the command of the valiant earl Harold, who, readily obeying the
king's orders, quickly pursued Griffin and Algar, and boldly entering
the Welsh borders encamped beyond Straddele; but they, knowing
him to be a brave and warlike man, dared not risk a battle, but
retreated into South Wales.   On discovering this, Harold left
there the greater part of his army with orders to manfully repel the
enemy if circumstances should require; and returning with the
remainder to Hereford, encircled it with a broad and deep ditch,
and fortified it with gates and bars.   Meanwhile messengers crossed
to and fro between the parties, and Griffin, Algar, and Harold,
and their attendants, met at a place called Biligesleagea, and peace
being mutually agreed upon, they determined to become firm
friends; whereupon earl Algar's fleet sailed to Chester and waited
there to receive the pay which he had promised to them; but the
earl went to the king, and received his earldom from him.   At
that time Tremerin, the pious Welsh bishop, died; he was for a
long time vicar of Aethelstan, bishop of Hereford, after the latter
became incapable of performing his episcopal duties, for he was
blind for thirteen years.   Heremann, bishop of Wiltshire, taking
offence that the king would not allow him to transfer the episcopal
see from the town of Ramsbury to the abbey of Malmesbury, resigned his bishopric, and going beyond sea, became a monk at
St. Bertin, and remained in the monastery there for three years.

A.D. 1056.   Aethelstan, bishop of Hereford, a man of great
sanctity, died on the 4th of the ides of February [10th Feb.],
at an episcopal vill called Bosanbirig; his body was carried to
Hereford, and buried in the church which he himself had built
from the foundation.   He was succeeded by Leovegar, earl Harold's
chaplain, who, on the 16th of the kalends of June [16th June] in
the same year was, together with his clerks, and sheriff Agelnoth,
and many others, slain by Griffin, king of the Welsh, at a place

called Clastbirig, after having held the bishopric for [1]eleven weeks and four days. On his death, the bishopric of Hereford was committed to Aldred, bishop of Worcester, until a bishop could be appointed: this same bishop Aldred afterwards, in conjunction with earls Leofric and Harold, mediated a peace between king Eadward and Griffin, king of the Welsh. [2]Herimann, archbishop of Cologne, died, and was succeeded by Anno. Marianus, setting out on a pilgrimage to his heavenly country, came to Cologne, and on Thursday, the kalends of August [1st Aug.], became a monk there in the monastery of the Scots dedicated to St. Martin. Earl Agelwin, (that is, Odda,[3]) the cherisher of churches, the entertainer of the poor, the defender of widows and orphans, the overthrower of tyrants, the guardian of virginity, died on the 2d of the kalends of September [31st Aug.], at Deorhyrste, having been made a monk shortly before his death by Aldred, bishop of Worcester; but he was buried in the monastery of Pershore with great ceremony. Agelric, bishop of Durham, voluntarily resigned his bishopric, and retired to his monastery of Peterborough, where he had been brought up and made a monk, and passed twelve years there. His brother Agelwin, a monk of the same monastery, succeeded him in the bishopric.

[4]The emperor Henry died on the 3d of the nones of October [5th Oct.], and was buried at Spires, where his father had been buried. Henry, the 96th emperor of the Romans, son of the last Henry, reigned fifty years.

A.D. 1057. Pope Victor died on the 5th of the kalends of August [28th July]. Eadward the etheling, son of king Eadmund Ironside, in obedience to the commands of his uncle, king Eadward, returned to England from Hungary, where, as we have before mentioned, he had been sent into exile long previously. For the king had determined to make him heir to the kingdom: but he died at London shortly after his arrival. Earl Leofric (son of earl Leofwin) of blessed memory, and worthy of all praise, died in a good old age, at his own vill of Bromley, on the 2d of the kalends of September [31st Aug.], and was buried with great state at Coventry. Among his other good deeds in this life, he and his wife, the noble countess Godgiva, (who was a devout worshipper of God, and one who loved the ever-virgin St. Mary,) entirely constructed at their own cost the monastery there, well endowed it with land, and enriched it with ornaments to such an extent, that no monastery could be then found in England possessing so much gold, silver, jewels, and precious stones. Moreover, the monasteries of Leominster and Wenlock, and the monasteries of St. John the Baptist and St. Werburg the Virgin at Chester, and the church which Eadnoth, bishop of Lincoln [Dorchester], [had built] at a celebrated place, called in English St. Mary's Stow, but in Latin

---

[1] This is the reading of A. and B.; the old editions read "twelve."
[2] This and the following sentence are from Marianus.
[3] These three words are introduced in B. between the lines.
[4] This passage is derived from Marianus, as is also the first sentence under the year 1057.

St. Mary's Place, were by them enriched with many valuable ornaments. They also endowed the monastery of Worcester with lands, and added to the buildings of that of Evesham, and gave to it divers ornaments and lands. As long as he lived, this earl's wisdom stood the kings and people of England in good stead. His earldom was given to his son Algar. Heca, bishop of the South Saxons, died, and Agelric, a monk of Christ's Church in Canterbury, was elected in his place. The before-mentioned earl Radulph died on the 12th of the kalends of January [21st Dec.], and was buried in the abbey of Peterborough.

A.D. 1058. ¹Stephen, abbot of Monte Cassino, was pope, being the 147th. On the Saturday before Palm Sunday [10th April], the city of Paderborn, and two monasteries, namely, that of the bishop and that of the monks, were destroyed by fire. In the monastery of monks there was a monk named Paternus, a Scottish anchorite of many years' standing; he had predicted the conflagration, yet would by no means leave the place, but was burned in his cell, and through these flames he passed to the cool shades of bliss: and some wonderful things are told concerning the spot where he died. "Immediately after this occurrence, on Monday after the octaves of Easter [27th April], as I was leaving Cologne for Fulda, in company with the abbot of Fulda, for the purpose of entering my cell, I prayed on the mat whereon he was burned." Thus saith Marianus, the Scottish anchorite.

Algar, earl of the Mercians, was a second time outlawed by king Eadward; but assisted by Griffin, king of the Welsh, and supported by the Norwegian fleet, which came to him unexpectedly, he soon recovered his earldom by force. ²On the 30th of March, pope Stephen died: he was succeeded by Benedict, who sent the pall to Stigand, archbishop of Canterbury. Agelric was ordained bishop of the South Saxons; and abbot Siward was consecrated bishop of Rochester. Aldred, bishop of Worcester, dedicated the church which he had built from the foundation in the city of Gloucester, with great ceremony, to Peter, prince of the apostles; and afterwards, with the king's permission, appointed Wulstan, a monk of Worcester of his own ordination, to be abbot thereof. Then, having resigned the bishopric of Wilton, which had been committed to his governance, and restored it to Herimann, whom we have mentioned before, he crossed the sea, and journeyed to Jerusalem by way of Hungary; a thing which no English archbishop or bishop was known to have done before.

A.D. 1059. Nicholas, bishop of Florence, was chosen pope, and Benedict was ejected. ³On Saturday in Mid-lent, being the 3d of the ides of March [13th March], Marianus the anchorite, in company with Sigefrid, abbot of Fulda, was consecrated priest beside the corpse of St. Kilian, at Wurtzburg; and on Friday after our Lord's Ascension, being the 2d of the ides of May [14th May], he entered his cell in Fulda for ten years. Liupold, archbishop of

---

¹ Marianus has supplied the whole of the narrative under this year.
² The passage ending with the word "Benedict" is from Marianus.
³ The remainder of the year is from Marianus.

Mentz, died on the 7th of the ides of December [7th Dec.] : Sigefrid succeeded him.

A.D. 1060.   Henry, king of the Franks, died, and was succeeded
by his eldest son, Philip. Duduc, bishop of Wells, died, and
was succeeded by Gisa, the king's chaplain : they were both
natives of Lorraine. Kinsi, archbishop of York, died at York
on the 11th of the kalends of January [22d Dec.] : his corpse
was taken to the monastery of Peterborough, and buried there
with great ceremony. On Christmas-day, Aldred, bishop of
Worcester, was chosen archbishop in his stead, and the bishopric
of Hereford, which had been committed to his charge on account
of his industry, was given to Walter, the queen's chaplain; a native
of Lorraine.

[1] On Christmas-day, which fell on a Sunday, Sigefrid, abbot of
Fulda, left Fulda for the king's court, and, with the consent of the
pope's legate, Alexander, who was shortly afterwards made pope,
received the staff of the archbishopric of Mentz, on the day of our
Lord's Epiphany. Widrat, dean of Fulda, succeeded him in the
abbacy.

A.D. 1061.   Aldred, archbishop of York, went to Rome, in
company with earl Tosti, and received the pall from pope Nicholas: [2]
[3] Maiolus, abbot of the Scots, died at Cologne : Foilan was his
successor. Pope Nicholas died. Alexander succeeded as pope,
being the 149th.

A.D. 1062.   The reverend Wulstan was made bishop of Worcester.
This favourite of God was born in that part of the Mercian territory lying within Warwickshire, of religious parents, his father's
name being Eatstan, and his mother's Wulgeova ; but he became
a proficient in literature and ecclesiastical duties in the noble
monastery of Peterborough. Both his parents were so devout,
that long prior to their deaths they took the vows of chastity, and
separated, rejoicing to finish their lives in the habit of holy conversation. Incited by these examples, and chiefly instigated by his
mother, he quitted the world, and in the same monastery of
Worcester where his father had also lived in God's service, received
the monastic habit and grade from the venerable Brihteag, bishop
of that church, who also ordained him to the grades of deacon and
priest ; and straightway entering on a severe and strictly religious
life, both in watching, fasting, prayer, and all kinds of virtues, he
quickly became an object of admiration. Hence, on account of
his strictness, he was at first appointed master and warden of the
children : and afterwards, in consequence of his skill in the church
offices, the elders appointed him to be chanter and treasurer of the
church. The custody of the church being thus committed to him,
he embraced the opportunity of serving God with less restraint,

---

[1] The whole of this passage is from Marianus.

[2] " There too Gisa was by the same pope ordained bishop of Wells, and Walter
was ordained bishop of Hereford. Until John, the successor of Gisa, all the
bishops of Wells had their see at Wells, in the church of St. Andrew the apostle."
A. addition.

[3] The remainder of the year is from Marianus.

giving himself up to a contemplative life, going into the church
day and night to pray and read the Bible, and diligently mortifying
his body by fasts of two and three days' duration.   So devoted was
he to sacred vigils, that not only would he keep himself awake
during the night, but day and night also ; and, what we would
hardly believe unless we had heard it from his own mouth, passing
four days and four nights without sleep : so that his parched up
brain would be in great danger if he did not hasten to satisfy the
demands of nature with a taste of sleep.   And when the urgency of
nature at last compelled him to sleep, he did not pamper his limbs
by resting on a bed or coverings, but would lie down for a short time
on one of the benches of the church, resting his head on the book
which he had used for praying or reading.   Some time afterwards,
the reverend man was, on the death of Agelwin, prior of the
monastery, appointed by bishop Aldred to be prior and father of
the congregation ; this office he filled in a laudable manner, by no
means abating the austerity of his former behaviour, but rather
increasing it, in order to give to others the example of a good life.
Then, after the lapse of some years, Aldred, bishop of Worcester,
being elected to the archbishopric of York, all the clergy and laity
unanimously elected him to be bishop ; the king having given them
permission to make their own choice.   For it chanced there were
present at that election two ambassadors from the apostolic see ;
namely, Armenfred, bishop of Sedunum, and another person.
They were sent by our lord the pope Alexander to Eadward, king
of the English, to receive his replies on certain ecclesiastical
matters, and by the king's orders were staying during nearly the
whole of Lent at Worcester, waiting for the answer to their embassy
until the meeting of the king's court at the ensuing Easter.   These
men noticing his praiseworthy behaviour during their stay, not only
agreed to his election, but were the chief promoters of it, both
among the clergy and the laity, and by their authority made his
election sure.   He obstinately refused, exclaiming that he was
unworthy, and with an oath declaring that he would rather be
beheaded than be advanced to such an high office : and when,
notwithstanding the frequent arguments of many pious and venerable
persons, he could by no means be brought to consent, he was at
last severely taken to task by the anchorite Wulsi, a man of God
who was well known to have lived in seclusion for more than forty
years.   By his influence, and in consequence of having been
alarmed by a divine oracle, he yielded an assent with great sorrow
of heart, and his election having been canonically confirmed on the
feast-day of the Decollation of St. John the Baptist [29th Aug.],
and the bishopric entered upon, he was consecrated on the Sunday
when the nativity of St. Mary is celebrated by the church [8th
Sept.], and so in the splendour of his life and virtues, he shone
forth as bishop of Worcester.   So he was consecrated bishop by
the venerable Aldred, archbishop of York ; Stigand, archbishop of
Canterbury, being then interdicted by the pope from exercising
the episcopal function, because he had presumed to take the archbishopric while archbishop Rotbert was still living : notwithstanding

which, Wulstan made his canonical profession to Stigand, the aforesaid archbishop of Canterbury, and not to Aldred, who had ordained him.   Moreover, Stigand so managed, that the said archbishop of York who ordained Wulstan was ordered to promise, in the presence of the king and his nobles, that he would not thereafter put forth any claim to ecclesiastical or secular dominion over him, neither by reason that he was consecrated by him, nor by reason that he had been one of his monks before his consecration.   This ordination of Wulstan occurred when he was more than fifty years old, in the twentieth year of the reign of king Eadward, and in the fifteenth indiction.

A.D. 1063.   After Christmas-day, Harold, the valiant earl of the West Saxons, took by king Eadward's command a small troop of horsemen, and leaving Gloucester, where the king was then staying, went in all haste to Rudelan,[1] with the determination to slay Griffin, king of the Welsh, on account of his frequent forays in the English marches, and the many insults which he offered to his lord, king Eadward.   But Griffin, when he heard of his coming, fled with his men, and, taking ship, escaped, though with great difficulty.   Harold, when he heard of his flight, ordered his palace and his ships and implements of navigation to be burned, and then returned the same day.   But about Rogation Week [26th May], he set out from Bristol with a naval force, and circumnavigated a great part of Wales.   Then his brother, earl Tosti, met him by the king's command, and having united their forces, they began to lay waste that part of the country.   The Welsh were thus compelled to give hostages and submit, and promised to pay tribute to him ; they also outlawed and renounced their king Griffin.

A.D. 1064.   [2]The great paschal cycle began at this time, in the second indiction.   The archbishop of Mentz, and the bishops of Utrecht, Bamberg, and Ratisbon, accompanied by more than seven thousand men, rich and poor, made a pilgrimage to Jerusalem, shortly after the feast-day of St. Martin [11th Nov.].   Whenever the bishops halted, they wore their palls on their shoulders ; and they ate and drank out of gold or silver cups.   At the report of their wealth, the Arabites assembled, and slew many of them on Good Friday [9th April].   Those who managed to escape took refuge in a deserted castle, called Caruasalim, and, shutting the gates, defended themselves with sticks and stones against the darts of the Arabites, who demanded their money, or in default threatened to slay and plunder them.   Then a very brave soldier, who was determined that no peril should prevent him from beholding our Lord's sepulchre, left the castle : the Arabites immediately took him prisoner, stretched him on his back upon the ground in the form of a cross, nailed his hands and feet to the earth, and cutting him open from the pit of his stomach to his throat, exposed all his entrails.   Having torn him limb from limb, their chief hurled a stone at him, and the others did the same : then they said to his companions, who were spectators of the transaction from the

---

[1] Ruddlan, in Flintshire.
[2] This long passage is from Marianus.

castle, "Thus you shall be served unless you give us all your money." The Christians promised to do so, and then the leader of the Arabites and sixteen of his followers, armed with swords, entered the castle. So the said leader found the bishops sitting in great state, and noticing that Gunther, the bishop of Bamberg, excelled the rest in height and shapeliness, fancied that he was the chief man among the Christians, and putting a thong round the bishop's neck, in the same manner as the heathens are accustomed to hold their criminals, he said, "You and all your property shall be mine." But the bishop said to him by means of an interpreter, "What will you do to me?" He answered, "I will suck the bright blood from that throat of yours, and then I will hang you up like a dog in front of the castle." The bishop thereupon seized him by the head, and with one blow of his fist felled him to the ground, and his followers were all put in fetters. When those outside found this out, they made an assault on the castle; but the prisoners were suspended from the walls opposite the assailants, and regard for their safety put a stop to the attack. Then those thieves began to quarrel about the money which they had previously taken from the Christians, and a great many died by each other's hands. Meanwhile, the prince of Ramala, at the request of those Christians who had managed to escape, came with a strong force, on the second day of Easter [12th April], and put the Arabites to flight : and then, after accepting fifty gold pieces from the Christians, he and an Arabite chief who was at war with his lord, the emir of the Saracens, conveyed them to Jerusalem, and thence to their ships. Thus this Christian host was so wasted away, that out of seven thousand and more only two thousand returned home.

Griffin, king of the Welsh, was slain by his subjects on the nones of August [5th Aug.], and his head, and his ship's beak, with its ornaments, were sent to earl Harold, who immediately forwarded them to king Eadward. King Eadward afterwards gave Wales to his [Griffin's] brothers, Blethgent and Rithwalan, who swore fealty to him and earl Harold, and promised to always obey their behests by land and by sea, and pay properly all which the country had previously paid to preceding kings.

A.D. 1065. The reverend Agelwin, bishop of Durham, disinterred the bones of St. Oswin, formerly king of Bernicia, from his tomb in the monastery which lies at the mouth of the river Tyne, where they had lain for four hundred and fifteen years, and deposited them in a chest with great ceremony. In July, Harold, the valiant earl of the West Saxons, gave orders for the erection of a large building at a place called Portascith [Portskewith], in Wales, and gave directions that it should be well stocked with meat and drink, in order that his lord, king Eadward, might pass some time there in hunting. But Cradoc, son of Griffin, king of the South Welsh, (whom Griffin, king of the North Welsh, had slain, and whose territory he had invaded some few years before,) marched there with as many men as he could get together; on the feast-day of St. Bartholomew [24th Aug.], and massacred nearly all the workmen and superintendents, and carried off all the effects

which had been transported thither.   Shortly after the feast-day of
St. Michael the archangel, to wit, on Monday, the 3d of October,
the Northumbrian thanes Gamelbearn, Dunstan the son of Athel-
neth, Glonieorn the son of Heardulf, entered York with two
hundred soldiers, and, in revenge for the execrable slaughter of the
noble Northumbrian thanes Gospatric (whom queen Eadgitha had
ordered to be treacherously slain in the king's court, on the fourth
night after the feast of our Lord's Nativity [28th Dec.], on account
of [a quarrel which he had with] her brother Tosti), and Gamel,
the son of Orm, and Ulf, the son of Dolfin (whom earl Tosti, while
at York, the year before, had caused to be treacherously slain in
his own chamber, although there was peace between them), and
also on account of the heavy tribute which he unjustly laid on the
whole of Northumbria, they on the same day, first of all, stopped
in their flight his Danish house-carls Amund and Reavensuart, and
put them to death outside the city walls, and on the following day
slew more than two hundred of his tenants, on the north side of
the river Humber : they also broke open his treasury, and retired,
carrying off all his effects.   After that, nearly all the men in his
earldom assembled, and went to Northampton, to meet Harold,
earl of the West Saxons, and others, whom the king, at Tosti's
request, had despatched to restore peace between them.   There
(as also afterwards at Oxford), on the feast-day of the apostles
Simon and Jude [28th Oct.], when earl Harold and the rest
attempted to bring about an accommodation between them and
earl Tosti, they all unanimously refused, and outlawed him and all
who had taken part with him in his unjust government; and, after
the feast of All Saints [1st Nov.], with the concurrence of earl
Eadwin, they banished Tosti from England : whereupon he
presently went, in company with his wife, to Baldwin, count of
Flanders, and passed the winter at St. Omer.   After this, king
Eadward's health began gradually to fail : however, at Christmas,
he held his court as well as he was able, at London, and on
the feast-day of the Holy Innocents [28th Dec.] he caused the
church [of Westminster], which was entirely of his own building,
to be dedicated with great splendour to St. Peter, the prince of
apostles.[1]

   A.D. 1066.   On Thursday, the vigil of our Lord's Epiphany
[5th Jan.], in the fourth indiction, the pride of the English, the
pacific king Eadward, son of king Aethelred, died at London,
having reigned over the Anglo-Saxons twenty-three years, six
months, and twenty-seven days : the next day he was buried in
kingly style, amid the bitter lamentations of all present.   After his
interment, the subregulus Harold, son of earl Godwin, whom the
king had nominated as his successor, was elected king by the chief
nobles of all England; and on the same day was crowned with great

---

   [1] " Cedric, abbot of Abingdon, after he had ruled with honour the house in-
trusted to him, and had brought it back from the memory of the prince of the
apostles to his own, died, exhausted by a long sickness ; whereupon Eadred, who
had discharged the office of provost in the same monastery, succeeded to the
dignity of abbot."   B. addition.

ceremony, by Aldred, archbishop of York. On taking the helm
of the kingdom, he immediately began to abolish unjust laws and
make good ones; to patronise churches and monasteries; to pay
particular attention and yield reverence to bishops, abbots, monks,
and clerks; to show himself pious, humble, and affable to all good
men: but he treated malefactors with the utmost severity, and
gave general orders to his earls, ealdormen, sheriffs, and thanes to
imprison all thieves, robbers, and disturbers of the kingdom; and
he himself laboured by sea and by land for the protection of his
country.

On the 8th of the kalends of May [24th April] in this year, a
comet was seen not only in England, but, it is said, all over the
world, and shone for seven days with exceeding brightness. Shortly
afterwards earl Tosti returned from Flanders and landed at the
Isle of Wight. After making the islanders pay tribute and stipend,
he departed and went pillaging along the sea-coast until he arrived
at the port of Sandwich. As soon as king Harold, who was then
at London, heard this, he assembled a large fleet and an army of
cavalry, and he prepared to go in person to the port of Sandwich.
When Tosti was informed of this he took some of the shipmen of
the place, willing and unwilling, and bent his course towards
Lindesey, where he burned many vills and put many men to
death. Thereupon Eadwin, earl of the Mercians, and Morcar,
earl of the Northumbrians, hastened up with an army and expelled him from that part of the country. Departing thence he
went to Malcolm, king of the Scots, and remained with him
during the whole of the summer. Meanwhile king Harold arrived
at the port of Sandwich, and waited there for his fleet. When it
was assembled, he crossed over with it to the Isle of Wight, and
inasmuch as king Eadward's cousin William, earl of the Normans,
was preparing to invade England with an army, he watched all the
summer and autumn for his coming; and in addition distributed
a land force at suitable points along the sea-coast. But about the
feast-day of the Nativity of St. Mary [8th Sept.] provisions fell
short, so the naval and land forces returned home.

After this Harold Harvagra,[1] king of the Norwegians, and brother
of St. Olaf the king, arrived on a sudden at the mouth of the river
Tyne, with a powerful fleet, consisting of more than five hundred
large ships. Earl Tosti, according to previous arrangement, joined
him with his fleet. They hastened their course and entered the river
Humber, and then sailing up the river Ouse against the stream,
landed at a place called Richale. King Harold, on hearing this,
marched in haste towards Northumbria; but before his arrival the
two brothers, earls Eadwin and Morcar, at the head of a large
army, fought a battle with the Norwegians on the northern bank
of the river Ouse near York, on Wednesday, being the vigil of the
feast-day of St. Matthew the apostle [20th Sept.], and they fought
so bravely at the onset that many of the enemy were overthrown.
But after a long contest the English were unable to withstand the

. [1] Here Florence is in error; Harold Hardrada, and not Harold Harfagr, was
the ally of Tostig.

attacks of the Norwegians, and fled with great loss; and more
were drowned in the river than slain in the field. The Norwegians
remained masters of the field of carnage, and having taken one
hundred and fifty hostages from York, and leaving there one
hundred and fifty of their own men as hostages, they went to their
ships. Five days afterwards, that is, on Monday, the 7th of the
kalends of October [25th Sept.], as Harold, king of the English,
was coming to York with many thousand well-armed fighting men,
he fell in with the Norwegians at a place called Stamford-bridge,
slew king Harold and earl Tosti, with the greater part of their
army, and gained a complete victory; nevertheless, the battle was
stoutly contested. He, however, permitted Olaf, the son of the
Norwegian king, and Paul, earl of Orkney, who had been sent off
with a portion of the army to guard the fleet, to return home without
molestation, with twenty ships and the remains of the army; first,
however, taking hostages and oaths [of submission] from them.

In the midst of these things, and when the king might have considered that all his enemies were subdued, it was told to him that
William, earl of the Normans, had arrived with a countless host of
horsemen, slingers, archers, and foot-soldiers, having brought with
him powerful auxiliaries from all parts of Gaul, and that he had
landed at a place called Pefnesea [Pevensey]. Thereat, the king
at once, and in great haste, marched his army towards London;
and though he well knew that some of the bravest Englishmen had
fallen in his two [former] battles, and that one half of his army had
not yet arrived, he did not hesitate to advance with all speed into
South Saxony against his enemies; and on Saturday the 11th of
the kalends of September [22d Oct.], before a third of his army
was in order for fighting, he joined battle with them nine miles
from Hastings, where they had fortified a castle. But inasmuch
as the English were drawn up in a narrow place, many retired
from the ranks, and very few remained true to him; nevertheless
from the third hour of the day until dusk he bravely withstood the
enemy, and fought so valiantly and stubbornly in his own defence,
that the enemy's forces could hardly make any impression. At
last, after great slaughter on both sides, about twilight the king,
alas! fell. There were slain also earl Girth, and his brother earl
Leofwin, and nearly all the nobility of England. Then earl William
returned with his men to Hastings.

Harold reigned nine months and as many days. On hearing of
his death, the earls Eadwin and Morcar, who had withdrawn themselves and their men from the conflict, went to London and sent
their sister queen Algitha to Chester; but Aldred, archbishop of
York, and the said earls, with the citizens of London and the
shipmen, were desirous of elevating to the throne Eadgar the
etheling, nephew of king Eadmund Ironside, and promised that
they would renew the contest under his command. But while
numbers were preparing to go out to fight, the earls withdrew their
assistance and returned home with their army.

Meanwhile earl William was laying waste South Saxony, Kent,
South Hamptonshire, Surrey, Middle Saxony, and Hertfordshire,

and kept on burning the vills and slaying the natives until he came to a vill called Beorcham.   There archbishop Aldred, Wulstan, bishop of Worcester, Walter, bishop of Hereford, Eadgar the etheling, earls Eadwin and Morcar, the chief men of London, and many more came to him, and, giving hostages, surrendered and swore fealty to him.   So he entered into a treaty with them; yet, nevertheless, he permitted his army to burn the vills and keep on pillaging.   But when the feast of our Lord's Nativity [25th Dec.] drew nigh, he went to London with his whole army in order that he might be made king.   And because Stigand, the primate of all England, was accused by the pope of having obtained the pall in an uncanonical manner, he was anointed king at Westminster with great ceremony on Christmas-day (which in that year fell on a Monday) by Aldred, archbishop of York, having previously (for the archbishop had made it a condition) sworn at the altar of St. Peter the apostle, in the presence of the clergy and people, that he would defend the holy churches of God and their ministers, and would also rule justly and with royal care the people who were placed under him, and would ordain and maintain right law, and utterly prohibit all spoliation and unrighteous judgments.

A.D. 1067.   When Lent [21st Feb.] arrived, king William returned to Normandy, taking with him Stigand, archbishop of Canterbury, Aegelnoth, abbot of Glastonbury, Edgar, etheling, the earls Edwin and Morkar, Waltheof, son of duke Siward, the noble Agelnoth, governor of Kent, and many others of the chiefs of England; and leaving his brother Odo, bishop of Bayeux, and William Fitzosberne (whom he had created earl of Hereford), as wardens of England, he gave orders to strengthen the forts in different places.

Wulfwius, bishop of Dorchester, died at Winchester, but was buried at Dorchester.

At that time lived a very powerful thane, Edric, surnamed the Forester, the son of Aelfric brother of Edric Streona, whose land, because he refused to surrender himself up to the king, the garrison of Hereford and Richard Fitz-Scrob frequently devastated; but as often as they sallied out against him they lost many of their knights and esquires.

Wherefore Edric, having summoned to his assistance the kings of the Welsh, Blethgent and Rithwalan, about the Assumption of St. Mary [15th Aug.], laid waste the province of Hereford, up to the bridge over the river Lucge, and brought back great spoil. After this, the winter being near, king William returned from Normandy into England, and imposed on the English an insupportable tax.   Then invading Devonshire, he besieged and speedily reduced the city of Exeter, which the citizens and a few English thanes held against him.   But the countess Gytha, the mother of Harold, king of the English, and sister of Sweyn, king of the Danes, escaped with many others from the city, and sought refuge in Flanders; and the citizens surrendered to the king, having interchanged right hands.   Siward, nineteenth bishop of Rochester, died.

A.D. 1068. After Easter [23d March], the countess Matilda came from Normandy into England, and on the day of Pentecost [11th May] was consecrated queen by Aldred, archbishop of York. After this, Marleswein and Gospatric, and all the nobler Northumbrians, to avoid the severity of the king, and dreading the imprisonment which so many had suffered, sailed to Scotland, with Eadgar, etheling, his mother Agatha, and his two sisters Margaret and Christina, and wintered there under the protection of Malcolm, king of Scots. Now king William came with his army to Nottingham, and having strengthened the castle there, proceeded to York; where having fortified two castles and placed five hundred men in them, he gave orders that the castles in the city of Lincoln and in other places should be fortified.

While these events were taking place, the sons of king Harold, Godwin, Eadmund, and Magnus, landed in Somerset, on their return from Ireland, and Eadnothus, late stallere to king Harold, met them, and giving them battle, was slain, with many others; and they, having gained the victory, and carried away a considerable spoil from Devon and Cornwall, returned to Ireland.

A.D. 1069. [1]Marianus, after a seclusion of ten years in Fulda, by command of the bishop of Mentz and the abbot of Fulda, came to Mentz, on the 3d of the nones of April [3d April], being the Friday before Palm Sunday [5th April]. Two of the sons of Harold, about the Nativity of St. John Baptist [24th June], coming again from Ireland with sixty-four ships, landed at the mouth of the Tavy, and fought a great battle with Brian of Brittany; after its termination they returned to the place whence they had come.

[2]Marianus, on the 6th of the ides of July [10th July], being the Friday in the Nativity of the Seven Holy Brethren, entered into seclusion in the same city, near the chief monastery.

Before the Nativity of St. Mary [8th Sept.], Harold and Canute, sons of Sweyn, king of the Danes, and their uncle, earl Asbiorn, with earl Thurkill, coming from Denmark with two hundred and forty ships, landed at the mouth of the Humber, where they were joined by Eadgar, etheling, earl Waltheof, and Marleswein, and many others, with the fleet which they had assembled. Aldred, archbishop of York, being much affected with grief at their arrival, fell into a dangerous sickness, and in the tenth year of his archiepiscopate, Friday, on the 3d of the ides of September [11th Sept.], as he had prayed of God, he departed this life, and was buried in the church of St. Peter. On the eighth day after this, namely, on Saturday, the 13th of the kalends of October [19th Sept.], the Normans who kept the forts set fire to the houses adjacent to them, fearing that they might be of use to the Danes in filling up the trenches; and the flames spreading, attacked the whole of the city, and entirely consumed it, together with the monastery of St. Peter.

But this was most speedily followed by a heavy infliction of the divine vengeance. For on Monday, before the whole of the city was entirely burnt, the Danes arrived with their fleet, and on the

[1] This passage respecting Marianus is extracted from his own Chronicle.
[2] Also from Marianus.

same day destroyed the forts; and having put to the sword upwards of three thousand of the Normans (one William Malet, with his wife and two children, and a very few others, being spared), they returned to their ships with a large amount of plunder.

When king William received intelligence of this, he at once assembled his army, and hastening, with an angry heart, into Northumbria, ceased not, during the whole winter, to lay waste the land, to murder the inhabitants, and to inflict numerous injuries.

Meanwhile he sent messengers to the Danish earl, Asbiörn, and engaged to present him secretly with a large sum of money, and to grant permission to his army to forage freely along the sea-coast, on condition that he would depart, without giving battle, at the end of the winter. But the Dane, too greedy of money, to his great dishonour, agreed to the terms proposed to him.

On account of the devastations of England by the North-men, (which were confined to Northumbria and other provinces, in the preceding year, and in the present and following years extended throughout nearly the whole of the country, but were most severe in Northumbria and the adjoining provinces,) so great a famine prevailed that men were forced to consume the flesh of horses, dogs, cats, and even that of human beings.

A.D. 1070.   By the advice of William, earl of Hereford, and some others, during the time of Lent, king William commanded the monasteries of the whole of England to be searched, and the money which the richer English, by reason of the severity and the depopulation of the land, had deposited in them, to be seized and carried to his treasury.

In the octaves of Easter [4th April], a great council was holden at Winchester, in the presence and by the command of king William, and by consent of pope Alexander, whose authority was represented by his legates, Earmenfred, bishop of Sion, and John and Peter, presbyter cardinals of the apostolic see. In this council Stigand, archbishop of Canterbury, was degraded on three grounds; because he was unlawfully holding the bishopric of Winchester, together with his own archbishopric; and because, during the life of archbishop Robert, he had not only taken possession of the archbishopric, but for some time during the celebration of the mass had worn his pall, which had been left at Canterbury after his violent and unjust banishment from England; and because he had afterwards received the pall from Benedict, who had been excommunicated by the Holy Roman Church for having simoniacally obtained possession of the apostolic see. His brother, Aegelmar, bishop of the East Angles, was also deposed. A few abbots were also there degraded, the king promoting the deprivation of the English, and filling up their places by persons of his own nation, in order to confirm his power in a kingdom which he had but newly acquired. He also deprived of their honours certain persons, both bishops and abbots, whom neither the ecclesiastical councils nor the civil laws could convict of any open crime, and to the end of their lives held them in confinement, induced solely by mistrust, as we have said, of losing his newly acquired kingdom. In this council also, while

the rest were trembling in anticipation of the loss of their own
honours, as though they had penetrated the intentions of the
king, the venerable Wulfstan, bishop of Worcester, courageously
demanded the restitution of many of the appurtenances of his see
which had been retained by archbishop Aeldred in his own power,
when he was translated from Worcester to York, and which, by his
death, had passed into the hands of the king; and insisted on
justice being done to him, not only by those who presided in the
council, but also by the king himself. But because the church of
York, not having a pastor who could plead her cause, was dumb, it
was adjudged that the dispute should remain undecided until the
appointment of an archbishop, who could defend her, when, as
there would be an opponent to reply to his argument, a more clear
and just decision would be elicited from their mutual statements
and answers. Thus, therefore, the matter remained for the present.
On the day of Pentecost [23d May], the king, at Windsor, gave
the archbishopric of York to the venerable Thomas, canon of
Bayeux, and the bishopric of Winchester to his chaplain, Walchelin;
by whose mandate, on the morrow, the aforesaid Aermenfrid,
bishop of Sion, held a synod, the cardinals, John and Peter, having
returned to Rome. In this synod, Aegelric, bishop of the South
Saxons, was uncanonically deposed, and soon after placed in confinement at Mearlesbeorge by the king, though he was innocent of
any crime; many abbots were also deposed. After their deprivation, the king gave the bishopric of the East Angles to Arfast,
and that of the South Saxons to Stigand, his chaplain; Stigand
transferred his see to Chichester, the capital of his diocese; the
king also gave abbeys to some Norman monks. And because the
archbishop of Canterbury was deposed, and the archbishop of York
dead, by command of the king, in the octave of Pentecost [31st
May], Walchelin was ordained by the same Aermenfrid, bishop
of Sion.

  The feast of St. John Baptist [24th June] being near, earl
Asbiörn went to Denmark with the fleet which had wintered in the
Humber, and his brother Sweyn outlawed him because he had
taken a bribe from king William against the wishes of the Danes.
That valiant man, Edric, surnamed the forester, (of whom we made
mention above,) was reconciled with king William. After this, the
king summoned from Normandy Landfranc, abbot of Caen, by
birth a Lombard, a man of varied learning, skilled in all liberal
arts, and in divine and secular knowledge, of exceeding prudence
in counsel, and in the management of state affairs; on the day of
the Assumption of St. Mary [15th Aug.] the king appointed him
archbishop of Canterbury, and caused him to be consecrated, on
Sunday, the feast of St. John Baptist [24th June], at Canterbury.
He was consecrated by Giso, bishop of Wells, and Walter, bishop
of Hereford, who were both ordained at Rome by pope Nicholas.
when Aeldred, archbishop of York, took the pall; for they avoided
ordination at the hands of Stigand, then archbishop of Canterbury,
knowing him to have received the pall uncanonically. Bishop
Heriman, who had now transferred the seat of his bishopric from

Shirburn to Salisbury, was also present at his consecration, with some others. Afterwards Landfranc consecrated Thomas, archbishop of York. These things being done, there being now a bishop who could plead for the church of York, the cause of the reverend Wulfstan, bishop of Worcester, was again mooted, and finally, by the aid of God's grace, concluded in a council holden in a place called Pedreda, in presence of the king, Landfranc, archbishop of Canterbury, and the bishops, abbots, earls, and chiefs of all England. For all the stratagems by which Thomas and his supporters were busily attempting to lower the church of Worcester, and to render her the subject and slave of York, being crushed by the just judgment of God, and the clearest documentary evidence, and totally annihilated, not only did Wulfstan regain the possession which he had publicly demanded, but he resumed his church in the enjoyment of those liberties which its first founders, St. Aethelred, Osher, viceroy of the Hwiccii, and the other kings of Mercia, Kenred, Aethelbald, Offa, Kenulf, and their successors, Eadward the elder, Aethelstan, Eadmund, Edred, Eadgar, had conferred upon it.

Aegelwine, bishop of Durham, was taken by the men of king William, and thrust into prison; where, refusing to eat from excessive sorrow of heart, he died of grief and starvation. On the death of Siward, bishop of Rochester, Arnostus, monk of Bec, succeeded to the see, and was himself succeeded by Gundulf, a monk of the same church.

A.D. 1071. Landfranc and Thomas went to Rome, and received the pall from pope Alexander. Earls Edwin and Morkar, because king William sought to put them in confinement, escaped secretly from his court, and for some time continued in rebellion against him; but when they saw that their enterprise had not turned out successfully, Edwin determined to go to Malcolm, king of the Scots, but was killed on the journey, in an ambush laid by his own people. But Morkar, and Aegelwine, bishop of Durham, Siward, surnamed Barn, and Hereward, a most valiant man, with many others, took ship, and went to the isle of Ely, desiring to winter there. When the king heard of this, he blocked up every outlet on the eastern side of the island by his sailors, and commanded a bridge of two miles in length to be constructed on the western side. And when they saw that they were thus shut in, they gave up resistance, and all except the valiant Hereward, who made his escape through the fens, with a few others, surrendered to the king; who at once sent bishop Aegelwine to Abingdon, where he was placed in confinement, and died the same winter. As for the earl and the rest, who were scattered throughout England, he placed some in confinement, and permitted some to go free, with the loss of their hands or eyes.[1]

A.D. 1072. After the Assumption of St. Mary [15th Aug.],

[1] " Aldred, abbot of Abingdon, was placed in custody in the castle of Walingford; but after some time he was removed thence, and committed to the keeping of Walcheline, bishop of Winchester, in which he continued as long as he lived. He was succeeded in his abbacy by Athelelm, a monk of Jumiege." Lamb. MS.

William, king of the English, having Edric the Forester in his retinue, invaded Scotland with a naval force and an army of cavalry, in order to reduce it to his own power; and Malcolm, king of Scots, met. him in a place called Abernithiei, and became his vassal. Aegelric, late bishop of Durham, departed this life at Westminster, whither king William had sent him into confinement, on Monday, the ides of October [15th October]. Walcer, a native of Lorrain, succeeded Aegelwine in the see of Durham.

A.D. 1073. William, king of the English, reduced to his own power the city called Maine, and the province belonging to it, principally by the aid of the English whom he had taken with him out of England. Eadgar Aetheling came out of Scotland through England into Normandy, and was reconciled to the king.

A.D. 1074. Roger, earl of Hereford, son of William, earl of the same province, gave his daughter in marriage to Ralph, earl of the East Angles, against the command of the king; and while he was celebrating the nuptials with much magnificence, along with a great multitude of nobles, at a place called Yxninge, in the province of Cambridge, he formed a conspiracy, in which most of the party oined, against the king, and they compelled earl Waltheof, whom they had insidiously surprised, to join them in the plot. As soon as he was able, however, he went to Landfranc, archbishop of Canterbury, and accepting penance for his compulsory oath, by his advice applied to king William, who was then in Normandy, and having related the affair from beginning to end, voluntarily threw himself upon the royal clemency. But the chiefs of the conspiracy, intent upon the advancement of their plot, retired to their castles, and began by every exertion, with the aid of their supporters, to excite the rebellion. But Wulfstan, bishop of Worcester, with a great military force, Aegelwy, abbot of Evesham, with his followers, and having procured the assistance of Urso, earl of Worcester, and Walter de Lacy, with their forces, and a large number of the people, prepared to prevent the earl of Hereford from crossing the Severn and joining earl Ralph and his army. Odo, bishop of Bayeux, the king's brother, and Geoffrey, bishop of Coutances, with a great force, both of English and Normans, ready for action, met the earl himself encamped near Cambridge. But he, perceiving that his plan was frustrated, and moreover fearing the superior numbers of his opponents, escaped secretly to Norwich, and, leaving his castle to the care of his wife and his knights, embarked from England for Lesser Brittany; his adversaries pursuing him, and killing or maiming in various ways those of his followers whom they were able to capture. Then the leaders laid siege to his castle, until the proclamation of peace by the permission of the king allowed his countess and her people to depart from England. These things being done, the king returned in the autumn from Normandy, and put earl Roger in confinement, and delivered earl Waltheof to custody, though he had implored his mercy.

Eadgyth, sister-in-law to king Harold, once king of the English, died at Winchester on the 14th of the kalends of January [19th Dec.].

Her body was brought to London by command of the king, and buried with honour near the body of her husband, king Eadward, at Westminster, where the king at the ensuing Nativity held his court; and of those who had rebelled against him, he outlawed some and disgraced others, by putting out their eyes or cutting off their hands; but he committed to closer confinement the earls Waltheof and Roger, who had been condemned by a judicial sentence.

A.D. 1075. Earl Waltheof, by order of king William, being brought outside of the city of Winchester, was beheaded with cruel indignity, and buried in the place of his execution; but in process of time, by the ordinance of God, his body was exhumed, carried with great honour to Croyland, and honourably buried in the church. This man, while yet in the enjoyment of life, being placed in close confinement, lamented without ceasing and with extreme bitterness the unrighteous actions of his past life. He earnestly sought to appease his God by vigils, prayers, fastings, and almsgiving; men desired to blot out the remembrance of him on earth; but we firmly believe that he is now rejoicing with the saints in heaven, on the testimony of archbishop Landfranc of pious memory, from whom he received the sacrament of penance after his confession, who declared that not only was he guiltless of the crime laid to his charge, the conspiracy mentioned above, but that, like a true Christian, he had lamented with tears of penitence the other sins which he had committed; and he added that he himself should esteem himself happy could he enjoy, after his own departure, the blessed repose of the earl. After this the king crossed the sea, and entering Lesser Brittany, besieged the castle of earl Ralph, which was called Dol, until Philip, king of the French, expelled him.

A.D. 1076.

A.D. 1077. Robert, the eldest son of the king, (because he was not permitted to possess Normandy which had been assigned to him in the presence of Philip, king of the French, before the arrival of William in England,) went to France, and, with the assistance of Philip, committed great and frequent ravages in Normandy; he burned the towns, put to death the people, and gave his father no little annoyance and anxiety.

A.D. 1078.

A.D. 1079. Malcolm, king of Scots, after the Assumption of St. Mary [15th Aug.], laid waste Northumbria as far as the great river Tyne, killing many men, capturing more, and returning with great spoil. King William, while engaged with his son Robert before the castle of Gerberoi, which king Philip had offered to him, was wounded by him in the arm and unhorsed; but the son recognising his father's voice, hastily dismounted, and bidding him mount his own charger, permitted him to depart. And many of the king's men having been slain, and some few taken prisoners, and his son William and many others wounded, he commenced a retreat. The venerable Robert, who had received the order of priesthood by the ministry of Wulfstan, bishop of Worcester, was consecrated at Canterbury bishop of Hereford, by Landfranc, archbishop of Canterbury, on Sunday the 4th of the kalends of January [29th Dec.].

A.D. 1080. Walcher, bishop of Durham, a native of Lorrain, was slain by the Northumbrians on Thursday, the 2d of the ides of May [14th May], at Gateshead, in revenge for the murder of Liulf, a thane of noble birth. This man held many possessions by hereditary right throughout England; but because in all parts of the land the Normans were at that time continually giving vent to their ferocity, he withdrew himself with all his people to Durham, by reason of the sincere affection which he bore to the holy Cuthbert, who (as he was wont to narrate to Aldred, archbishop of York, and other religious persons) very often appeared to him both in his sleeping and waking hours, and revealed to him as to his faithful friend all that he wished to be done, under whose protection he had lived for a long time, sometimes in the town, sometimes on the possessions which he held on those districts. The arrival of this person was not unpleasing to bishop Walcher, who was greatly devoted to the same saint in all things. For this reason he became so much beloved by the bishop, that he would not transact or arrange the weightier matters of his secular business without his advice. Wherefore his chaplain, Leobwin, whom he had so much exalted that scarcely anything was moved in the bishopric or in the county without his consent, goaded on by envy, and puffed up with excess of pride by reason of his own power, arrogantly opposed himself to the aforesaid Liulf, treating as if they were worthless his judgments and counsels, and by every means striving to bring them to nothing. Frequently, also, arguing with him in the presence of the bishop, not without threats, did he provoke him to anger by opprobrious words. One day it happened that when this same Liulf, having been called to the council by the bishop, had decided in all cases lawfully and justly, Leobwin obstinately opposed him and exasperated him by contumelious speeches. And because he was answered more harshly than ordinarily was the case, he at once left the court, and calling to him Gilebert, to whom the bishop, as being his own kinsman, had committed the government of the county of Northumbria, he earnestly prayed that he would avenge him, and as soon as possible would hasten the death of Liulf. Gilebert at once agreeing to his iniquitous request, having collected the soldiers of the bishop and of Leobwin himself, set out one night for the town where Liulf then lived, and wickedly slew him in his own house with nearly all his household. When he first heard this, the bishop, sighing deeply from his very heart, tore his hood from his head, and casting it on the ground, said sorrowfully to Leobwin, who was present, "This has been done, O Leobwin, by thy artful dealings and most foolish machinations; and I would have thee know that for a surety thou hast destroyed both me, thyself, and all my household by the sword of thy tongue." Saying this he hastily withdrew into his castle, and immediately sending messengers through Northumbria, he took great care to inform all that so far from having been privy to the death of Liulf, he had outlawed from

Northumbria his murderer and all his companions, and was prepared to purge himself according to the pope's judgment. Then
the bishop and the relatives of the deceased (after having sent messengers to and fro, and peace being mutually given and accepted)
appointed a place and day on which to meet and confirm the
same. When the day arrived they met together in the appointed
place; but the bishop was unwilling to plead with them in the
open air, but entered into a church there with his clergy and the
more honourable of his knights; and having held a council, sent out
to them from among his people once and again those who were to
make peace with them. But they would by no means acquiesce in
the required conditions, because they held it certain that Liulf had
been put to death by the bishop's orders; for not only had
Leobwin, on the very next night after the murder of his relative,
taken Gilebert and his companions into his house with friendly
familiarity, but had received him as before into his favour and
family. Wherefore they at first put to death all those of the
bishop's party who were found out of doors, a few saving themselves by flight. Seeing this, in order to satisfy the fury of his
enemies, the bishop ordered the aforesaid Gilebert, his kinsman,
for whose life they were seeking, to go out of the church, the
guard following close upon him as he went out ; but forthwith
they were attacked upon all sides by the enemy with sword and
spear, and in a moment destroyed, only two Englishmen being
spared by reason of consanguinity. Leofwin, the dean of Durham, because he had often given much assistance to the bishop
against them, and the other clergy, they slew as soon as they came
forth. But the bishop, when he saw that their fury could not be
mitigated by any means short of the death of the chief and author
of all the calamity, Leobwin, requested him to go forth ; being
entirely unable to prevail upon him, he proceeded himself to the
gates of the church, and begged that his own life might be spared.
This being refused, he covered his head with the border of his
robe, went forth, and soon perished by the swords of his enemies.
Then they commanded Leobwin to come forth, and when he
refused, they set fire to the walls and roof of the church. But he,
choosing rather to end his life by fire than sword, bore the flames
for some time. At length, half burnt, he leaped from the building,
and having been dashed in pieces he died a wretched death, paying
the penalty of his wickedness. To revenge the detestable murder
of these men, king William in the same year laid waste the province of Northumbria.

A.D. 1081. William, abbot of the monastery of St. Vincent
the Martyr, being elected by king William, received the bishopric
of Durham, and on the nones of January [5th Jan.] was consecrated
by archbishop Thomas.

A.D. 1082. King William placed his brother Odo, bishop of
Bayeux, in confinement in Normandy.

A.D. 1083. A dire dispute arose between the monks of Glastonbury and their unworthy abbot Turstan, whom, despite his want of
discretion, king William had elevated from being a monk of Caen,

to the dignity of abbot of Glastonbury. Among his other foolish exploits, he despised the Gregorian chant, and attempted to compel the monks to relinquish it, and to learn to sing that of one William of Fécamp. When they, who had grown old in the practice of the Roman church, in this, as in other ecclesiastical ceremonies, received his proposal with hesitation, on a sudden, at the head of a military force, without their knowledge, he one day broke into the chapter-house and pursued the terrified monks, who fled into the church, as far as the altar. The roods, and images, and shrines of the saints, were pierced by the spears and arrows of his band; he himself speared and killed one of the monks who was embracing the holy altar, and put to death a second, who lay pierced with arrows at its foot; the rest, compelled by necessity, bravely defended themselves with the benches and candlesticks of the church, and though severely wounded, they succeeded in driving back all the soldiers out of the choir. The result of this was, that of the monks there were two killed, and fourteen wounded, and even of the soldiers a few injured.

The matter was brought to a judicial investigation, and when it was clear that the greater share of the blame belonged to the abbot, the king removed him, and placed him in his own monastery in Normandy. Most of the monks were dispersed through bishoprics and abbacies, and placed in custody by command of the king. After his death, the abbot purchased back his abbacy from his son, king William, for five hundred pounds, and wandering about for some years over the possessions of his church, at length finished his days in misery, far from the monastery itself, as he well deserved. On Thursday, the 4th of the nones of November [2d Nov.], queen Matilda died in Normandy, and was buried at Caen.

A.D. 1084. William, king of the English, took six shillings from every hide throughout England.

A.D. 1085. Eadmund, abbot of Pershore, a man of rare probity and piety, died in a good old age, on Sunday, the 17th of the kalends of July [15th June], and was honourably buried by the venerable Serlo, abbot of Gloucester; Turstan, monk of Gloucester, succeeded him. In the same year, Canute, king of the Danes, with a great fleet, and aided by his father-in-law, Robert, earl of Flanders, prepared to invade England. Wherefore king William, levying soldiers, footmen, and archers, to the number of many thousands, from the whole of France, and taking some out of Normandy, returned in the autumn to England, and dividing his army, gave orders to his bishops, abbots, earls, barons, sheriffs, and officers, to supply them with provisions. But when he ascertained that his enemies had been checked, he sent back a part of his army, and kept a part with him through the whole of the winter; and on the day of the Nativity of our Lord [25th Dec.], held his court at Gloucester, where he gave bishoprics to three of his chaplains, namely, to Maurice the see of London, to William that of Thetford, to Robert that of Chester.

A.D. 1086. King William caused all England to be described; namely, the quantity of land possessed by each of his barons, the

number of knights' fees, the number of hides of land, the number of villeins, the number of beasts, yea, the amount of ready
money which each possessed in all his kingdom, from the greatest
to the least, and how much rent each property was able to return :
and the land was sorely vexed with the murders which proceeded
therefrom.   In the week of Whitsuntide [24th May], the king
honoured his son Henry with knighthood at Westminster, where he
was holding his court.   Not long afterwards he commanded that
his archbishops, bishops, abbots, earls, barons, sheriffs, with their
knights, should meet him at Salisbury, on the kalends of August
[1st Aug.] ; when they were there, he compelled their knights to
swear fealty to him against all men.   At that time Eadgar, etheling, having obtained permission of the king, went over sea with
two hundred knights, and proceeded to Apulia ; his sister, the
maiden Christina, entered the monastery, which is called the
monastery of Rumsey, and assumed the dress of a nun.   In the
same year there was a murrain among beasts, and a great tempest.

A.D. 1087.   In this year many perished, at first from fever, and
then from famine.   Meanwhile a destructive fire consumed nearly
all the principal cities of England, and the church of St. Paul the
Apostle, with the greater and better part of London.   The Danes
martyred their king, Canute, on Saturday, the 6th of the ides of
July, in a certain church.   Stigand, bishop of Chichester, Scolland,
abbot of St. Augustine's, Alsi, abbot of Bath, and Turstan, abbot
of Pershore, died.   Before the Assumption of St. Mary [15th Aug.],
king William came with an army into France, burned the town
which is called Mathantum [Mantes], and all the churches situated
therein, and two recluses, and thence returned into Normandy ;
but on the journey a dreadful disease of the bowels seized him,
which grew more and more serious from day to day.   Now when,
as his sickness became worse, he perceived that the day of his
death was near, he released his brother Odo, bishop of Baieux, earls
Morkar and Roger, Siward, surnamed Barn, and Wulnoth, brother
of king Harold, whom he had kept in confinement from boyhood,
and all whom he had delivered into custody in England or in
Normandy.   Then he consigned the kingdom of England to his
son William, and granted the earldom of Normandy to his first-
born Robert, who was then absent in France : and so, supported
by the heavenly viaticum, on the 5th of the ides of September [9th
Sept.], having reigned over England twenty years, ten months, and
twenty-eight days, he rendered up at once his life and his kingdom.
He lies at Caen, in the church of St. Stephen the Protomartyr,
which he himself had built and endowed.   His son William
hastened to England, taking with him Wulnoth and Morkar ; but
as soon as he arrived at Winchester, he put them into custody as
before, and on Sunday, the 6th of the kalends of October [26th
Sept.], he was consecrated king at Westminster by Landfranc,
archbishop of Canterbury.   Then, returning to Winchester, he
divided the treasure of his father, in pursuance of his commands,
among some of the principal churches of England, giving to some
ten, to others six marks of gold, to others less ; he also com-

manded that forty pence should be given to each of the churches in his cities and towns ; and that crosses, altars, shrines, copies of the Gospels, candlesticks, sacred vessels, pipes [for the wine in the Holy Communion], and various ornaments, received in exchange for jewels, gold, silver, and precious stones, should be divided among the more important churches and monasteries. His brother Robert also returning into Normandy, liberally divided among the monasteries, churches, and poor, the treasures which he had found, and this he did for the repose of his father's soul. Moreover he released from custody Ulf, son of Harold, once king of the English, and Duncan, son of Malcolm, king of Scots, and honoured them with knighthood, and permitted them to depart.

A.D. 1088.   In this year great dissension arose between the nobles of England ; for one part (and that the lesser) of the Norman nobles favoured king William, but the greater part adhered to Robert, earl of Normandy; being desirous of summoning him into the kingdom, and either of delivering his brother to him alive, or of depriving him of his power by putting him to death. The leaders of this execrable business were Odo, bishop of Baieux, who was also earl of Kent, Robert his brother, the earl of Mortain, both of whom were brothers, by the mother's side only, of king William the elder. Along with his nephew Robert, earl of Northumberland, there participated in this design Geoffrey, bishop of Coutance, Roger, earl of Shrewsbury, and (what was worse still) William, bishop of Durham ; for at that very time the king was guided by his sagacity, as if he were a trustworthy adviser, for he was of good counsel, and by his advice was the whole realm of England managed. These men had great influence in this land by reason of their worldly wealth. Every day the multitude of their fellow-soldiers and accomplices in the conspiracy increased. They began to discuss this execrable plot during the season of Lent, and concluded that they could burst into open rebellion after Easter [16th April]; for they withdrew themselves from the court, and fortifying their castles, ravaged the land with fire, sword, and slaughter. An accursed deed was this, a war worse than a civil war ! For fathers were fighting against their sons, brothers against brothers, friends against kinsmen, the aliens against the aliens. Meanwhile the bishop of Baieux, having fortified Rochester, sent into Normandy, exhorting earl Robert to come with all speed into England, informing him of what was being done, and declaring that a kingdom was ready for him, and, if he were not wanting to himself, a crown also. Struck with the strange news, the earl with exultation informed his friends, and, full of triumph, like one already secure of victory, spurred on his followers to the plunder; he sent auxiliaries into England, to his uncle, bishop Odo, promising to follow with all speed as soon as he shall have assembled a larger force. When they arrived, the defence of Rochester was entrusted to them by Odo, the command being assumed by Eustace the younger, earl of Boulogne, and Robert de Belesme. When the news of this affair reached the ears of the king, he was troubled with an unusual anxiety; but, relying (like a brave man) on his claim to the crown and the courage of his soldiers, he employed his royal authority and sent messengers to summon those whom he believed to be faithful to himself, and he then marched to London to settle the details of the war, and to provide necessaries for the expedition. Having assembled an army of horse and foot, though of moderate size, consisting principally of Englishmen, and of as large a number of Normans as he was able for the present to collect, and making laws and promising rewards to his supporters, he put his trust in the mercy of God. He determined to march to Rochester, where he heard the army had assembled in the greatest numbers; for he had been informed that bishop Odo was there with his men and the foreign force. Marching thither, at the very commencement of his journey, he found that Tunbridge, which was under the command of Gilebert Fitz Richard, held out against him; he besieged it, reduced it in two days, and forced Gilebert, who was wounded, to surrender with his garrison. The fame of this success reached the ears of Odo, who, after having held a consultation with his friends, left Rochester, and proceeded with a few followers to the castle of his brother, Robert, earl of Mortain, which is called Pevensey. Finding his brother there, he exhorted him to remain, promising him that they would be secure, and that while the king was busy in reducing Rochester, the earl of Normandy would come over with a large army, would set them and their men at liberty, and would take possession of the kingdom, after handsomely rewarding all his supporters. The king, having reduced Tunbridge, and accepted the fealty of the inhabitants, leaving Gilebert behind him by reason of his wound, and placing the castle under guard, was about to depart for Rochester, as he had intended, when he heard that his uncle had left that place and had gone to Pevensey.

Having taken wholesome counsel, he pursued him with his army as far as Pevensey, hoping that he would more speedily terminate the war, if he could first subdue the chiefs of the rebellion. He pushed forward, he prepared his engines, and laid siege to both his uncles : the position was strongly fortified ; but he laboured daily to reduce it. Meanwhile, throughout England the storm of war raged in every direction ; the people of Rochester carried fire and slaughter against the inhabitants of Canterbury and London; for archbishop Landfranc and nearly all the nobles of that province were with the king. Roger, a partisan of Robert, was in his castle of Arundel, expecting the arrival of the earl. Geoffrey, bishop of Coutance, was in Bristol castle, having with him his nephew, Robert de Mulbray, an accomplice in his conspiracy and treachery, a man skilled in the art of war, who assembled an army and attacked the city of Bath, which was on the king's side ; and when he had burned and plundered it, he then crossed over into Wiltshire, and laid waste the towns. After a great slaughter of the inhabitants, he at length reached Ilchester, and laid siege to it, and attempted to reduce it. Those who were attracted by the hope of plunder and the love of victory, fought outside the town ; those who were within the walls resisted, having due regard for the safety of their persons and their property. At length the cause of necessity triumphed, and Robert retired in sorrow, disappointed of the victory. William de Eu invaded the province of Gloucester, plundered the royal town of Berkeley, and did great mischief everywhere with fire and sword.

Now, while these evils were being perpetrated on every side, Bernard de Newmarket, Roger de Lacy, who had just marched against the king at Hereford, Ralph de Mortimer, all of them conspirators, with the men of earl Roger of Shrewsbury, having assembled a great army of English, Normans, and Welshmen, made an inroad into the province of Worcester, declaring that they would burn the city of Worcester itself, spoil the church of God and St. Mary, and take heavy vengeance on the loyal inhabitants. On hearing this, the reverend father Wulfstan, bishop of Worcester, (a man of great piety and dove-like simplicity, one beloved of God and the people whom he ruled in all things, constant and faithful to the king, as his earthly lord,) was exceedingly troubled; but soon recovering confidence by the mercy of God, already, like another Moses, prepared himself to stand manfully by his people and his city. While they made ready their arms to repel the enemy, he poured forth supplications for the impending danger, exhorting his people that they despair not of God's assistance, since He fights neither with sword nor spear. Meanwhile the Normans taking counsel, entreat the bishop to remove from the church into the castle, affirming that they would be the more secure by reason of his presence, if a greater danger should happen to attack them; for they loved him greatly. But he (such was his kindness of disposition) assented to their request, moved by his fidelity to the king, and his affection to themselves. Meanwhile the episcopal household was courageously preparing for the contest; the garrison and the whole of the citizens assembled, declaring that they would meet the enemy on the other side of the Severn, provided always that the bishop's licence be obtained. Being armed and ready, they met him on his way to the castle, and begged the licence which they desired; to whom, assenting freely, " Go," said he, " my children, go in peace, go in security, with the blessing of God and mine. Trusting in the Lord, I promise you this day no sword shall injure you, no mishap, no adversary. Be firm in your allegiance to the king, manfully fighting for the safety of the people and the city." With these words, they eagerly crossed the bridge, and beheld the enemy approaching rapidly at a distance. Among them already raged the madness of war; for, despising the commands of the bishop, they had burnt many portions of his territory. When he heard this, the bishop was stricken with great sorrow, beholding the destruction of the property of the church; and taking counsel, launched against them, by the advice of all who were present, a heavy anathema. A wonderful thing, proclaiming most clearly the power of God and the goodness of the man, came to pass : for immediately the enemy, who were wandering scattered over the fields, were stricken with so great a weakness in their limbs, and enfeebled by such blindness of the outward eye, that they were hardly able to bear their arms; they could neither recognise their friends, nor distinguish those who were attacking them from the opposite party. While blindness deceived them, confidence in God and the bishop's benediction comforted our men. So stupified were they that they knew not how to escape, neither did they seek any means of defence ; but by the will of God, being given over to a reprobate mind, they fell an easy prey into the hands of their enemies. The footmen were slain, the horsemen captured—English, Normans, and Welshmen—the rest just escaping by a feeble flight. Those who were faithful to the king, along with the household of the bishop, joyfully exulting, returned without loss to their own homes ; thanking God for the safety of the property of the church, thanking the bishop for the wholesomeness of his counsel.

A.D. 1089.   Landfranc, archbishop of Canterbury, died on Thursday, the 9th of the kalends of June [24th May]. In the same year, on Saturday, the 3d of the ides of August [11th Aug.], about the third hour, there was a great earthquake throughout all England.

A.D. 1090. William the younger, the king of England, desirous of depriving his brother Robert of the province of Normandy, and of reducing it under his own dominion, took possession first of the castle of Walter de St. Valéry, and the castle of Odo de Albemarle, and next of other castles, and placed men in them to ravage Normandy ; seeing which, and having discovered the unfaithfulness of his allies, earl Robert sent messengers to Philip, king of the French, his lord, and caused him to come into Normandy, and he and the king besieged one of the castles in which his brother's soldiers were stationed. When news of this was brought to king William, he secretly sent a large sum of money to king Philip, and earnestly entreated him to raise the siege and to return home.

A.D. 1091. In the month of February, king William went over to Normandy, in order to take it from his brother Robert ; but while he was sojourning there peace was concluded between them, on condition that the earl should freely give up to the king the earldom of Eu, the monastery of Féchamp, the abbey situated on Mount St. Michel, Cherbourg, and the castles which had revolted from him ; that the king on his part should reduce to his obedience the province of Maine, and the castles in Normandy which were then resisting earl Robert, should restore their lands in England to the Normans who had lost them by their adherence to that earl, and should assign him a certain quantity of land in England to be agreed upon between them. In addition to this, it was agreed that if the earl should die without a legitimate son, the king should be his heir ; and in like manner, if it should happen that the king died, the earl should be his heir. Twelve barons on the part of the king, and twelve on the part of the earl, confirmed this treaty by oath. Meanwhile their brother Henry, with all the soldiers he was able to get together, entered Mount St. Michel, some of the monks assisting him ; and he laid waste the king's land, and captured some and spoiled others of his people. Wherefore the king and the earl assembled an army, and laid siege to the Mount, during the whole of the season of Lent, and frequently gave battle to the prince, and lost some of their men and horses. But the king grew tired of the long siege, and withdrew unappeased, and not long after deprived Eadgar, etheling, of the possessions which the earl had granted him, and expelled him from Normandy. Meanwhile, in the month of May, Malcolm, king of Scots, invaded Northumbria with a great army, intending, if he had good success, to proceed farther, and to attack the inhabitants of England. But God decreed that it should not be so, wherefore his attempt was frustrated ; nevertheless before he returned, the army carried away with it a considerable spoil out of Northumbria. When the king heard of this, he returned to England with his brother Robert in the month of August, and not long after he set out for Scotland, with a large fleet and an army of horsemen, to subdue king Malcolm ; but before he reached Scotland, a few days before Michaelmas [29th Sept.], nearly all the fleet was lost, and many of his horsemen perished from cold and hunger. King Malcolm met him in the district of Loidis with his army. Earl Robert seeing this, summoned to him Eadgar, etheling, whom the king had expelled from Normandy, and who was then living with the king of Scots ; and relying on his aid, he concluded a peace between the two kings, on condition that Malcolm should obey William in the same manner as he had obeyed his father ; and that William should restore to Malcolm twelve towns which he had held under his father in England, and should pay him yearly the sum of twelve marks of gold. But the peace between them did not last very long. And the earl also reconciled Eadgar himself with the king.

On Thursday, the 1st of the ides of October [15th Oct.], a violent stroke of lightning struck the tower of Winchcombe church, making a large hole in the wall near the roof; after having split one of the beams, it cut off the head of an image of Christ, which was violently struck and thrown to the ground, and the right leg broken. An image of St. Mary, which was standing near the rood, was also struck to the ground. A thick smoke of a stifling odour then burst forth and filled the whole church, lasting until the monks of the house had gone the round of the offices of the monastery, singing psalms, and bearing holy water and incense and the relics of the saints. Moreover on Friday, the 16th of the kalends of November [17th Oct.], a violent whirlwind coming from the south-west, shook and threw down more than six hundred houses and very many churches in London. In the church of St. Mary, called At the Bow, it killed two men, and taking up the roof and its beams, and whirling it about hither and thither through the air, at length drove six of the beams, in the same order as that in which they lay in the roof itself, so deep into the earth that no more than the seventh or eighth part of them remained visible, their length being as much as twenty-seven or twenty-eight feet.

After this the king returned from Northumbria through Mercia, into Wessex, and kept the earl with him nearly up to the Nativity of the Lord [25th Dec.], but would not perform the conditions of the treaty which had been made between them. The earl being vexed thereat, returned to Normandy on the 10th of the kalends of January [23d Dec.], with Eadgar, etheling. There were, as it was reported in England, at this time two who called themselves Roman pontiffs, mutually at variance between themselves, and so drawing after them the church of God, they divided it internally; namely, Urban, first called Odo, bishop of Ostia, and Clement, who was called Wibert, archbishop of Ravenna: which thing, to say nothing of the rest of the world, so occupied the attention of the church of England for many years, that from the time of the death of Gregory, who was called Hildebrand, up to the present, the church would obey no man for pope. Italy and Gaul had already accepted Urban as the vicar of St. Peter.

A.D. 1092. The city of London was almost entirely consumed by fire. Osmund, bishop of Salisbury, dedicated the church which he had built in Sarum castle, with the assistance of Walchelin, bishop of Winchester, and John, bishop of Bath, on Monday, the nones of April [5th April]. Remigius, who by the licence of king William the elder had transferred the seat of his bishopric from Dorchester to Lincoln, was desirous of dedicating the church, worthy to become an episcopal see, which he had built there, because he felt that the day of his death was fast approaching; but Thomas, archbishop of York, opposed him, declaring that the church had been built within his diocese. But king William the younger, in consideration of money which Remigius had given him, commanded all the bishops of England to assemble and dedicate the church on the 7th of the ides of May [9th May]; but two days before the appointed time, by the hidden judgment of God, Remigius himself departed from the world, and by reason of this the dedication of the church was postponed. When this had been done, the king went into Northumbria, and repaired the city which is called in the British language Cairleu, and in Latin Lugubalia [Carlisle], and built a castle therein; for this city, like some others in those parts, had been destroyed two hundred years before by the pagan Danes, and had remained deserted up to this time.

A.D. 1093. King William the younger, being stricken with a serious illness in the royal vill called Alwestan, hastened to Gloucester, and lay there in a feeble state through the whole of Lent. When he thought that he was on the verge of the grave, as his barons also intimated to him, he promised to God that he would amend his life, that he would no more sell nor tax the churches, but that he would defend them by his royal power, that he would repeal unrighteous laws, and enact those which were righteous. Moreover he gave to Anselm, abbot of Bec, who was then staying in England, the archbishopric of Canterbury, and to his chancellor Robert, surnamed Bloet, the bishopric of Lincoln. But it was not permitted to Anselm to receive anything from the archbishopric, beyond that which the king had commanded to be given to him, until the tribute, which he had received from it every year since the death of Landfranc, should be fully discharged. Res, king of the Welch, during the Easter week, was slain in battle near the castle of Brecknock. From that day kings ceased to reign in Wales. Malcolm, king of Scots, on the day of the feast of St. Bartholomew Apostle [24th Aug.], met the king in the city of Gloucester, as had previously been agreed upon by their ambassadors, in order that the peace between them might be renewed, and a firm friendship established, as some of the nobles of England desired; but each of them departed before any reconciliation had taken place : for William disdained, by reason of his excessive pride and pomp, either to see Malcolm or to speak with him. Moreover he desired to compel him to do him homage in his own court, according to the judgment of his own barons only; but Malcolm was by no means willing to do this, except in the confines of his own kingdom, where the kings of Scotland were accustomed to do homage to the kings of England, and according to the judgment of the chief men of both kingdoms. After this a very wonderful sign appeared in the sun ; and Roger, earl of Shrewsbury, and Guy, abbot of the monastery of St. Augustine, and Paul, abbot of the monastery of St. Alban, died. In the same year also died Robert, earl of Flanders, a man of great valour ; and his eldest son Robert succeeded him. Malcolm, king of Scots, and his eldest son Eadward, with many others, were slain in Northumbria on the feast of St. Brice [13th Nov.], by the soldiers of Robert, earl of Northumbria. When she heard of their death, Margaret, queen of Scots, was so heavily affected with sorrow, that she suddenly fell into a serious sickness. Without delay, she summoned the priests, entered the church, and having confessed her sins to them, caused herself to be anointed with oil and strengthened with the heavenly viaticum, beseeching God with the most earnest and heartfelt prayers, that He would not suffer her to live longer in this world of trouble. Nor was it very long before her prayers were heard ; for in three days after the death of the king, she was released from the bonds of the flesh, and passed (as we believe) to the joys of eternal salvation. While she lived, she was a faithful labourer in deeds of piety, justice, peace, and charity ; she was frequent in prayer ; she kept her body in subjection by vigils and fastings ; she endowed churches and monasteries, loved and honoured the servants and handmaidens of God, broke bread to the hungry, clothed the naked, gave lodging, clothing, and food to the strangers who came to her, and loved God with all her soul. After her death, the Scots chose Donald, brother of king Malcolm, for their king, and drove out of Scotland all the English who were of the king's court. When he heard these things, Duncan, son of king Malcolm, besought and entreated king William, under whom he then served, to grant him his father's kingdom, and swore allegiance to him ; and so he hastened into Scotland with a multitude of English and Normans, and expelled his uncle Donald from the kingdom, and then reigned in his stead. Then some of the Scots assembled, and murdered nearly all his men, and he himself with difficulty escaped with a few. But after this they suffered him to reign, on condition that he would introduce no more

English or Normans into Scotland, and would permit them to serve him.   Nearly all the bishops of England assembling, among whom Thomas, archbishop of York, was the chief, they consecrated as their archbishop Anselm, abbot of Bec, on the day before the nones of December [4th Dec.].   In the same year William, earl of Eu, overcome by a great greed of gold, and seduced by the magnitude of the honour which was promised, deserted from his natural lord Robert, earl of Normandy, to whom he had sworn fealty, and coming to England to king William, that great traitor surrendered himself to his power.

A.D. 1094.   Arfast, who had been first the chaplain to William when earl, and then to William when king, and in process of time bishop of Hereford, being now dead, as well as his successor William, Herbert, surnamed Losinga (an appellation which his power of flattery had lately obtained for him), from being prior of Féchamp and abbot of Ramesey, was made bishop of Thetford by purchasing the see; his father Robert, with the same surname, being intruded on the abbacy of Winchester.   But repentance wiped out the erring impulse of youth ; for proceeding to Rome in his stricter years, and there laying aside the simoniacal staff and ring of his office, by the indulgence of that merciful see he was again permitted to receive them.   But when he returned home, he translated his episcopal seat to a town renowned for its trade and resort, called Norwich, and instituted there a congregation of monks.   King William went to Hastings, and caused to be dedicated there the church of Battle, and afterwards returned to Normandy; he came to a conference with his brother according to the terms of the peace established between them, but departed unappeased.   The earl proceeded to Rouen.   The king returned to Eu, and took up his quarters there, and having assembled soldiers from all parts by bribes and promises of gold, silver, and lands, he induced the nobles of Normandy to desert his brother Robert, and surrender themselves and their castles into his power ; and as they were ready to do his will, he distributed his soldiers over the castles, as well those which he formerly possessed as those which he now had purchased.   Meanwhile he took the castle called Bures, and sent some of the earl's men who were taken in it to England there to be imprisoned ; and others he confined in Normandy ; and in many ways vexing his brother, he strove to disinherit him.   But Robert, driven by necessity, brought his lord, Philip king of the French, with his army into Normandy ; and the king besieged the castle of Argentan, and on the very day of the commencement of the siege, captured without shedding a drop of blood, seven hundred of the king's knights, with twice as many esquires, and all the garrison in the castle, and commanded them to be kept prisoners until they were ransomed ; after which he returned to France.·   But earl Robert besieged the castle of La Houlme, until William Peverel, and eight hundred men who were defending it, surrendered to him.   When this was made known to the king, he sent messengers into England, and ordered twenty thousand footmen to be despatched into Normandy for his assistance.

When they were assembled at Hastings, preparing to cross the sea, Ralph Passeflambard, by order of the king, took away the money which had been given to them for their support, namely ten shillings each, and commanded them to march home again; the money he sent over to the king. Meanwhile all England was vexed by a heavy and unremitting tax, and by a mortality among the inhabitants, during the present and following year. In addition, first the North Welch and then the West and South Welch, threw off the yoke of slavery with which they had long been weighed down, and thus gaining confidence they strove to regain their liberty. A multitude of them assembled and destroyed the castles which had been fortified in West Wales, burned many towns in the counties of Chester, Shropshire, and Hereford, carried off spoil, and put to death many of the English and Normans. They also destroyed the castle in the Isle of Man, and reduced the island itself to subjection. Meanwhile the Scots treacherously put to death their king Duncan, and some others, by the advice and persuasion of Donald, and again appointed him their king. After this king William, on the 4th of the kalends of January [29th Dec.], returned to England, and led an army into Wales to subdue the Welch, and lost there many men and horses.

A.D. 1095. The venerable and excellent man Wulfstan, bishop of the holy church of Worcester, from youth set apart to the service of God, after many hard struggles, by which (for the sake of gaining the glory of the heavenly kingdom), with great devoutness and humility, he had earnestly served God, in the night of Saturday the 18th of January, in the middle of the seventh hour, departed this life, in the year 5299 from the beginning of the world, according to the certain evidence of holy Scripture, in the 529th of the ninth great cycle, in the 476th of the ninth cycle from the beginning of the world, in the 1084th from the passion of the Lord according to the Gospel, and the 1066th according to the calculation of Beda, according to Dionysius 1061, in the 741st from the arrival of the Angles in Britain, in the 498th from the arrival of St. Augustine, in the 103d from the death of St. Oswald archbishop, in the 302d of the eleventh great paschal cycle, and in the 502d of the tenth from the beginning of the world, in the 4th of the second solar cycle, in the 3d of the bissextile cycle, in the 13th of the second of the cycle of 19 years, in the 10th of the second lunar cycle, in the 5th of the hendecad, in the 3d of the indictional cycle, in the 18th lustrum of his own life, and in the 3d year of the 7th lustrum of his pontificate.

In a wonderful manner, in the very hour of his departure, he appeared in a vision to that friend of his whom he had especially loved, Robert, bishop of Hereford, in the town called Cricklade, and commanded him to hasten to Worcester in order to bury him. God suffered no man to remove from his finger the ring along with which he had received the pontifical benediction, that after death the holy man might not seem to deceive his people, for he had often said to them that he would never lose it during his life, nor even on the day of his burial.

On the day before the nones of April [4th April], at night, stars were seen, as it were, to fall from the sky. Walter, bishop of Albano, legate of the holy Roman church, sent by pope Urban, came to England before Easter, bringing the pall for which king William had sent in the preceding year; and, according to agreement, on Sunday, the 4th of the ides of June [10th June], it was laid by him on the altar of the blessed Saviour at Canterbury, thence it was taken by Anselm, and humbly kissed by all in reverence to St. Peter. Robert, bishop of Hereford, a man of great piety, died on Tuesday, the 6th of the kalends of July [26th June]. Wulfstan, bishop of Worcester, on the 30th day after his departure out of this world, reappeared to him in a vision, and sharply reprimanded him for his negligence and idleness, admonishing him to apply himself to the reformation of his own life and that of the people committed to his charge, as watchfully as he was able; and that if he would do this, he told him that he would soon obtain a pardon from God for all his sins. And he added that he would not long sit in the seat in which he then sat, but that if he would be more watchful, he should feast with him in the presence of God. For both these fathers were mutually attached to one another by strong affection in the love of God; and therefore it is credible that he who had first gone from this life to God should feel a solicitude for the beloved one whom he had left in the world, and should have done his utmost endeavour that they both might the more speedily rejoice together in the presence of God.

Robert de Mowbray, earl of Northumberland, and William de Eu, with many others, made an attempt to deprive king William of his kingdom and his life, and to establish Stephen de Albemarle, the son of his aunt, on his throne, but without success: for the king, as soon as he knew it, assembled his army from every part of England, and besieged for two months the castle of the aforesaid Robert, which was situated near the mouth of the river Tyne. Meanwhile, by the capture of a small fortress, he made prisoners of nearly all the best soldiers of the earl, and put them into confinement. Then he took the castle itself, and placed into safe custody the brother of the earl and the knights, whom he found within. After this he raised a castle before Bamburgh, that is, the city of Queen Bebba, into which the earl had escaped, and this he called Malveisin, and having garrisoned it, returned to the country south of the Humber. After his departure, they who were watching at Newcastle, promised earl Robert that they would allow him to enter, if he would come secretly. And he joyfully acceded, and went out by night for the purpose with thirty men. This becoming known, the knights who kept the castle followed him, and sent messengers to the guard of Newcastle to inform them of his departure; being ignorant of this, on the Lord's-day he made his attempt, which failed, for he was detected. Wherefore he fled to the monastery of St. Oswin, king and martyr, where, on the 6th day of the siege, he was severely wounded in the leg, while engaged in resisting the enemy, of whom many were killed and many wounded; while of his own men some were wounded and all taken prisoners, he himself taking refuge in a church, from which he was brought forth and placed in confinement. Meanwhile the Welch destroyed the castle of Montgomery, and put to death some of the men of Hugh, earl of Shrewsbury, who were there. The king, enraged at this, speedily commanded an invasion, and led an army into Wales after the feast of St. Michael [29th Sept.], where he lost many men and horses. Returning thence, he ordered earl Robert to be brought before Bamborough, and commanded his eyes to be put out, unless his wife and his kinsman Moreal would surrender his castle. And this they did, being compelled by such a necessity. Whereupon the earl was sent to Windsor, put in close confinement, and Moreal disclosed the cause of his treason to the king.

A.D. 1096. William, bishop of Durham, died at Windsor in the court of the king on Wednesday, being the kalends of January [1st Jan.], but was buried at Durham. In the octave of the Epiphany [13th Jan.] a council was holden at Salisbury, where the king condemned William de Eu, who had been vanquished in duel, to lose his eyes, and to be emasculated; he ordered also that his steward William de Alderi, the son of his aunt, and privy to his treason, should be hanged; and he placed in confinement earl Odo of Champagne, the father of Stephen aforesaid, Philip, the son of Roger, earl of Shrewsbury, and some others concerned in his treason.

Pope Urban came into France, and holding a synod at Clermont during Lent, exhorted the Christians to make an expedition to Jerusalem to subdue the Turks, Saracens, Turcopolites, and other pagans; and in the very synod itself, Raymond, earl of St. Giles, and many with him, were forthwith signed with the cross of Christ, and solemnly vowed to undertake the pilgrimage for the love of God, and to accomplish what the pope had exhorted. When this was heard, the rest of the christian world dwelling in Italy, Germany, France, England, vied with each other in preparing for the expedition. Their leaders were Aymer, bishop of Le Puy, the bishop of Ostia, with many other bishops, Peter the monk, Hugh the Great, the brother of Philip, king of France, Godfrey, duke of Lorrain, Stephen, earl of Chartres, Robert, earl of Normandy, Robert, earl of Flanders, the two brothers of duke Godfrey, Eustace, earl of Boulogne, and Baldwin, earl Raymond aforesaid, and Boemund, son of Robert Wiscard.

Samson was consecrated as bishop of Worcester by Anselm, archbishop of Canterbury, at London, in the church of St. Paul, on Sunday, the 17th of the kalends of July [15th June].

After this Robert, earl of Normandy, when intending to set out for Jerusalem with the other crusaders, sent messengers to England, and besought his kinsman king William to renew the peace between them, and to lend him ten thousand marks of silver, as security for which he was willing that he should have the province of Normandy. In order to meet his demands, William commanded that each of the nobles of England should lend him money in proportion to his ability, as speedily as possible. Wherefore the bishops, abbots, abbesses, broke up the gold and silver ornaments of their churches, the earls, barons, and sheriffs spoiled their knights and villeins, and presented the king with a large sum of money. And William crossed the sea in the month of September, made peace with his brother, lent him six thousand six hundred and sixty-six pounds, and received Normandy as security.

A.D. 1097. William, king of the English, returned to England during Lent; and after Easter [5th April] he invaded Wales for the second time with an army of horsemen and infantry, intending to massacre all the male inhabitants; but he was unable to capture or kill any one of them, but lost some of his own men, and many horses. After this he sent Eadgar, etheling, with an army into Scotland, to expel his uncle Donald who had usurped the throne, and to establish in his stead Eadgar, son of king Malcolm, his cousin.

The Christians took the city of Nice on Saturday, the 13th of the kalends of July [19th June]. A star, called a comet, was visible for fifteen days from the 3d of the kalends of October [29th Sept.]. Some affirmed that they saw at that time a strange sign in the heavens, as it were burning, and in the form of a cross. Soon after a dissension arose between the king and archbishop Anselm, because from the time at which he had been made archbishop, he had not been suffered to hold a synod, nor to correct the evil practices which had grown up throughout England; the latter crossed the sea, and after having remained for a time in France, he proceeded to Rome to pope Urban. The king himself, about the feast of St. Andrew [30th Nov.], set out from England into Normandy. Baldwin, abbot of the monastery of St. Edmund, a man of exceeding piety, by birth a Frenchman, and well skilled in the art of medicine, died in a good old age on Tuesday, the 4th of the kalends of January [29th Dec.], and rests in the middle of the choir in the principal church.

A.D. 1098. Walchelin, bishop of Winchester, died on Sunday, the 3d of the nones of January [3d Jan.]. And Thurold, abbot of the monastery of St. Peter of Burh, and Robert, abbot of New-minster, died. In the summer, William the younger, king of the English, reduced the city of Maine, and a great part of that province. Meanwhile, Hugh, earl of Chester, and Hugh, earl of Shrewsbury, invaded the island of Mevania, commonly called Anglesege, with an army, and slew many of the Welch whom they captured therein, and blinded others, having previously cut off their hands and feet; and then emasculated them. And they brought forth from his church a certain priest, advanced in years, named Kenned, from whom the Welch received advice in the matters in which they were engaged; and having emasculated him and put out one of his eyes, they cut off his tongue; but on the third day, by the mercy of God, his speech was restored to him. At that time Magnus, king of Norway, son of king Olave, son of king Harold Hardrada, after having subdued the Orkneys, came hither with a small fleet. When he was attempting to land, Hugh, earl of Shrewsbury, came out against him with a large force on the very sea-shore, and, as it is reported, he fell, having been hit by an arrow sent from the hand of the king, about seven days after he had so cruelly treated the aforesaid priest.

The city of Antioch was taken by the Christians on Wednesday, the 3d of the nones of June [3d June], where, after a few days, the spear with which the Saviour of the world was pierced while suspended on the cross (being revealed by Andrew the apostle, the mildest of saints), was discovered in the church of St. Peter the apostle. The Christians, filled with courage by this discovery, on Monday, the 4th of the kalends of July [28th June], took with them the spear, sallied out of the city, and giving battle to the Pagans, drove back at the point of the sword Curbara, chief of the chivalry of the soldan of Persia, Turks, Arabs, Saracens, Publicans, Azimati, Persians, Agulani, and the people of many other nations ; they put many thousands of them to death, and by the blessing of God gained a complete victory. An unusual light continued to shine during nearly the whole of the night of the 5th of the kalends of October [27th Sept.]. In the same year the bones of the king and martyr Canute were taken out of the tomb, and placed in a shrine with honour. Roger, duke of Apulia, having assembled a large army, besieged the city of Capua, which had revolted from him. Pope Urban, accompanied in obedience to his command by Anselm, archbishop of Canterbury, proceeded to the council which he intended to hold at Bari on the kalends of October [1st Oct.]; in which council many points of catholic faith were discussed by the successor of the apostles with eloquence and reason. Here a question being mooted on the part of the Greeks (who were desirous to prove by the authority of the evangelists that the Holy Spirit proceeded only from the Father), the aforesaid Anselm so discussed, argued, and summed up the question, that there was no one in the council who did not admit that he was fully satisfied.

A.D. 1099. Pope Urban, in the 3d day in Easter week [10th April], held a great council at Rome, in which various laws having been repealed, and new ones enforced against the enemies of holy church, with the consent of the whole council he launched the sentence of excommunication against all laymen giving and all persons receiving at their hands the investitures of churches, and against all those who should consecrate any one to the discharge of the duties of a preferment so given. He also excommunicated all those who subjected themselves to laymen out of regard to any ecclesiastical dignity ; for he said that it was accursed, that hands which had been exalted to so lofty an eminence as to create by their impress the all-creating God (a power granted to none of the angels), and to offer Him, for the salvation and redemption of the whole world, in the presence of the most high God the Father, should be debased to such a depth of ignominy as to become in subjection to the hands of those persons who day and night are polluted by immodest contacts, or defiled by the unlawful effusion of blood and by rapine. " So be it, so be it," was exclaimed by all, and so with this the council finished. After this the archbishop proceeded to Lyons.

William the younger, king of the English, returned from Normandy into England, and held a court in the feast of Pentecost [29th May], and gave the bishopric of Durham to Ralph, whom he had appointed extortioner over the whole kingdom, and whom Thomas, archbishop of York, soon after consecrated there. On Thursday, the ides of July [15th July], Jerusalem was taken by the Christians, and afterwards on the 11th of the kalends of August [22d July], on the same day of the week, Godfrey, duke of Lorraine, was elected king by all the army. Pope Urban died on Thursday, the 4th of the kalends of August [29th July]. The Christians fought a battle with Amiravis, the commander of the army, and second in power in the kingdom of the king of Babylon, before the city of Ascalon, the day before the ides of August [12th Aug.], on the same day of the week, and by the blessing of Christ he obtained the victory. Paschal, a venerable man, who had been ordained priest by pope Hildebrand, was elected pope by the people of Rome on the ides of August [13th Aug.], and on the following day, namely, on Sunday the 19th of the kalends of September [14th Aug.], was consecrated. On the 3d nones of November [3d Nov.], the sea rose over the shore and overwhelmed many towns, drowning men and innumerable oxen and sheep. Osmund, bishop of Salisbury, died on the 3d nones of December [3d Dec.].

A.D. 1100. Pope Clement, who was also called Wibert, died. On Sunday, the ides of July [15th July], the church which abbot Serlo, of pious memory, had constructed from its foundation at Gloucester, was dedicated with great honour by bishops Samson of Gloucester, Gundulf of Rochester, Gerard of Hereford, and Harvey of Bangor. On Thursday, the 4th of the nones of August [2d Aug.], in the eighth indiction, William the younger, king of England, while engaged in hunting in the New Forest, which is called Ytene in the English tongue, was struck and killed by an arrow, carelessly aimed by a Frenchman, Walter, surnamed Tirell; and he was brought to Winchester, and buried in the old minster in the church of St. Peter. And no wonder, if (as common report affirms) the Almighty should thus have exhibited his power and his anger. For in times long past, (for instance, during the reigns of king Edward, and the other kings of England his predecessors,) this same tract of land abounded in churches and in inhabitants who honoured God; yet this notwithstanding, by command of king William the elder the men were expelled, their houses reduced almost to ruins, and the churches destroyed, and thus the land was rendered fit only for the habitation of wild beasts; and hence, as it is believed, the cause of this misfortune. For even the brother of William the younger, namely Richard, had fallen long before in the same forest; and a short time before, his cousin Richard, the son of Robert earl of Normandy, while he was hunting, was also killed by an arrow, shot by one of his knights. In the place where the king fell, in former times a church had been built, but it was destroyed, as we have said, in the time of his father.

During the reign of this king, (as we have partly mentioned above,) many signs appeared in the sun, moon, and stars; the sea often overflowed the shore, drowning men and cattle, and destroying many towns and houses; in the district called Barrucsire, a short time before his death, blood flowed from a fountain for three

weeks; and the devil frequently appeared in the woods in a horrible
form to many Normans, and spoke with them much concerning
the king, and Ralph, and some others.   Nor is it to be wondered
at; for in their time law was almost silenced, and money ruled
supreme in all appeals to justice.   In their time, some men obeyed
the will of the king rather than justice; and Ralph—disregarding
the ecclesiastical law and all the rules of his order, for he was a
priest,—received from the king, first the abbeys, and then the
bishoprics, whose pastors had recently died, that he might put
them up for sale; and from this source he was enabled to pay a large
sum of money annually to the king, and as his cunning and shrewd-
ness were great, in a short time he so increased, that the king appointed him pleader and taxer for the whole kingdom.   When he
had at length acquired this power, he pillaged all the richer Englishmen in the kingdom, by depriving them of their goods and lands :
and he unceasingly oppressed the poorer by a heavy and unjust tax,
and, in many ways,—both before he obtained his bishopric and
even while he possessed it,—did he vex both great and small, even
up to the time of the king's decease ; for on the very day of his
death, he held in his own hands the archbishopric of Canterbury,
and the bishoprics of Winchester and Salisbury.   This king reigned
thirteen years, all but thirty-eight days; his younger brother Henry
succeeded him; and on Sunday, the nones of August [5th Aug.],
was consecrated king in Westminster, by Maurice, bishop of
London.   On the day of his consecration he made free the holy
church of God, which in his brother's time had been sold and
placed to farm; he removed all the evil customs and unjust
exactions, by which the kingdom of England had been oppressed ;
he established a firm peace in his dominions, and commanded its
preservation ; he restored the law of king Eadward to all in
common, with the emendations which his father had made; but he
retained in his own hands the forests, which he had established and
of which he had taken possession.   Not long after he committed
to custody in the Tower of London, Ralph, bishop of Durham, and
recalled Anselm, archbishop of Canterbury, from France.   Meanwhile Robert, earl of Flanders, and Eustace, earl of Boulogne,
returned home from Jerusalem, and were followed by Robert, earl
of Normandy, with his wife, whom he had married in Sicily.
During this, Henry, king of England, assembled the chief men of
England at London, and took to wife Mathilda, daughter of Malcolm, king of the Scots, and queen Margaret; she was consecrated
queen and crowned by Anselm, archbishop of Canterbury.   On
Sunday, being the feast of St. Martin [11th Nov.], Thomas, archbishop of York, a man of venerated memory, and extraordinary
piety, affable and beloved by all, departed this life at York, on
Sunday, the 14th of the kalends of December [18th Nov.], and
was succeeded by Gerhard, bishop of Hereford.

A.D. 1101.   Ralph, bishop of Durham, after Christmas, with
great cunning made his escape from prison, crossed the sea, and
going over to Robert, count of Normandy, persuaded him to invade
England.   And many of the nobles of this land sent messengers to

him, and prayed him to come speedily to England, promising him the crown of England. The city of Gloucester was consumed by fire, with the chief monastery, and others, on Friday, the 8th of the ides of June [6th June]. Robert, earl of Normandy, assembled a great number of horsemen, archers, and footmen, and collected his ships at a place called in the Norman tongue, Ultresporte. When the king gained intelligence of this, he ordered his sailors to guard the sea, and to see that no one approached England from the coast of Normandy. And having assembled an immense army from the whole of England, he encamped not far from Hastings in Sussex; for he thought for certain that his brother would land on that part of the coast. But by the advice of bishop Ranulph, earl Robert so worked upon the minds of some of the king's sailors by promises of all kinds, that, setting aside their allegiance, they deserted to his enemies, and became their pilots to England. All being ready, Robert embarked with his army, and about the feast of St. Peter ad Vincula [1st Aug.], he landed in a place called Portesmuth; and straightway marching his army to Winchester, he encamped in a convenient position. When his arrival was known, some of the English nobles deserted to him, as they had previously intended; others concealed their intentions and remained with the king; but the bishops, the mercenary soldiers, and the English remained faithful to him, agreeing among themselves that they were ready to go to battle with him. The wiser men of both sides, having taken wholesome counsel together, brought about a peace between the brothers, on condition that the king should pay annually to the earl a sum of three thousand marks, that is, two thousand pounds of silver, and should restore freely to every one the honours which he had formerly possessed in England and might have lost by reason of his allegiance to the earl; while it was agreed that Robert should make restitution to all who had been deprived of honours in Normandy in the king's cause, and this he was to do free of all cost. The peace being concluded, the king's army returned home; but part of the earl's returned to Normandy, and part remained with him in England. Godfrey, king of Jerusalem, the powerful duke of Lorraine, son of Eustace the elder, earl of Boulogne, died, and lies buried in the church of the Golgotha. After his death, the Christians unanimously chose his brother Baldwin for their king. Robert de Belesme, earl of Shrewsbury, son of earl Roger, began to fortify with a wide, deep, and lofty wall, the bridge which Aegelfled, queen of the Mercians, had built during the reign of her brother Eadward the elder, on the western bank of the river Severn, in a place called in the Saxon tongue, Brycge. And this he did against the king, as the issue proved. He commenced the construction of another also in Wales, in a place called Caroclove.

A.D. 1102.   The aforesaid Robert, earl of Belesme, who at that time governed the county of Ponthieu, and possessed many castles in Normandy, fortified strongly, against king Henry, the city of Shrewsbury, the castle therein, and the castles of Arundel and Tyckyll, supplying them with provisions, machines, arms, horse-soldiers, and footmen. He also hastened the completion of the walls and towers of the castles of Brycge and Caroclove, by carrying on the works night and day; and he excited the Welchmen, who were in subjection to him, to the more prompt, faithful, and speedy performance of his wishes, by awarding to them with a liberal hand honours, lands, horses, arms, and gifts of all sorts. His project, however, was speedily interrupted, for his designs being discovered and clearly published, the king declared him to be a public enemy. Wherefore, having assembled together as many Welchmen and Normans as they could muster, he and his brother Arnold laid waste a part of the county of Stafford, and carried away into Wales many horses and cattle, and some few men. But the king without delay besieged his castle of Arundel, and after having erected fortresses before it, he went away. Then he commanded Robert, bishop of Lincoln, to besiege Tyckyll with a part of his forces; and he himself besieged Brycge with the army of nearly all England, and began to construct there machines and a fortress. Meanwhile he very easily bribed the Welch, by moderate presents, in whom Robert had great confidence, to break their oaths, and to desert from him and join against him. Within thirty days the city and all the castles having been surrendered, he subdued his enemy Robert and drove him ignominiously out of England; and punished his brother Arnold shortly afterwards for his perfidy by a similar expulsion.

After this the king was at London, at Michaelmas [29th Sept.], with all his nobles, ecclesiastical and secular; where he invested two of the clergy with bishoprics, namely, Roger, his chancellor, with the see of Salisbury, and Roger, his larderer, with that of Hereford. Here also archbishop Anselm held a great council on questions pertaining to the christian faith, in which he associated with himself Gerard, archbishop of York, Maurice, bishop of London, William, bishop elect of Winchester, Robert, bishop of Lincoln, Samson, bishop of Worcester, Robert, bishop of Chester, John, bishop of Bath, Herbert, bishop of Norwich, Ralph, bishop of Chichester, Gundulf, bishop of Rochester, Harvey, bishop of Bangor, and the two recently invested bishops, viz. Roger, bishop of Salisbury, and Roger, bishop of Hereford ; Osbern, bishop of Exeter, was detained by infirmity, and unable to attend the meeting. In this council many abbots, both French as well as English, were deposed and deprived of the preferments of which they had unjustly become possessed, or in which they had lived unrighteously ; namely, Guy, abbot of Pershore, Aldwin of Ramsey, the abbot of Tavistock, Haimoe of Cerne, the abbot of Micelenei, Aegelric of Middleton, Godric of Peterborough, Richard of Ely, Robert of St. Edmund's. Roger, bishop elect of Hereford, aforesaid, was taken ill at London, and died; and the queen's chancellor, named Reignelm, was promoted in his stead by a similar investiture. Henry, king of the English, gave Mary, the queen's sister, in marriage to Eustace, earl of Boulogne.

A.D. 1103. A great dissension arose between king Henry and archbishop Anselm, the archbishop refusing to consent to the

giving of investitures by the king, and to consecrate or com-
municate with those to whom the king had already given churches,
because the apostolic pope had interdicted this as well to himself
as to all others.   Wherefore the king commanded Gerard, the
archbishop of York, to consecrate the bishops to whom he had
given investitures, namely, William Giffard and Roger, who
was his chaplain, to whom the king had already given the
church of Salisbury.   Gerard performed the command of the
king, but William set both that and the benediction of archbishop Gerard at defiance, having regard to the justice of the
case.   Wherefore, by the command of the king, he was despoiled
of all his possessions and sent out of the kingdom; the others
remained unconsecrated.   But Reignelm shortly before this had
surrendered the bishopric of Hereford to the king, believing that he
had given offence to God in receiving the investiture of a church
from the hands of a layman.   After this the king held his court in
Easter [29th March], at Winchester.   Archbishop Anselm, after
the many insults and contumelies of all kinds which he had suffered, by the request of the king proceeded to Rome on the 5th of
the kalends of May [27th April], in accordance with an agreement
made between himself and the king, taking in his suite William,
bishop elect of Winchester, and the abbots who had been deprived
of their abbeys, namely, Richard, abbot of Ely, and Aldwin of
Ramsey.   Robert, earl of Normandy, came into England to confer
with his brother, and before he returned he remitted to William the
three thousand marks of silver which that king was bound to pay
annually to him according to their agreement.   In the province
called Berkshire, in a place called Heamstede, blood was seen by
many to flow out of the.ground.   In the same year, on the 3d ides
of August [11th Aug.], a great storm of wind arose, which caused
damage to the fruits of the earth throughout England, such as the
men then alive had never seen in past times.

A.D. 1104.   Walter, abbot of Evesham, died on the 13th of the
kalends of February [20th Jan.], and Serlo, abbot of Gloucester, on
the 4th nones of March [4th March].   Henry, king of the English,
held his court at Westminster at Whitsuntide.   On Tuesday, the
7th of the ides of June [7th June], four circles of a white colour
were seen round the sun, about the sixth hour, one under the
other, as if they had been painted.   All who saw it marvelled,
because such things had never been seen before by any one of
them.   William, earl of Moreton, was disinherited of all the land
which he possessed in England.   It would be difficult to describe
the misery which the land suffered at that time by reason of the
exactions of the king.   The body of St. Cuthbert the bishop, by
reason of the incredulity of certain abbots, during the pontificate of
bishop Ralph, was exhumed, and it, as well as the head of St.
Oswald, king and martyr, and of St. Beda, and the relics of many
saints, was found to be evidently uncorrupted.   This was done by
Ralph, abbot of Seez, afterwards bishop of Rochester, and by the
brethren of Durham, in presence of earl Alexander, brother of Eadgar,
king of Scots, afterwards king.   And because it was permitted to

him to be present at so sacred a ceremony, he gave many marks of gold and silver, and caused to be prepared a shrine, in which the sacred body, enveloped in new vestments, was honourably preserved.

A.D. 1105. King Henry crossed the sea, and nearly all the Norman nobles, as soon as he arrived, despising the earl, their lord, and unmindful of the allegiance which they owed him, grasped the gold and silver which the king had brought with him out of England, and surrendered to him their castles and the fortified cities and towns. And he burned Bayeux and the church of St. Mary there, and took Caen from his brother; he then returned to England, because he was unable to reduce the whole of Normandy, intending however to return next year with a larger supply of money, and subdue the remainder, to the disinheritance of his brother. Earl William de Moreteon injured the property and men of the king, wherever he could lay hands on them, in revenge for the loss of his possessions in England.

A.D. 1106. Robert, earl of Normandy, came to England to confer with his brother Henry, whom he found at Northampton. Then the earl requested him to restore what he had taken from him in Normandy; but the king said no to everything; and the earl retired enraged, and crossed the sea. In the Friday of the first week of Lent, the 14th of the kalends of March [16th Feb.], in the evening, an extraordinary star appeared, and shone for twenty-five days, in the same form and at the same hour, between the south and west. It was itself small and dim, but the light which issued from it was exceedingly clear, and a brilliancy like a large beam darted into the star itself from the east and north. Many affirmed that they saw at that time several extraordinary stars. On Holy Thursday two moons were visible at night, shortly before daybreak, one in the east and one in the west, both being full, and on that day the moon was fourteen days old. In this year arose a most execrable dissension between the emperor of Germany and his son. Henry, king of England, crossed the sea before the month of August, proceeding into Normandy, and nearly all the Norman chiefs surrendered to him, except Robert de Belesme, William de Moreteon, and a few others who remained steady to earl Robert.

Henry, king of England, on the Assumption of St. Mary [15th Aug.], came to Bec, where he and archbishop Anselm met, and all the disputes which had hitherto divided them at length came to a peaceable termination. Not long after this the archbishop, by the command and request of the king, returned to England. An army was assembled, and the king marched to a castle belonging to the earl of Moreteon, called Tenercebrei, and besieged it. While he was thus engaged, earl Robert, the king's brother, came up against him with his army on the vigil of St. Michael [28th Sept.], and with him Robert de Beleasme, and William, earl of Moreton; but the right and the victory were on the king's side. Robert, earl of Normandy, William, earl of Moreteon, and Robert de Stuteville were taken prisoners there; but Robert de Beleasme escaped by flight. William Crispin and many others were also taken prisoners.

After this the king subdued the whole of Normandy, and governed it according to his own will, intelligence of which he sent by letters to archbishop Anselm.

A.D. 1107. Eadgar, king of Scots, died on the 8th of the ides of January [6th Jan.], and his brother Alexander succeeded him. Peace having been established in Normandy under the rule of the king, and Robert, earl of Normandy, and William, earl of Moreton, having been sent on to England in custody, the king returned to his kingdom before Easter [14th April]. In the kalends of August [1st Aug.] an assembly of all bishops, abbots, and nobles of the kingdom was held in London in the king's palace, and for three days, in the absence of archbishop Anselm, the question of ecclesiastical investitures was fully entered into between the king and the bishops, many striving to persuade him to act according to the custom of his father and brother, and not in obedience to the precept of the apostolic see ; for pope Paschal, standing firm to the sentence which had been published upon this point, had conceded all those things which pope Urban had interdicted, together with investitures. By this means the pope had brought the king to an agreement with himself upon the question of investitures. At a later period, in the presence of Anselm and of a multitude of the people, the king granted and ordained that from that time forth no person should ever be invested, by the giving of the pastoral staff or the ring, with any bishopric or abbey in England, by the king, or indeed by any layman whatever. Anselm, on his part, conceded that no bishop elect should be deprived of consecration by reason of the homage which he had done to the king. Gerard, archbishop of York, placing his hand in the hand of Anselm, in accordance with his wish, promised, on his fealty, that he would show to him and his successors in the archbishopric, the same submission and obedience as the bishop elect of Hereford had promised to himself before his consecration to the church of Hereford. The following bishops elect, namely, William of Winchester, Roger of Salisbury, Reignelm of Hereford, William of Exeter, and Urban of Glamorgan, in Wales, came at the same time to Canterbury ; and on Sunday, the 3d of the ides of August [11th Aug.], all these individuals were consecrated by Anselm. The suffragan bishops of the same see, namely, Gerard, archbishop of York, Robert, bishop of Lincoln, John of Bath, Herbert of Norwich, Robert of Chester, Ralph of Chichester, and Ranulph of Durham, all assisted him in the service. There was certainly no person of that day who remembered in past times the election and ordination at one time of so many bishops in England, except in the time of Eadward the elder, when archbishop Pleigmund ordained in one day seven bishops to seven churches. In this year Maurice, bishop of London, Richard, abbot of Ely, Robert, abbot of St. Edmund's, Miles Crispin, Robert Fitz Haimon, Roger Bigod, and Richard de Redvers, the king's councillors, departed this life.

A.D. 1108. Gundulf, bishop of Rochester, died, on the nones of March [7th March]. Henry, king of England, having established peace, enacted a law that if any man were caught in theft or robbery, he should be hanged. He also enacted that debased and false money should be corrected with great severity; condemning those who were caught in the making of false coin, to lose, without the possibility of bail or ransom, their eyes and the lower parts of their bodies. And since it frequently happened that coin, upon examination, was found to be bent, broken, and therefore rejected, he enacted that no penny or halfpenny (which he also ordained should be round), and even no farthing should be entire.[1] From which edict great advantage followed to all the kingdom, for the king caused these secular changes to be made for the relief of the burdens of the land. Gerard, archbishop of York, died, and Thomas, the cousin by the father's side, of his predecessor Thomas, succeeded him.

These following statutes were made concerning archdeacons, priests, deacons, subdeacons, and canons of whatever rank, by Anselm, archbishop of Canterbury, and Thomas, archbishop elect of York, with him, and all the bishops of England, in presence of the glorious king Henry, by assent of his barons, in the year 1108. " It is enacted that priests, deacons, and subdeacons shall live chastely, and shall not have any women in their houses, except those connected with them by the closest relationship, according to what the holy Synod of Nice has declared. Those priests, deacons, or subdeacons, however, who, after the interdict of the Council of London, have retained their wives, or married others, if they be desirous of again celebrating mass, are to separate from them entirely, and neither to suffer them to enter their own houses, nor are they themselves to visit these women; they are not knowingly to meet in any house, nor are such wives to reside within the boundary of the church; and if it be necessary, for any legitimate purpose, to hold converse with them, they are to meet out of doors in the presence of two lawful witnesses.

" If, by the testimony of two or three lawful witnesses, or the common report of his parishioners, any of the clergy be accused of the violation of this statute, he shall purge himself in the presence of proper witnesses of his own order: six if he be a priest, four if a deacon, two if a subdeacon. He who fails in this purgation shall be judged a transgressor of the sacred statute.

" Those priests who, contemning the sacred altar and holy orders, shall prefer to live with women, are to be removed from their divine office, deprived of all ecclesiastical preferment, placed without the choir, and declared infamous.

" Those rebel and contumacious persons who have not left their wives, and yet presumed to celebrate mass, shall be called to satisfaction; and if they neglect to appear in eight days, they shall be excommunicated.

" The same sentence, including the relinquishment of women, the avoidance of their conversation, and the imposition of censure, if the statute be transgressed, embraces all archdeacons and canons.

" All archdeacons shall swear that they will not receive money to overlook the infraction of this law, nor allow priests whom they

---

[1] This sentence is obscure, and possibly is corrupt; although the MSS. afford no means of correcting it by giving it a different interpretation.

know to have wives, to sing mass or to appoint substitutes. Deans shall do the same.

" The archdeacon or dean who refuses to swear to this, shall lose his archidiaconate or his deanery.

" Priests who decide to leave their wives and to serve the holy altar of God, shall be suspended for forty days, during which time they shall appoint substitutes, and shall suffer a penance prescribed by their bishops."

Philip, king of France, died, and his son Louis succeeded him. Henry, king of England, crossed the sea.   Archbishop Anselm, in accordance with the request of the king, consecrated Richard, the elect of London, as bishop of that diocese in his chapel at Paggaham, William, bishop of Winchester, Roger, bishop of Salisbury, Ralph, bishop of Chichester, and William, bishop of Exeter, assisting him in the service ; the accustomed profession of obedience and sub-mission being first of all made from the said bishop. After this he came to Canterbury, and consecrated Ralph, abbot of Seez, to the church of Rochester, in place of Gundulf, on the 3d of the ides of August [11th Aug.], William, bishop of Winchester, Ralph, bishop of Chichester, and Richard, bishop of London, assisting him. This Richard, after the custom of his ancestors, honoured on the same day his mother-church of Canterbury with a magnificent gift.

A.D. 1109.   Anselm, archbishop of Canterbury, died at Canter-bury on Wednesday the 11th of the kalends of May [21st April], and was buried with due honour on the following day, being Holy Thursday.   Henry, king of England, returned about rogation week to England, and held his court at Westminster in Whitsuntide [13th June].   Thomas, archbishop elect of York, was consecrated by Richard, bishop of London, at London, on the 5th of the kalends of July [27th June], and afterwards on Sunday, being the kalends of August [1st Aug.], he received at York the pall which the pope had sent to him; and on the same day consecrated Turgod, prior of Durham, to the bishopric of St. Andrew's, in Scotland, which is called Cenrimunt.   In the same year the king changed the abbey of Ely into an episcopal see, and appointed Hervey, bishop of Bangor, to that church.   A comet was seen about the milky way in the month of December, its tail being directed to the north.

A.D. 1110.   Henry, king of England, gave his daughter to Henry, king of the Germans.   In the same year many signs appeared throughout England.   A severe earthquake was felt at Shrewsbury.   The river called Trent was dried up at Nottingham from the morning up to the third hour of the day, for the space of a mile, so that men walked dry-foot on its bed.   A comet appeared on the 6th of the ides of June [8th June], and was visible for three weeks.   Henry, king of the Germans, came to Rome, took pope Paschal, and put him in confinement, but afterwards made peace with him at the bridge of the Via Salaria, where they celebrated the feast of Easter in the Campus.

In this form the reconciliation between the king and the pope was made; and this is the oath of the king:—

" I, king Henry, will set free, on next Thursday or Friday, the lord pope; and the bishops and cardinals, and all the captives and hostages who have been taken for or with him, I will cause to be safely conducted within the gates of the city beyond the river Tiber : I will never again take or permit to be taken those who remain in the allegiance of the lord the pope Paschal, and I will keep peace and security with the Roman people, and of the city beyond the Tiber and island, through me and mine, in persons and in things, provided they keep peace with me. I will faithfully aid the lord the pope to keep his position as pope quietly and securely. I will restore the patrimonies and possessions of the Romish church which I have taken away, and I will faithfully aid her to recover and keep all which she ought to possess, as my ancestors have done ; I will obey our lord the pope, having regard to the honour of my kingdom and empire, in the same manner as catholic emperors have obeyed catholic Roman pontiffs. All these things will I faithfully observe without fraud or deceit."

These are the jurors on the part of the king : Frederic, archbishop of Cologne, Gebehard, bishop of Trent, Burchard, bishop of Munster, Bruno, bishop of Spires, Albert, chancellor, earl Herman, Frederic, count palatine, earl Berengar, earl Frederic, marquis Boniface, Albert, earl of Blandry, earl Frederic, earl Godefrid, marquis Warnerius.

A second convention between the pope and the king:—" Our lord the pope Paschal, being the one hundred and fifty-sixth pope, is willing to concede to king Henry and his kingdom, and will confirm and corroborate this his privilege under anathema, that it shall be lawful for the king, after the election of a bishop or abbot without simony, with the royal assent, to invest him with a ring and staff. And the bishop or abbot so invested by the king, shall freely accept consecration from the bishop to whom the right shall pertain. If any be elected by the clergy and people, except he be invested by the king, he shall not be consecrated; and archbishops and bishops shall have the liberty of consecrating those invested by the king. In none of these things shall the lord the pope molest king Henry, nor his kingdom, nor his empire."

This is the oath on the part of the pope :—

" Our lord the pope Paschal shall not molest our lord the king Henry, nor his empire, nor his kingdom, touching the investiture of bishoprics or abbacies, nor for any injustice done to himself and his people, nor shall he do any evil to him or any other person in this cause ; and he shall by no means pronounce an anathema against the person of the king, nor shall it remain in the power of the pope to refuse him coronation, as is contained in the agreement ; and he shall aid to the best of his power the kingdom and empire of the king by the influence of his office : and this the pope shall do without fraud and treachery."

These are the names of those bishops and cardinals who, by the command of the pope, have confirmed the privilege and agreement by oath to the emperor Henry: Peter, bishop of Porto, Centius, bishop of Sabina, Robert, cardinal of St. Eusebius, Boniface, cardinal of St. Mark, Anastasius, cardinal of St. Clement, Gregory, cardinal of the Holy Apostles Peter and Paul; also Gregory, cardinal of St. Chrisogonus, John, cardinal of St. Potentiana, Risus, cardinal of St. Lawrence, Rainer, cardinal of Sts. Marcellus and Peter, Vitalis, cardinal of St. Balbina, Duuzo, cardinal of St. Martin, Theodbald, cardinal of John and Paul, John, deacon of St. Mary in Schola Græca.

This is the privilege of the lord the pope, which he granted to the emperor concerning the investitures of bishoprics :—

" *Paschal the Bishop, Servant of the servants of God, to his most beloved son in Christ, Henry, the glorious King of the Germans, and by the grace of God august Emperor of the Romans, greeting, and the apostolic benediction.* God's providence has decreed that a singularly close attachment should exist between your kingdom and the holy Roman church; your predecessors, in consequence of their honour and more abundant prudence, obtained the crown and empire of the city of Rome; to which dignity, dearest son, the Divine Majesty has advanced you by the ministry of our holy office. The prerogative of that dignity, which our predecessors have conceded to the catholic emperors, your predecessors, and have confirmed by writing, we also concede to you, our beloved friend, confirming it by this instrument; to wit, that you are permitted to confer upon the bishops or abbots of your kingdom, who have been elected without violence or simony, the investiture of the staff and ring; and that after the investiture they may canonically receive consecration from the bishop to whom that office may pertain. If any be elected against your assent, except he be invested by you, let him not be consecrated. Let bishops or archbishops have liberty from you of consecrating bishops or abbots canonically. For your predecessors out of their royal possessions have so amply endowed the churches of their kingdom, that it is absolutely necessary that the same kingdom should be defended by abbots or bishops, and that the popular riots, which often happen in elections, should be subdued by the royal authority. Wherefore, by God's assistance, you ought to rely on your own prudence and carefulness to preserve the eminence of the Roman church and the safety of the rest by benefits and services. If any person, ecclesiastical or secular, shall audaciously attempt to pervert the import of this concession, let him be bound by the chain of an anathema, except he repent, and suffer the loss of his honours and dignities; and may the Divine Mercy preserve those who observe it, and grant you happily to reign to his honour and glory."

With these conventions and oaths between the lord the pope and the king, peace was made in the feast of Easter. Then the king came to Rome in the ides of April [13th April], and the pope having celebrated mass in the church of St. Peter, consecrated him emperor, and gave him and all his people absolution, and pardoned all the injuries which he himself had received. Henry, king of England, transferred into Wales the Flemings, who inhabited Northumberland, with all their furniture, and commanded them to inhabit the land called Ros. And he also commanded that the new monastery, which had been built by William, bishop of Winchester, within the walls of Winchester, should be rebuilt outside the walls; and soon after crossed the sea. In this year there was a very severe winter, a heavy famine, and a great mortality among men, a plague among animals, both beasts of the field and domestic animals, and a great destruction of birds.

A.D. 1111.

A.D. 1112. The decision of a council against the heresy concerning the investiture :—

In the thirteenth year of the pontificate of pope Paschal II., the fifth indiction, in the month of March, on the 15th of the kalends of April [18th March], a council was held at Rome, in the Lateran, in the Constantine church. In this council, when the pope had returned with his archbishops, bishops, cardinals, and a great multitude of clergy and laity, on the last day of the council, having made a profession of the catholic faith in the presence of all, in order that none might doubt of his belief, he said ; " I embrace all Holy Scripture, namely, the Old and New Testament, the law of Moses, and the holy prophets. I embrace the four gospels, the seven canonical epistles, the epistles of the glorious doctor the blessed Paul the apostle, the sacred canons of the apostles, the four general councils (even as I embrace the four gospels), namely, the councils of Nice, Ephesus, Constantinopole, and Chalcedon ; the council of Antioch, and the decrees of the holy fathers, pontiffs of Rome, especially the decrees of my lord pope Gregory VII., and pope Urban, of blessed memory. What they accepted, I accept ; what they held, I hold ; what they confirmed, I confirm ; what they condemned, I condemn ; what they rejected, I reject ; what they interdicted, I interdict ; what they prohibited, I prohibit, in all and through all ; and in these things I will always persevere."

When he had finished, Gerard, bishop of Engoulesme, legate in Acquitain, rose for all ; and by the common assent of pope Paschal and all the council, he read as follows :—" All we, assembled in this sacred council with the lord the pope, do, by censure canonical and authority ecclesiastical, by the judgment of the Holy Spirit, condemn, and judge to be void and of no effect, and altogether quash, and (lest it have any authority or efficacy) totally repudiate the privilege, (which is no privilege, but ought rather to be called a violation of the law,) that, namely, which, for the liberation of prisoners and the church, has been extorted from pope Paschal by the violence of king Henry ; and it is therefore condemned, because it contains the clause, that one canonically elected by the clergy and people, unless he be first invested by the king, shall not be consecrated ; which is against the Holy Spirit and the canonical institutions."

When this charter had been read, the whole council exclaimed at once, " Amen, Amen ! so be it, so be it !" The archbishops who were present with their suffragans, were these : John, patriarch of Venice, Semies of Capua, Landulf of Benevento, those of Amalfi, Reggio, Otranto, Brindisi, Capsa, Gyrontium ; and of the Greeks, Risano, and the archbishop of San Severino ; the bishops, Centius of Savona, Peter of Porto, Leo of Ostia, Cono of Palestina, Girard of Engoulesme, Galo of Leon, legate for the archbishops of Bourges and Vienne, Roger of Volturara, Geoffrey of Sienna, Roland of Pampeluna, Gregory of Tarragona, William of Troia, Gibin of Syracuse, legate for all the Sicilies, and other bishops to the number of nearly one hundred. Siguin and John of Toscolano, bishops, though at Rome on that day, were not present at the council. Afterwards, they read the condemnation of the privilege, and consented to it and accepted it.

Samson, the twenty-fifth bishop of Worcester, died on Sunday, the 3d of the nones of May [5th May]. Henry, king of England, placed earl Robert of Belesme in custody, in Carisbrook, in the month of October.

A.D. 1113. The city of Worcester, with its cathedral church, and all the other churches, and the castle, was consumed by fire, on Friday, the 13th of the kalends of July [19th June]. There perished in the flames one of the monks, who had been most useful to the monastery, with two servants, and fifteen citizens. Henry, king of England, returned to England in the month of July, and placed earl Robert de Belesme, whom he had brought over from Normandy, in the closest confinement at Warham. Thomas the prior, and Colemann, celebrated monks of St. Mary of Worcester, men of rare worth, departed this life, on Saturday, the 4th of the nones of October [4th Oct.].

> Thus by a common fate they pay the debt of nature;
> Yet theirs are the highest joys, theirs the most perfect peace;
> For with the saints they inherit the life which knoweth no end.

Teoulf, the king's chaplain, was made bishop of Worcester, on Sunday, the 5th of the kalends of January [28th Dec.], at Windsor.

A.D. 1114. Mathilda, daughter of Henry, king of the English, on the 8th of the ides of January [6th Jan.], was married at Mayence, to Henry, emperor of Rome, and consecrated queen. Thomas, archbishop of York, died on Tuesday, the 6th of the kalends of March [24th Feb.]. Ralph, bishop of Rochester, on Sunday, the 6th of the kalends of May [26th April], was elected to the archbishopric of Canterbury, at Windsor. The city of Chichester, with the principal monastery, was burnt, on Tuesday, the 3d of the nones of May [5th May], by negligence. Thurstan, the king's chaplain, was elected on the day of the Assumption of St. Mary [15th Aug.], at Winchester, to the archbishopric of York. Arnulf, abbot of Burgh, was elected bishop of Rochester. Henry, king of England, after he had led an army into Wales, crossed the sea, before the Feast of St. Michael [29th Sept.]. The river called Medewege became so shallow for many miles, on the 6th of the ides of October [10th Oct.], that even in the middle of the stream the smallest vessels were quite unable to keep afloat from want of water. The Thames, on the same day, suffered the same failure; for between the bridge and the Royal Tower, even under the bridge, the water was so shallow, that not only horses but a great multitude of men and boys crossed on foot, the water scarcely reaching up to their knees. This want of water lasted from the middle of the preceding night to the middle of the following night. We have heard, from credible sources, that a similar want of water was experienced on the same day at Yarmouth, and in other places throughout England.

A.D. 1115. In this year the winter was so severe, that nearly all the bridges in England were ruined by the frost. The emperor Henry, after he had laid siege to Cologne for a long time, and had lost many of his men in a pitched battle, made peace by oath in the city of Nussa. Ralph, archbishop of Canterbury, on Sunday, the 5th of the kalends of July [27th June], assumed the pall at Canterbury, where the bishops of all England were assembled, at the hands of Anselm, legate of the holy Roman church. And on the same day Teoulf, bishop of Worcester, was consecrated with great honour. Wilfrid, bishop of St. David, died in Wales; up to his time the bishops had been Britons. In the octave of the apostles St. John and St. Paul [6th July], a great council was celebrated at Châlons, by Cono, cardinal of the Roman church ; in which he excommunicated the bishops who were not present at the council; he also degraded some, and deprived many abbots of their staffs and deposed them from their seats, interdicting them from the exercise of the ecclesiastical office. Henry, king of the Romans, returned to England, in the middle of July. Bernard, the queen's chancellor, was elected bishop of St. David's in Wales, on Saturday, the 14th of the kalends of October [18th Sept.], and on the same day was promoted to the priesthood, by William, bishop of Winchester, at Southwark, and on the morrow, in the presence of the queen, he was consecrated bishop at Westminster, by archbishop Ralph. Regnelm, bishop of Hereford, died on the 6th of the kalends of November [27th Oct.], in whose stead Gosfrid, the king's chaplain, was elected. Ralph, archbishop of Canterbury, ordained at Canterbury, on St. Stephen [26th Dec.], Arnulf to the see of Rochester, and Gosfrid to Hereford.

A.D. 1116. Griffin ap Rees ravaged Wales in the spring, and burned the castles, because king Henry would not give him a portion of the land of his father. An assembly of nobles and barons of all England was held at Salisbury, on the 14th of the kalends of April [19th March], and they did homage and swore allegiance in the presence of king Henry to his son William. The dissension which had continued for a whole year between Ralph, archbishop of Canterbury, and Thurstan, archbishop elect of York, was mooted here. This archbishop elect, on receiving admonition from the pope to do that which he was bound to do to the church of Canterbury, and to receive his benediction according to ecclesiastical customs, made answer that he was willing to accept the benediction, but that he would by no means make the profession which was demanded of him. But king Henry, when he understood that Thurstan still remained in his disobedience, openly declared that he should either follow the custom of his predecessors, both in making the profession and in other matters belonging of ancient right to the church of Canterbury, or that he should entirely lose both the archbishopric of York and the benediction. When he heard this, being led astray by the impulse of his temper, he renounced the archbishopric, promising the king and archbishop that he would never claim it while he lived, and that he would make no demand for it whoever was put in his place.   Owen, king of Wales, was slain, and Henry, king of England, crossed the sea; Thurstan, archbishop elect of York, accompanying them, in the hope that he might recover the investiture of his archbishopric, and obtain the benediction from the archbishop by the royal command without the exaction of the required profession.   About the month of August, Anselm returned from Rome, having brought the pall from Rome for the archbishop of Canterbury; and he came to Normandy, bringing letters from the apostolic see, by which there was conceded to himself the office of legate in England, which he intimated to the kingdom of England by his letters.   Hereupon, by the advice of the queen and some of the nobles of England, Ralph, archbishop of Canterbury, after the feast of the Nativity of St. Mary [8th Sept.], crossed the sea, went to the king, whom he found residing at Rouen; and having carefully discussed with him the business on which he had come, point by point, by his advice he set out on his journey to Rome.

A.D. 1117.   By command of king Henry, a new building was commenced at Cirencester.   In Lombardy a great earthquake took place, and, according to the testimony of those who knew about it, it lasted for a space of forty days, during which time many buildings were thrown down ; and, what is wonderful, a large town was suddenly moved from its own position, and may be now seen to stand in a place far removed from other towns.   While some men of patrician rank were assembled in a tower at Milan, for the transaction of state affairs, a voice at the door resounded in the ears of all, calling one of them by name, and entreating him to come forth at once.   When he delayed, a form appeared before them, and by earnest prayers prevailed upon him to leave.   As soon as he was gone the tower suddenly fell, and buried all who were present in its ruins.   Robert, bishop of Stafford [Coventry], and Gilebert, abbot of Westminster, died on the 8th of the ides of December [6th Dec.].

HERE ENDS THE CHRONICLE OF FLORENCE OF WORCESTER.

HERE BEGINS THE CONTINUATION OF
THE CHRONICLE OF FLORENCE OF WORCESTER.

A.D. 1118. POPE PASCHAL, of holy memory, died on the 14th of
the kalends of February [19th Jan.], and a certain John, a native of
Cajeta, succeeded him, his name being changed to Gelasius. .He
was bred up for a monk in the monastery of Mount Cassino from
infancy, and when he attained man's estate became chancellor to
the venerable apostolic popes Desiderius, Urban, and Paschal. The
king of Germany, who was also emperor of Rome, hearing that the
pope had departed this life, hurried to Rome, and appointed as
pope the bishop of Braga, who-had been excommunicated in the
preceding year at Beneventum by Paschal, when Gelasius left the
city; and he then called him Gregory, instead of his former name,
Maurice. Mathilda, queen of England, died at Westminster on
the kalends of May [1st May], and was honourably buried in the
monastery itself. Many of the Normans who had sworn allegiance
to king Henry went over to Louis, king of France, and his chiefs,
who were the adversaries of the king, thus not fearing to set aside
the claims of their natural lord. The aforesaid pope Gelasius
came over sea to Burgundy, and his arrival was immediately made
known to the whole of France. On the nones of July [7th July],
Florence of Worcester, the monk, died. His deep knowledge and
great industry have rendered this Chronicle of chronicles pre-
eminent over all others.

> The earth covers his body, may his soul find rest in heaven,
> And reign for ever there with the saints in the presence of God.

After the dedication of the church at Momerfeld by Gosfrid,
bishop of Hereford, all who had come to that service set out to
return home; but the air which had been before remarkably serene,
became clouded, and a great storm of thunder and lightning arose,
and some of those on their journey back, being overtaken by it
and unable to return, rested in a certain spot at which they happened to have arrived. They were five in number, three men and
two women; one of the latter was killed by a stroke of lightning,
and the other having been set on fire from the middle down to the
soles of the feet, perished miserably, the men alone scarce escaping
with their lives. Five of their horses also were struck and killed.

A.D. 1119. Pope Gelasius died, and was buried at Cluny;
Guy, bishop of Vienne, succeeded him, whose name was changed
to Calixtus. Gosfrid, bishop of Hereford, died on the 3d of the
nones of February [3d Feb.], and Herbert, of Norwich, on the

11th of the kalends of August [22d July]. A war having arisen between Henry, king of England, and Louis, king of France, and the earl of Anjou, and the earl of Flanders, king Henry, seizing the opportunity, took the initiative in making peace with the earl, and accepted his daughter in marriage for his son William, whom he had already made the heir of all his kingdom. The earl of Anjou went to Jerusalem. After this king Henry, by the advice of his nobles, made peace with the king of France, by which his son William received Normandy, to be held of the king of France. The king also made peace not only with his nobles, who had unjustly and unfaithfully deserted him, but also with the earl of Flanders. An earthquake was felt in many places in England on Sunday, the 4th of the kalends of October [28th Sept.], about the third hour of the day. Pope Calixtus appointed a general council at Rheims on the 13th of the kalends of November [20th Oct.], where there was a great assembly of archbishops, bishops, abbots, and princes of different provinces, and an immense multitude of clergy and people. The bishops of England, who were then staying with the king in Normandy, namely, William of Exeter, Ranulph of Durham, Bernard of St. David's, and Urban of Glamorgan, and the bishops and abbots of Normandy, were sent by the king himself to the council. Ralph, archbishop of Canterbury, was not able to attend by reason of sickness. Thurstan, archbishop elect of York, sought permission of the king to go thither, and at length obtained it, pledging his faith that he would, on no account, accept the episcopal consecration from the pope. Bound by this promise, he hastened on his journey, and came to the pope; and soon, setting aside his promise, by the aid of bribes he brought the Romans over to his own side, and through them besought the pope that he would with his own hand consecrate him bishop. And he was consecrated to the archbishopric of York, and many of the bishops of France were present at his consecration. The bishops of England, however, had not yet come to the council; but when they became acquainted with what had been done, they told it to the king. And he being very indignant hereat, forbade Thurstan and his people to return either into England or Normandy, or indeed to any of his dominions.

A.D. 1120. Ralph, archbishop of Canterbury, returned to England on Sunday the 2d of the nones of January [4th Jan.], and on Sunday the 2d of the nones of April [4th April] he consecrated a venerable clerk named David, who was chosen to the bishopric of Bangor by king Griffin and the clergy and people of Wales; and at this consecration were present Richard, bishop of London, Robert of Lincoln, Roger of Salisbury, and Urban of Glamorgan. Henry, king of England, after having concluded everything prosperously and according to his wishes, returned from Normandy into England. His son William followed him, and embarked attended by a great company of nobles, soldiers, boys, and women. When they had put out of port, relying on the extraordinary calmness of the weather, and were proceeding on the voyage, in a short time the ship in which they were sailing struck upon a rock, and all who were on board (except one peasant who escaped by the wonderful mercy of God, and he, as it is related, not even worthy to be mentioned by name) were swallowed up by the waves. The most noble of these were William, the king's son, Richard, his brother, Richard, earl of Chester, Otthuel, his brother, William Bigod, Geoffrey Riddel, Walter de Everci, Geoffrey, archdeacon of Hereford, the countess of Perch, daughter of the king, the countess of Chester, the king's niece, and many others, whom we pass by for brevity's sake. This shocked and distressed the mind of the king (who had reached England after a prosperous voyage), and of all who heard it, and caused them to ponder upon the hidden judgments of a just God.

A.D. 1121. Henry, king of England, having now been a widower for a long time (and that he might no longer lead an improper life), by the advice of Ralph, archbishop of Canterbury, and the nobles of the kingdom, whom he assembled together at London, on the Epiphany of our Lord [6th Jan.], determined that he would choose for his wife Adelaide, daughter of Godfrey, duke of Lorrain, a maiden adorned with the comeliness of a modest countenance. Messengers are despatched ; and they brought the future queen, with great state, from the parts beyond the sea, to the court of the king. Meanwhile, two clerks were elected to the government of churches which had been vacant for some time, namely, Richard, who was keeper of the royal seal under the chancellor, and Robert, whose duty it was to serve the king in the care of his bread and drink. The former of these was made bishop of Hereford, the latter of Chester. Herbert, also, monk of the abbey of Westminster, was appointed abbot of the same place. Richard was elected on Friday, the 7th of the ides of January [7th Jan.], and on Sunday, the 17th of the kalends of February [16th Jan.], was consecrated bishop at Lambeth, by Ralph, archbishop of Canterbury, with the assistance of Richard, bishop of London, Robert of Lincoln, Arnulph of Ro- chester, Urban of Glamorgan, Bernard of St. David's. The maid aforesaid, being elected queen, was espoused to the king on Satur- day the 4th of the kalends of February [29th Jan.], by William, bishop of Winchester, by command of Ralph, archbishop of Canter- bury ; and on the morrow, namely, on the 3d of the kalends of February [30th Jan.], was consecrated queen by the same arch- bishop, and crowned. After this the archbishop came to Abingdon, with the king, and on Sunday, the 3d of the ides of March [13th March], he consecrated the aforesaid Robert to the bishopric of Chester ; William, bishop of Winchester, William of Exeter, Urban and Bernard, Welsh bishops, being present and assisting in the consecration. After a few days, a certain member of the chapel royal, named Everard, was elected to the bishopric of Norwich, and consecrated at Canterbury, by Ralph, archbishop of Canterbury, on the 2d of the ides of June [12th June], Arnulph, bishop of Ro- chester, Richard of Hereford, and Robert of Coventry, assembling for this purpose. Pope Calixtus, having collected forces from all parts, took the above-mentioned Maurice, surnamed Burdinus, whom the emperor had established, by the name of Gregory, in the apostolic see; and contumeliously thrust him into a monastery, after having stripped him of all his honours. , Henry, king of England, led an army against the Welsh, and, taking hostages from them, reduced the whole of Wales to his own dominion.   A certain clerk, an Irishman by birth, and by name Gregory, being chosen bishop of Dublin by the king, the clergy, and the people of Ireland, came to England, that he might be ordained, according to ancient custom, by the archbishop of Canterbury, primate of England; whereupon by the command of the archbishop, Roger, bishop of Salisbury, promoted him to the rank of the deaconship and priesthood, at his castle called Devizes, on Saturday, the 11th of the kalends of October [21st Sept.].   He was ordained bishop on Sunday, the 6th of the nones of October [2d Oct.], at Lambeth, by Ralph, archbishop of Canterbury; and Richard, bishop of London, Roger of Salisbury, Robert of Lincoln, Everard of Norwich, and David of Bangor, were present at his consecration.   The principal church at Tewksbury was consecrated with great pomp, by Teoulf, bishop of Worcester, Richard of Hereford, Urban of Glamorgan, and the aforesaid Gregory of Dublin, on Monday, the 9th of the kalends of November [24th Oct.].

A.D. 1122.   The city of Gloucester, with the principal monastery, for the second time were destroyed by fire, on Wednesday, the 7th of the ides of March [9th March], in the twenty-second year of the reign of king Henry; the former conflagration happened in the first year of his reign, on Thursday, the 11th of the kalends of June [22d May].   Ralph, the twenty-fifth archbishop of Canterbury, departed this life at Canterbury, on Thursday, the 14th of the kalends of November [19th Oct.].   John, bishop of Bath, died on the 4th of the kalends of January [29th Dec.]; during his lifetime he had sold all the town of Bath to king Henry, for five hundred pounds.

A.D. 1123.   Robert, the eighteenth bishop of Lincoln, in the month of January, while at Woodstock, when on horseback, and holding a conversation with king Henry, suddenly lost his speech and sank to the ground; he was carried away to an house, where he died.   Ranulph, also, the king's chancellor, departed this life in a miserable manner.   William, canon of St. Osgith's of Chiche, was elected to the archbishopric of Canterbury, at Gloucester, where the king held his court, on the Purification of St. Mary [2d Feb.]; and he was consecrated archbishop of Canterbury, by William, bishop of Winchester, with the assistance of many others, on the 14th of the kalends of March [16th Feb.].   With his assent, in Lent, the bishopric of the city of Lincoln was given to Alexander, archdeacon of Salisbury.   Afterwards the same archbishop William (in company with Thurstan, archbishop of York, Bernard, bishop of St. David's, Sigefrid, abbot of Glastonbury, and Anselm, abbot of St. Edmund) went to Rome for his pall.   Alexander, king of Scots, died on the 7th of the kalends of May [25th April].   Henry, king of England, after the feast of Pentecost [3d June], went over sea.   William, archbishop of Canterbury, having received the pall from pope Calixtus, and Thurstan, archbishop of York, with his companions, returned from Rome, and joined the king, who was staying in Normandy. And not long after this, archbishop William returned to England, and on the 11th of the kalends of August [22d July], being then at Canterbury, he consecrated Alexander, bishop of Lincoln ; and on the 7th of the kalends of September [26th Aug.], and in the church of St. Paul apostle, at London, he consecrated Godefrey, the queen's chancellor; bishop of Bath. Teoulf, the twenty-sixth bishop of Worcester, died on Saturday, the 13th of the kalends of November [20th Oct.], at his vill of Hantun. Robert, abbot of Tewkesbury, departed this life on the 6th of the ides of December [8th Dec.]. David, brother of Alexander, king of the Scots, succeeded him in the kingdom.

A.D. 1124. Arnulf, the twenty-third bishop of Rochester, died in the month of March. Galeran, count of Mellent, was captured in Passion-week by the soldiers of king Henry, in Normandy, and was placed, with many others, in close confinement at Rouen. Gosfrid, abbot of the new monastery of Winchester, died. The reverend prior of the church of Worcester, named Nicholas, died on Wednesday, the 8th of the kalends of July [24th June]. May he, by the mercy of God, rejoice in the kingdom of heaven ! William, archbishop of Canterbury, as the king had commanded, crossed the sea. Pope Calixtus died, and was succeeded by Honorius, bishop of Ostia.

A.D. 1125. The coiners who were taken in England with false money, suffered the cruel sentence of the king, by amputation of their right hands, and the loss of the lower parts of their bodies. Afterwards, in consequence of a change in the value of money, all things became dear ; whence a severe famine arose, and reduced a great multitude of men nearly to death. Simon, the queen's chancellor, and Sigefrid, abbot of Glastonbury, men of remarkable piety and probity, were elected (when they were in Normandy) to be bishops ; Simon to the bishopric of Worcester, and Sigefrid to that of Chichester. Hugh, archdeacon of two bishops of Worcester, namely, Samson and Teoulf, a man of great prudence, died on the 12th of the kalends of April [21st March]. The feast of Easter having ended [29th March], Simon and Sigefrid, the bishops elect, came to England, in company with archbishops William and Thurstan, and a Roman cardinal, by name John ; and Sigefrid was ordained bishop of the church of Chichester, by archbishop William, on the 2d of the ides of April [12th April]. There were present at his ordination the Roman cardinal, Thurstan, archbishop of York, Everard of Norwich, Richard of Hereford, Bernard of St. David's, David of Bangor, Urban of Glamorgan, and John, bishop elect of Rochester. Simon, bishop elect of Worcester, was received at Worcester by the clergy and people with a festive procession, on the 8th of the ides of May [8th May], being the day of the Ascension of the Lord ; and on the 10th of the kalends of June [23d May] he was ordained priest at Canterbury, by William, archbishop of Canterbury. The emperor Henry died, and was buried at Spires, where his grandfather also lies.

Lothair, the ninety-eighth emperor of the Romans, reigned thirteen years. Simon, bishop elect of Worcester, accompanied by

Godfrey, bishop of Bath, came to Canterbury, and was ordained priest on the Saturday in Whitsun-week [17th May], by William, archbishop of Canterbury, and on the next day was consecrated with great pomp bishop of the holy mother church of Worcester; and along with him John, archdeacon of Canterbury, was ordained bishop of Rochester. At their consecration were present Richard, bishop of Hereford, David of Bangor, Godfrey of Bath, Sigefrid of Chichester. When Simon of Worcester came to the seat of his bishopric, a great multitude of the people assembled; after which he was received by a honourable procession, and enthroned with the celebration of a mass in honour of the Holy Trinity. On the same day, that is, on the 9th of the kalends of June [24th May], that servant and faithful friend of God, in all his house, by name Benedict, who in the preceding year had been elected abbot of Tewkesbury, (one who had been brought up there in the monkish habit from a boy, and in process of time, by the permission of Wulfstan the bishop, from whom he had already taken all the ecclesiastical orders, having become in peace and love one of the monks of Worcester,) was consecrated by the same new bishop, Simon, to the office of abbot of the church of Worcester. There were present at the consecration of the same bishop, the following; namely, Richard of Hereford, Godfrey of Bath, David of Bangor, and his diocesans, the abbots, Guy of Pershore, William of Gloucester, Godfrey of Winchelcumbe, and instead of his abbot, who was prevented by sickness, Dominic, prior of Evesham, Walcer, the prior of Malvern, to whom the words of the Psalmist may be applied, "The Lord sendeth out the fountains in the valleys, and the whole assembly who met the priest in procession." These same ecclesiastics also received the said Benedict in procession.

A synod was celebrated at London, in the church of the blessed chief of the apostles at Westminster, on the 9th of September, that is, on the 5th of the ides, where, after the discussion of many causes, these canons, seventeen in number, were published and confirmed by all. John de Crema presided in this synod; he was cardinal priest of the holy and apostolic church, of the title of Saint Crisogonus, being the legate of pope Honorius in England, with William, archbishop of Canterbury, and Thurstan, archbishop of York, and the bishops of different provinces, twenty in number, and about forty abbots, and an innumerable multitude of the clergy and the people. These are the canons :—

The first canon.—Following in the footsteps of the holy fathers, by our apostolic authority we forbid the ordination of any person in the church for money.

II. We interdict the exaction of any fee for the chrism, for oil, for baptism, for penance, for the visitation of the sick or unction, for the communion of the Body of Christ, or for burial.

III. Moreover we ordain, and decree by apostolic authority, that in the consecration of bishops, or the benedictions of abbots, or the dedications of churches, no cope, nor tapet, nor napkin, nor basin, nor anything else whatever, shall be exacted by violence, unless it shall be spontaneously offered.

IV. No abbot, no prior, no monk or clerk shall accept a church, tithe, or any ecclesiastical benefice from the gift of a layman, without the assent and authority of his own bishop. If he shall presume to do this, the donation shall be void, and he himself shall be subjected to the canonical censure.

V. We enact, moreover, that no person shall claim for himself a church or prebend by paternal inheritance, or shall appoint a successor to himself in any ecclesiastical benefice, which if he presume to do, we forbid that it have any effect, saying with the Psalmist, " O my God, make them like a wheel, and (as they have said) Let us possess the sanctuary of God as an inheritance."

VI. Furthermore we enact, that clerks who hold churches or ecclesiastical benefices, and avoid ordination, in order to be able to live more freely in the world; and after having been urged thereto by their bishops, should they still continue to contemn promotion to orders, they shall be deprived of their churches and benefices.·

VII. None but a priest shall be promoted to the dignity of dean or prior; none but a deacon to the rank of archdeacon.

VIII. No person shall be ordained priest or deacon except on a definite title. Whoever shall have been ordained absolutely shall lose his assumed dignity.

IX. No abbot, no clerk or layman whatever, shall presume to eject any person ecclesiastically ordained to a church, without the sentence of his own bishop. He who shall presume to do otherwise will subject himself to excommunication.

X. No bishop shall presume to ordain or adjudge the inhabitants of another diocese, for each stands or falls to his own master; nor is any one bound by a sentence which is not pronounced by his own judge.

XI. No person shall presume to take into communion one who has been excommunicated by another. If he shall have knowingly done this, he shall himself be deprived of christian communion.

XII. We command, also, that two archdeaconries or preferments of different ranks shall not be assigned to the same person.

XIII. We prohibit by apostolic authority all priests, deacons, subdeacons and canons, from cohabiting with wives, or concubines, and with all women generally, except it be in the case of a mother, a sister, an aunt, or those women who are removed from all suspicion. Whoever shall be proved by confession or conviction to have violated this decree, let him suffer the loss of his own orders.

XIV. We altogether prohibit usury and filthy gain to all sorts of clerks. Whoever shall have confessed or have been convicted of such a crime, is to be degraded from the orders which he holds.

XV. We command the excommunication of fortune-tellers, soothsayers, and dealers in all kinds of auguries, and those who consent to them, and we brand them with perpetual infamy.

XVI. We forbid the contraction of marriages as well between those connected by blood as those connected by affinity. If any such shall have been joined together in marriage, they are to be separated.

XVII. We forbid not only the acceptance of the testimony of husbands accusing their own wives of consanguinity, but further that of the witnesses whom they may bring forward; but let the ancient authority of the fathers be observed.

"Does this please you?" "It pleases us." "Does this please you?" "It pleases us." "Does this please you?" "It pleases us.'

This same cardinal, having left England, went to Normandy and finally returned to Rome. The archbishop William also, considering the church of the kingdom of England to have suffered a heavy scandal in the humiliation of the church of Canterbury, crossed the sea himself on his way to Rome, to obtain what aid he could in the management of his affairs which had fallen into disorder, and to prevent the further progress of the evil. He came, therefore, to Rome, and was honourably received by pope Honorius, who had succeeded Calixtus, and who committed to the archbishop the exercise of vicarial authority over England and Scotland, and appointed him legate of the apostolic see.

A.D. 1126. Henry, king of England, returned to England on the Nativity of our Lord [25th Dec.], and held his court with great magnificence in Windsor Castle, and there united together the nobility of the whole kingdom by his decree. Here, when the archbishop of York was desirous of crowning the king, thereby putting himself on an equality with the archbishop of Canterbury, herein following the example of his predecessors, he was repulsed by the judgment of all, and the general sentiment of all unanimously declared that the office of conferring the crown of the kingdom in no manner appertained to him. The bearer of the cross which he caused to be carried before him into the king's chapel, along with the cross which he carried, was thrust out of the chapel; for according to the judgment of the bishops and some prudent men skilled in ecclesiastical law, it was held to be a ruled point that it is not lawful for any metropolitan to bear a cross before him beyond the bounds of his own jurisdiction. When these festivities were concluded, the king and all the nobility proceeded to London, and there, by command of the king, archbishop William (being the legate of the Roman church), and all the other bishops of England, with the nobles of the land, on their allegiance and oath, bound themselves to the daughter of the king, that they would defend the kingdom of England for her behoof against all persons, should she survive her father; unless he, before his death, should beget a son in lawful wedlock, who in that case should succeed him. On the death of her husband, the emperor Henry, (who had lived in marriage with her for many years,) without children, she returned to her father, and resided in his court, as was becoming, with the greatest honour. On the death of the king's son William, (which we have above narrated,) there was none to succeed as legitimate heir of his kingdom, for which reason he transferred the rights of his kingdom to his daughter, the sister of this William, on the condition which we have mentioned. Henry, also, by the advice of his barons, granted to the church of Canterbury, and to William the archbishop, and to all his successors,

the custody and constableship of the castle of Rochester to hold
for ever ; and he gave them permission to make in the same castle
a fortification or tower of what kind soever they pleased, and have
and keep it for ever ; and that the soldiers who should be sent to
guard the castle should come in and go out as was convenient, and
should form the garrison of the same castle.   Robert, surnamed
Peccatum, bishop of Coventry, departed this life, and reposes at
Coventry.   Hugh, abbot of St. Augustine's, died.

A.D. 1127.   William, archbishop of Canterbury, assembled a
general council of all bishops and abbots, and of the religious
persons of England, at the monastery of St. Peter, situated in the
western part of London.   He himself presided at this council, as
archbishop of Canterbury and legate of the apostolic see, together
with William, bishop of Winchester, Roger of Salisbury, William of
Exeter, Hervey of Ely, Alexander of Lincoln, Everard of Norwich,
Seifred of Chichester, Richard of Hereford, Godfrey of Bath, John
of Rochester, Bernard of St. David's in Wales, Urban of Glamorgan
or Llandaff, and David of Bangor.   At this time Richard of London
and Robert of Chester were dead, and hitherto no person had
succeeded to their sees.   But Thurstan, the archbishop of York,
sent messengers and letters, and showed reasonable cause why he
could not be present at that assembly.   Ranulph, bishop of
Durham, on his way thither, was seized with sickness, and was
unable to complete the journey, as the prior of the church and the
clerks whom he had sent thither in support of the truth of his as-
sertion attested.   And Simon, bishop of Worcester, had gone over
sea to visit his relations, and had not yet returned.   Great multi-
tudes of clerks and laymen, as well of the rich as of the middle
orders, having collected there, the meeting was exceedingly numerous.   It sat for three days, namely, the 3d of the ides of May
[11th May], and the following day, and the fourth after that, the
17th of the kalends of June [16th May].   A few things were done
concerning secular affairs, some determined, some deferred, and
some, by reason of the tumult of the stormy crowd, withdrawn from
the ears of the judges.   We have thought it advisable to record in
this work the decrees and statutes which were passed by the common
consent of the bishops in this council, as they were publicly recited
and set forth.   They are these :—

I. We entirely prohibit, by the authority of the blessed Peter, the
chief of apostles, and our own, the buying or selling of ecclesiastical
benefices, or of any ecclesiastical preferments whatsoever.   Whoever shall have been convicted of having violated this statute, if he
be a clerk, either a regular canon or a monk, let him be degraded
from his orders : if a laic, let him be held outlawed and excommu-
nicate, and be deprived of his right over the same church or
preferment.

II. We entirely interdict, by apostolic authority, the ordination
or promotion of any person for money in the church of God.

III. We condemn the exaction of monies for the admission of
canons, monks, and nuns.

IV. None is to be appointed dean but a priest ; none arch-

deacon but a deacon.   If any person in orders below those here
specified be already nominated for those preferments, he is to be
admonished by the bishop that he proceed to the proper orders.
If in disobedience to the monition of the bishop he refuse to be
ordained, he is to be deprived of the dignity to which he had been
nominated.

V. We altogether forbid priests, deacons, sub-deacons, and all
canons, to cohabit with unlawful women.   If they will retain their
concubines (which God forbid) or their wives, they are to be
deprived of their orders, preferment, and benefice.   Parish priests
(if there be any such) we expel without the chancel, and pronounce
them infamous.   We command, by the authority of God and our
own, all archdeacons and ministers whose duty this is, with all
diligence and solicitude to eradicate this deadly evil out of the
church of God.   If they be found negligent in this, or (which
God forbid) if they be consenting thereto, they are, for the first
and second offence, to be sufficiently corrected by the bishop, and
for the third to be canonically punished with more severity.

VI. The concubines of priests and canons, except they shall
have been lawfully married there, shall be expelled from the parish.
If afterwards they be found in the same fault, in whosesoever
province they may be, they are to be taken by the ministers of the
church ; and we command, under pain of excommunication, that
they are not to be detained by any power lesser or greater, but to be
freely delivered to the minister of the church, and to be given
up to ecclesiastical discipline or custody.

VII. We prohibit under anathema any archdeacon from holding
different archdeaconries in different bishoprics ; let him retain that
only to which he was first appointed.

VIII. Bishops are to forbid the priests, abbots, monks, and priors
subject to them from holding farms.

IX. We command that tithes be wholly paid, for they are the
property of the most high God.

X. We forbid by canonical authority any person from giving or
receiving churches, or tithes, or other ecclesiastical benefices, without the consent or authority of the bishop.

XI. No abbess or nun is to use garments of higher value than
lambs-wool or cat-skin.

· King Henry, who was meanwhile residing in London, gave his
assent to the acts of this council, and permitted and confirmed by
his royal authority and power the statutes of the council which had
been celebrated at Westminster by William, archbishop of Canterbury, and the legate of the holy Roman church.   A certain Hugh,
of the see of Rochester, having been appointed abbot by William,
archbishop of Canterbury, in Chichester, on Sunday, the 2d of the
ides of June [12th June], was promoted to the rank of abbot of
St. Augustine's, an honour which he well deserved.   Richard,
bishop of Hereford, died at his vill called Dydelebrig, on Monday,
the 18th of the kalends of September [15th Aug.]; his body was
brought to Hereford, and buried in the church beside his predecessors.   Henry, king of England, went over sea.

A.D. 1128. Thurstan, archbishop of York, consecrated Robert (whom Alexander, king of Scotland, had intruded into the church of St. Andrews, at the petition of David, the brother and successor of Alexander,) bishop at York, in which office he had invited the assistance of Ranulph, bishop of Durham, and one Ralph, formerly ordained bishop of the Orkneys. This Ralph, having been ordained neither by the assent or election of the nobles of the land, nor the clergy, nor the people, was rejected by all and accepted by none as a bishop. He, because he was bishop of no city, attaching himself sometimes to York, sometimes to Durham, was supported by them, and employed by both as their vicar in the services of the bishoprics. Robert was consecrated by those persons, and, though he was a canon of York, was not permitted by the Scots to make profession of subjection or obedience to the church of York or its bishop. A certain canon of the church of Lyons, an honest and aged man, was elected to the bishopric of London; for Richard, bishop of the same city, was dead, and this man, named Gilebert, and surnamed Universalis, was appointed in his stead by king Henry and archbishop William, with the assent of the clergy and people. He was consecrated at Canterbury by the archbishop himself, in the mother church, on Sunday, the 11th of the kalends of February [22d Jan.], Seifrid, bishop of Chichester, and John of Rochester assisting and ministering to him in this office, in the presence of the abbots and other great and noble persons assembled at Canterbury for this purpose. His profession was first taken, after the custom of his ancestors, by which he promised that he would show to the archbishop and all his successors canonical subjection and obedience in all things.

Urban, bishop of Glamorgan or Llandaff,—because he considered that he had not been justly dealt with in disputes concerning certain matters, which in the general council of the past year he had mooted against Bernard, bishop of St. David's,—after the conclusion of the feast of the Purification of St. Mary [2d Feb.], crossed the sea, went to Rome, and communicated the cause of his journey to the pope, certain of his own people attesting the truth of his statement. The pope supported his cause by wishes and words, and directed letters to Henry, king of England, and archbishop William, and all the bishops of England, commanding them all, by virtue of his apostolic authority, to see that no person in anything opposed the just demands of Urban. The venerable Godefrey, abbot of Shrewsbury, died on Wednesday, the 9th of the kalends of April [24th March]. Gosfrid, prior of Canterbury, at the request of David, king of Scots, and with the assent of archbishop William, was elected abbot of a certain place in Scotland called Dunfermelin, and was ordained by Robert, bishop of the church of St. Andrews. Urban, bishop of Llandaff, returned to England after a prosperous journey, and by the king's command the apostolic mandates concerning him were put in force. One of the monks of the church of Shrewsbury, called Herbert, having been chosen abbot, was consecrated by archbishop William, at Lewes, and placed as abbot over the church of Shrewsbury. Hugh, abbot of Chertsey, died.   The count of Flanders, named William, surnamed Miser, was surrounded by his enemies and wounded, and his sufferings increasing, finished his life in a lamentable manner, on the 6th of the kalends of August [27th July], and was buried at St. Bertin.   Ranulph, bishop of Durham, died on the nones of September [5th Sept.] ; and Geoffrey, archbishop of Rouen, departed this life on the 4th of the kalends of December [28th Nov.].

A.D. 1129.   William, bishop of Winchester, died, on the 8th of the kalends of February [25th Jan.], and was buried at Winchester. In the month of July, Henry, king of England, returned from Normandy into England ; his nephew Henry, abbot of Glastonbury, was elected to the bishopric of Winchester, in the month of October, and consecrated by William, archbishop of Canterbury, on Sunday, the 15th of the kalends of December [17th Nov.].   Roger, nephew of Geoffrey de Clintun, archdeacon of Buckingham, was elected to the bishopric of Chester, ordained priest on the 12th of the kalends of January [21st Dec.], and on the following day was consecrated bishop, at Canterbury, by William, archbishop of Canterbury ; and Simon, bishop of Worcester, by command of the archbishop, afterwards enthroned him in the episcopal chair of Coventry.   A monk of Gloucester, a man of the highest piety, Reignold by name, was elected abbot, and ordained at Worcester, by the same Simon, bishop of Worcester, on Monday, the 6th of the kalends of February [27th Jan.].

A.D. 1130.   Hugh, abbot of Reading, was chosen archbishop of Rouen.   Christ Church, Canterbury, was dedicated with great pomp, by William, archbishop of the same city, on Sunday, the 4th of the nones of May [4th May] ; at the consecration of which were present the following : John bishop of Rochester, Gilebert of London, Henry of Winchester, Simon of Worcester, Alexander of Lincoln, Roger of Salisbury, Godfrey of Bath, Everard of Norwich, Sigefrid of Chichester, Bernard of St. David's, Audoen of Evreux (a continental diocese), and John of Seez.   On the 4th day after this, that is, on the nones of May [7th May], the city of Rochester was consumed by fire, the king being a spectator ; and on the following day, namely Ascension Sunday, the new church of St. Andrew was consecrated, by archbishop William, some of the aforesaid bishops assisting him in this service.   The prior of Lewes was elected abbot of the church of Reading, and afterwards ordained ; moreover, the prior of Winchester, Ingulfus, having been elected abbot of Abingdon, was ordained by Roger, bishop of Salisbury. William, abbot of Glastonbury, having voluntarily laid aside his pastoral duties, by reason of age, with the consent of the friars, elected a monk called Walter, who was ordained abbot on Sunday, the 3d of the nones of August [3d Aug.], by Simon, bishop of Worcester.   Serlo also, canon of Salisbury, was ordained abbot by the same bishop, at Blockeley, a vill belonging to the bishop, and was placed over the church of Cirencester.   Robert, prior of the church of Lanthony, being elected to the bishopric of Hereford, was consecrated at Oxford, by William, archbishop of Canterbury. Henry, king of England, went over the sea.

A.D. 1131. Reignold, the venerable abbot of Ramsey, died, on the 13th of the kalends of June [20th May], and William, abbot of Gloucester, and Hervey, bishop first of Bangor, and afterwards first bishop of Ely, died, on the 3d of the kalends of September [30th Aug.], in the ninth indiction.

A.D. 1132. A comet was visible for nearly five days, on the 8th of the ides of October [8th Oct.]. The greatest part of the city of London, with the mother church of St. Paul the apostle, was consumed by fire, in the week of Whitsuntide, which was on the 2d of the ides of May [14th May]. In the 33d year from the commencement of the reign of Henry, king of England, on Wednesday, and on the same day, according to the revolution of the year, on which his brother and predecessor, king William Rufus, was slain, and on which Henry himself, in the first year of his reign, had assumed the government, the following pheno-menon was seen. While the king was waiting near the sea-shore for the purpose of crossing over to the continent (the wind being frequently favourable to the passage), at length, on the day aforesaid, about noon, when he had come down to the sea-shore, and was about to cross, surrounded, as is the custom of kings, with troops of his soldiers, suddenly a cloud appeared in the air, which was visible, though not of the same size, throughout the whole of England. For in some places the day seemed to be only gloomy, but in others the obscurity was so great, that men had need of candle-light to do anything. Wherefore the king and his immediate attendants, and many others, wondering and raising their eyes to heaven, beheld the sun shining as it were in appearance like a new moon; but it did not long preserve one form or aspect, for some-times it was broader, sometimes narrower, sometimes more curved, sometimes straighter, now of its ordinary firmness, then again moving, and trembling and liquid like quicksilver. Some assert that an eclipse of the sun had taken place; if this be true, the sun was then in the head of the Dragon, and the moon in his tail, or the sun in his tail and the moon in his head, in the fifth sign, and the seventeenth degree of that sign. And the moon was then in her twenty-seventh day. On the same day, and about the same hour, many stars appeared. And on the same day, when the ships were at anchor near the shore, ready for the king's voyage, the sea being remarkably calm and a very moderate wind blowing, the great anchors of one of the ships were suddenly torn out of the ground as though by some violence, and the ship being set in motion, (to the wonder of many who attempted to hold her, but were unable,) moved the ship next to her, and thus eight ships were set in motion by some unknown forces, and all of them were injured. Many also said, that on the same day, and about the same hour, they had seen many churches in the province of York dripping as if by a profuse perspiration. All these things happened, as it has been said, on Wednesday, the 4th of the nones of August [2d Aug.]. And on the sixth day of the same week, namely, on the 2d of the nones of the same month [4th Aug.], in the morning, a great earthquake took place in many parts of England. Some people also said, that in the following week, on Tuesday, the 6th of the ides of the same month [8th Aug.], when the moon was three days old, they saw her first as she generally appeared at such an age, and after a short interval in the evening of the same day, they saw her full, after the manner of a shield, round and very brilliant. Many also said that on the same night they had seen two moons, distant from one another by about the length of a lance.

A.D. 1133. King Henry, however, crossed the sea, and left England for Normandy, never again to return alive, never again to see England. In the month of November, the city of Worcester, as was often the case, was burnt.

A.D. 1134. Robert, brother of king Henry, formerly earl of Normandy, was afterwards taken in war by him when in Normandy, at a certain castle called Tenercebrei, and for some time was placed in confinement in England; he died at Cairdif, was carried to Gloucester, and buried in the pavement of the church, before the altar, with great honour. Godfrey, bishop of Bath, died on the 17th of the kalends of September [16th Aug.]; he was succeeded, in due time, by a monk named Robert, a Fleming by descent, but born in England; Robert was made a bishop from a monk, for so Henry bishop of Winchester had arranged it before he became legate of the church of Rome, as he now is.

A.D. 1135. Henry, king of England, died on the 4th of the nones of December [2d Dec.], having reigned thirty-five years and four months, being in the sixty-ninth year of his age ; and Stephen, the son of his sister, being chosen to the kingdom of England, was consecrated king at London, on Sunday, the 13th of the kalends of January [20th Dec.]. Here also, by virtue of his royal prerogative, he graciously held his court at Christmas, along with all the nobles of England. After the conclusion of this holy festival, the body of king Henry, lately deceased, was brought from Normandy into England, and the king, attended by a great multitude of nobles, went to meet it; and by reason of the love which he bore to his uncle, he supported the bier on his royal shoulders, and with his barons caused the body to be carried to Reading. Amid the celebration of masses, divers precious offerings, alms given to a numerous multitude of poor persons, and obsequies properly celebrated, after his remains had been exposed on the bier, his tomb was erected according to custom in the principal church of the most blessed and glorious Virgin Mary, which king Henry himself, for the good of his soul, had endowed with lands, woods, meadows, pastures, and various ornaments; he was buried before the altar, with great pomp and honour. May king Henry, wealthy in earthly possessions, rescued from pain, enjoy the delights of heaven !

After his death, during the reign of Stephen, as well as long before, in every part of Normandy and England, the bond of peace was broken asunder, and the greatest disorder prevailed. Every man raised his hand against his neighbour; discord arose, and found its way into the residences of the nobles, and wasted the possessions of noble and ignoble. Every man spoiled another of his property: the strong oppresses the weak by force, prevents any complaint being made by threatening further violence; the man who resists is slain. The nobles of a wealthy land, rolling in riches, care little how unjustly the wretched poor are treated; they care only for themselves and their friends. They store their castles and towns with provisions, guard them with an armed military force; their chief fear is some political change, and thus they neglect to consider that this is in the hand of God, for " his ways are past finding out." Instead however of having everything settled peaceably, out of fear of the king, (whom every one ought to regard as an angry lion,) in many places, especially in Wales, depopulations and depredations never cease, and from this one might easily see that England was ruled by governors possessed of small prudence and feeble determination, nay, rather by injustice than justice. Amid dominant avarice and the worst self-seeking, there was no room for temperance, the mother of all virtue. Stephen, king of England, reached Devonshire with an army of horse and foot, with the intention of besieging the castle of Exeter, which Baldwin, surnamed Redvers, had fortified against him. At length the garrison surrendered, provisions having failed them; and after a treaty had been offered and accepted, Baldwin, with his wife and daughters, was outlawed and expelled from England. The venerable Ansger, abbot of Reading, died on the 6th of the kalends of February [27th Jan.], and Godfrey, bishop of Bath, on the 17th of the kalends of September [16th Aug.].

A.D. 1136. Immediately after the death of king Henry, on the 4th of the nones of December [2d Dec.], a serious battle took place on the kalends of January [1st Jan.], at Gower, between the Normans and Welsh, where five hundred and sixteen of both sides perished. Their bodies were horribly scattered about the field and devoured by wolves. Afterwards a great irruption was made by the Welsh, which was the occasion of a vast and wide-spread destruction of churches, towns, wheat, and cattle, a burning of castles and other fortified places, a slaughter, dispersion, and selling to foreign lands of numberless men, both rich and poor, among whom the noble and amiable Richard Fitz Gilebert was surprised and slain by an ambush of the Welsh on the 17th of the kalends of May [15th April], and his body was carried to Gloucester and honourably buried in the chapter-house of the brethren. Afterwards in the same year, a very bloody battle was fought at Cardigan, in the month of October, in the second week, in which there was so great a slaughter that (not taking into account the men who were carried away into captivity) there remained ten thousand women, whose husbands, with numberless children, had been either drowned, or burned, or put to the sword. And it was a wretched sight to see, when the bridge over the river Teuwi broke down, and a bridge consisting as well of human bodies as of the horses which had been drowned therein was made for those who went to and fro. William, archbishop of Canterbury, died at one of his vills, in the 15th year of his patriarchate, on the 12th of the kalends of December [20th Nov.], and was buried at Canterbury. Guy, abbot of Pershore, a man of great prudence, died on the nones of

August [5th Aug.].   Benedict, abbot of Tewkesbury, a man of great religion and chastity, died on the ides of March [15th March].

A.D. 1137.   Stephen, king of England, before Easter, which was on the 4th of the ides of April [11th April?], went over sea in the month of March, and sojourned in foreign parts.   Griffin ap Rees, king of Wales, was put to death by the artifice of his wife.   After the Welsh had suffered much in the defence of their native land, not only at the hands of the rich Normans, but also of the Flemings, and when many had fallen on both sides, they at length subdued the Flemings, and ceased not to commit devastations all round, burning the towns and castles, and murdering all who resisted them, innocent or guilty, indifferently.   One of these, a soldier named Paganus, a man, as it is related, of wonderful strength, when intending to capture and slay a party of Welsh freebooters, was thrust through the head with a lance, and died, and his body was taken to Gloucester, and is buried in the chapter-house of the brethren.   On the Friday in the week of Pentecost, which fell on the 6th of the ides of June [8th June], the city of York was burned, together with the principal monastery.   Not long after the city of Rochester was consumed.   On Thursday, the 4th of the kalends of August [29th July], the church of Bath, and in the same month of August the city of Leicester, were consumed. As we have learned from the relation of some credible witnesses, one day while the people were standing at the celebration of mass at Windsor, a light shone into the interior of the church; astonished at this, some persons went out of doors, and on looking upwards saw an extraordinary star shining in the heavens; and on their return they perceived that the light which they had noticed within the church, had descended from the star.   Miracle succeeded miracle.   Many beheld the cross which was standing over the altar moving and wringing its hands, now the right hand with the left, now the left hand with the right, after the manner of those who are in distress.   Next followed this miracle: the whole cross began to tremble, and for nearly half an hour streamed all over with perspiration, but returned afterwards to its former condition. At Southwell, an archiepiscopal town, while a grave was being prepared for an interment, the relics of some saints, and a glass vessel containing some very clear water, supported on uprights, which apparently protected it from being broken, were found; this being given to the sick and taken by them, they were restored to their former health.   The first of these miracles I relate as I heard it; the second was narrated to me by Henry, bishop of Winchester. Thurstan, archbishop of York, with Roger, bishop of Salisbury, and some other bishops and nobles of the kingdom, held a council at Northampton in the presence of many persons.

The see of Rome had now been disturbed for seven years by a double papacy, that of Gregory, who was also called Innocent, and of Peter, who was called Leo, in whose cause a war arose between Lothaire, emperor of the Romans, and Roger, duke of Apulia.   Both these men were wealthy, but one was the superior in religion and dignity; the other (to his own confusion) more liberal with his gold. But imperial dignity, as is meet and just, excels all kingly dignity in all things. Both appointed a pope at Rome. Lothaire affirmed that Gregory was canonically elected; Roger made a grant of the papacy of the city of Rome to Peter [surnamed] Leo. But this dissension between them being displeasing to the cardinals and the prefect of the city, for the love of gold they received as pope, first Gregory, to the expulsion of Leo, and then Leo, to the exclusion of Gregory. At length Gregory was established by Lothaire and ruled the apostolic see. Peter Leo, the whelp of the ancient Peter the Lion, sits at the Lateran, like another pope; but if ambition for the dignity stimulated both, neither was pleasing to God. While these things were happening in the world, they were preserved for the judgment of God, whose judgments are as a deep abyss. By reason of so great a dissension existing for so many years in the chief of all churches through the world, by the common advice of the princes a day was appointed, on which a battle was to be fought between the Romans and Apulians, in order that the all-powerful God, the judge of all men, may assign the victory to whom He shall please. The emperor Lothaire, though laid up with illness, having assembled an immense army, encamped in Apulia. Roger, having raised an army of many thousands of infantry and cavalry, met him. A battle was fought, God disposing the event so that the emperor and his army gained the victory and triumphed, and Roger and his army lost the battle and commenced a retreat; his crown, with which he had caused himself to be crowned king, adorned with gold and precious stones, and the royal spear blazing with gold, were at length discovered by treachery and delivered as an acceptable gift to the emperor, who, returning to his country not long after, lost his kingdom and his life. Louis, king of France, died, and his son Louis succeeded him. In the month of December, Stephen, king of England, returned to England; and on the Nativity of the Lord, held his court at Dunstaple, a town in Bedfordshire.

A.D. 1138. Conrad, the 99th emperor of the Romans, duke of Bavaria, the nephew of Henry the elder, who had for empress the daughter of Henry, king of England, reigned twelve years. In old times, a race coming from the north penetrated the land of Thuringia for the purpose of settling there; whereupon the inhabitants granted them a large portion of their territory, as these foreigners requested. The people increased and multiplied exceedingly. After the lapse of a long period they refused to pay the Thuringians the tribute which was due to them. As is the custom of this nation, an armed convention was hereupon held by both parties, in order that the debt might be demanded by the one, and discharged by the other. This was done once and again without a wound; on the third occasion it was agreed by both parties that they should peacefully meet without arms. A large body of the foreigners, perceiving the feebleness of the Thuringians, agreed that the land was ill ruled both in the council-chamber and the field of battle. On the appointed day they crowded to the discussion, carrying secretly with them long sheathed knives for their own defence. The question was discussed, not peacefully, but in anger. What need of more words? The Thuringians were conquered; the foreign and savage race triumphed; for having drawn their long knives, they slew many of the Thuringians. The old inhabitants were expelled from their land in disgrace, nearly all their country passed to those to whom inconstant fortune had given the victory. At length, the land which up to that time had been called Thuringia, was afterwards, by a change of name, called Saxony, from these long and victorious knives.

After the conclusion of the feast of the Nativity of our Lord, Stephen, king of England, besieged and took the castle of Bedford, as he had before that of Exeter, hereby preserving the meaning of his name. In consequence of the arrival of a messenger with intelligence of the irruption of the enemy, the devastation of the land, the burning of towns, the siege of castles and cities, he proceeded with a strong force to Northumberland, where he remained for a short time, and having with difficulty, though successfully, accomplished the object of his expedition, he returned. It was related by those who knew, that a dreadful irruption was made into Northumberland and the surrounding country, during nearly six months, by many enemies of different races. Many were captured, robbed, imprisoned, and tortured; ecclesiastics were put to death for the sake of the property of their churches, and scarce any one can compute the number of the slain either on our side or theirs. On the death of pope Leo, Innocent succeeded him, and all who had adhered to the side of Peter against him, came to him and were reconciled, after having made satisfaction in all things. This pope consecrated at Rome, on Easter-day [3d April], Alberic, abbot of Vercelli, as bishop of Ostia.

HOW THE DEVIL BECAME A MONK, BEING TAKEN IN THE SNARE OF
HIS OWN MALICE, WHILE IN THE SHAPE OF A BOY.

At this time a report flew to all parts that the following miracle had taken place. In the archbishopric of Treves there is a noble monastery, which is called Prum, dedicated in honour of SS. Peter and Paul, apostles, and founded in old times by Pepin, king of France, father of Charlemagne. In it the following extraordinary occurrence is related to have happened, which is attested by all who at that time were residing there. One morning, when the cellarer of the monastery had entered the wine-cellar with his servant for the purpose of procuring wine as usual for the sacrifice of the altar, he found one of the casks which he had left full on the preceding day emptied down to the bung-hole, and the wine spilled over the whole of the pavement. Lamenting the accident which had happened, he severely reprimanded the attendant who was standing by, saying, that he must have put in the spigot very negligently on the evening before, and that the damage had thus arisen. Having said this, he commanded him with threats to tell no person what had happened; for he was afraid that if the abbot were to hear of it, he would deprive him of his office and disgrace him. When it was evening, before the brethren went to rest, he again entered the cellar, and carefully closed the taps of the wine casks, and after shutting the door, went to bed. In the morning, as soon as he entered the cellar according to custom, he saw that another vessel had been emptied, as on the previous day, down to the bung-hole, and the wine was running about. Seeing this, and not knowing to whose negligence to blame the damage, he took the matter heavily to heart, marvelling greatly, and strictly commanding his servant to tell no man what had occurred. Before he went to bed that evening, he fastened all the bungs with the utmost care, and in sorrow and anxiety lay down to rest. Rising early in the morning, and opening the cellar, for a third time he saw that the bung had been taken out of a cask, and that the wine had streamed out of the hole. Being alarmed at this, (and not without cause,) and fearing to conceal any longer the common loss, he hastened to the abbot, and throwing himself at his feet, told him all that he had seen; the abbot, after taking counsel with the friars, commanded that the bung-holes of such barrels as contained wine should be anointed all round, towards the evening, with chrism; and this was accordingly done. At daybreak, the aforesaid friar, when he entered the cellar according to custom, found a marvellously little black boy sticking by the hands to one of the bungs; he speedily seized him, and bringing him before the abbot, " Behold," said he, " master, this little creature whom you see has caused us all the damage which we have suffered in our cellar :" saying which, he related to the abbot how he had found the dwarf sticking to the barrel. The abbot, astonished at the incredible dwarfishness of the urchin, after consultation, ordered that a monk's dress should be prepared for him, and that he should be brought up in the cloister with the scholars of his own age. This was done, and the boy, as the abbot had commanded, associated with the scholars day and night, never however taking drink or meat, and never speaking in public or private ; while the others were at rest by night or in mid-day, he sat upon his bed constantly weeping, and pouring forth incessant lamentations. Meanwhile, the abbot of another house, coming to pray in the monastery, was detained there for some days ; and while the scholars were frequently passed before him, while he sat with the abbot and the superiors of the house, the little boy, stretching forth his hands to him, cast a tearful glance at him, as if to make some request. When he repeated this frequently, the abbot, wondering at his smallness, asked of those who sat near him, for what purpose they kept so small a boy in the monastery with them? They, smiling, said, " Master, this small boy is not what you think him;" and they narrated to him the damage which he had done them, and how he had been found sticking by the hands to the bung of a cask; and how taciturn he had been, while coming in and going out among them. Hearing this, the abbot was afraid, and groaning deeply, said, " Expel him with all haste from your monastery, lest ye incur a greater loss, or run a more serious risk : for he is clearly a devil concealed in human form ; but by the mercy of God protecting you, through the merits of the saints, whose relics ye have here, he has been unable to injure you any further."

Forthwith, at the command of the abbot of the same church, the boy was produced; and as soon as they had stripped him of his monkish garments, he vanished from among them, as if it had been smoke.

Stephen, king of England, held a council at Northampton, in the octave of Easter, which was on the 4th of the ides of April [10th April], and archbishop Thurstan presided, together with the bishops, abbots, earls, barons, and all the nobles of England. In this council, an archdeacon, named Robert, being chosen by a few, was made bishop of the church of Exeter, at that time destitute of a bishop in consequence of the death of William de Warawast. Two abbeys were also given away, that of Winchcombe to a monk of Cluny, as it is related, a kinsman of the king, by name Robert; the other, that of York, to a monk. One of these, the elect of Winchecumbe, was ordained abbot of the church of Winchecumbe by the venerable bishop Simon, on the day of Pentecost, the 11th of the kalends of June [22d May]. The king having removed his troops from Northampton, went to Gloucester; his arrival having been expected, the citizens met him at a distance of more than five miles with great joy, and conducted him into their city with honour; and there, on the third Rogation day [10th May], he was received with the honours of a procession by the monks. There he laid his royal ring upon the holy altar, which was brought back to him on the same day by the royal chaplains, after the payment of fifty shillings. Then Milo, at that time his constable, conducted him to the palace with honour, where the citizens on the ensuing day swore allegiance to him. On the third day, which was [Holy] Thursday, the king returned with his court to the monastery, and was present at the solemnization of masses and processions in honour of our Lord's Ascension. After this festival was concluded, the king heard of a castle which was being fortified against him at Hereford, and marched thither with all speed; on his arrival there, he discovered that what he had heard was true. He remained in the same place for near four or five weeks, and sent orders through England that forces should come to his assistance, for the purpose of subduing all his enemies. While the king was there, the city of Hereford below the bridge of the Wye was burnt. Not long after, the lamentable conflagration of the city of Oxford reached the ears of the king and all his court. The garrison of Hereford, seeing that the king would gain a victory over them from the great magnitude of his army, entered into a treaty and surrendered themselves. And since he was, nay is, a king who loves peace and gentleness, he injured no person, but permitted his enemies to go free. The king took the town called Wibbeleage, which Geoffrey de Talbot, afterwards a fugitive, had held against him; by whose art and ingenuity in those parts the rebels had been upheld in their rebellion; and this and the aforesaid castle of Hereford he garrisoned with soldiers. Meanwhile, Alberic, bishop of Ostia, came to England as legate, to root up, destroy, build, and plant all things necessary. After letters from the apostolic see had been read before the king and the nobles of England, out of reverence of the apostolic see, he was at length received, though after some delay. Going the round of England, he observed all things, and kept in mind whatever ought to be corrected by the provision and appointment of a council. The king, after having resided for some time at Hereford, left it along with his people. After his departure, on Thursday, the 17th of the kalends of July [15th June], the whole city beyond the river Wye was burned by the aforesaid Geoffrey, none of our men, but seven or eight of the Welsh, having been killed. I omit saying anything of the blood-shed of many others, for I am ignorant on this point, but I pray

> That every Christian may repose in peace.
> If John offend, may he be corrected by the reader of these.

Then the king, the Nativity of St. John [24th June] being near, set out for Oxford, and hearing that the castle of Devizes was being fortified against him, sent messengers to the builder of the castle, Roger, bishop of Salisbury, then stationed at Malmesbury, and commanded him to come and speak with him. The bishop, it is said, set forth on this journey with great unwillingness, as though he should never return, and took with him his two nephews, the bishops of Lincoln and Ely, with a great assembly of soldiers, armed and mounted. Seeing this, the king, suspecting treason, ordered his men to arm and to be ready, if need should arise, to defend him. While the king was discussing various matters with the bishops, a great and furious tumult arose between the soldiers of both sides concerning their lodgings; when the king's soldiers ran to their arms, the bishop's men took flight, leaving all their armour behind them. Roger, bishop of Salisbury, with the bishop of Lincoln, and his son Roger, surnamed Pauper, was captured by the king; the bishop of Ely escaped, and having reached the castle of Devizes, he fortified it, and held it against the king.

While the king, being angry, was preparing to pursue him, he placed the captured bishops in custody, namely one of them, Roger, in a cow-house, in the oxen's rack, and the other under a vile shed, while he resolved to hang the third unless the castle were speedily surrendered to him. Seeing this, and fearing for his son's safety, Roger bound himself by an oath that he would neither eat nor drink until the king gained possession of the aforesaid castle, which he accomplished; for during three days he neither did the one nor the other. Thence the king advanced with his royal retinue, on his march to London. But Geoffrey de Talbot, deserting the peace-loving king with his followers, repaired to the son of the earl of Gloucester, who then held the castle of Bristol against the king, and offered himself for the defence of that place. One day, as if to give assistance to a certain straggler, but more, as it afterwards appeared, to reconnoitre Bath, with a view to its subsequent assault, in company with two valiant knights, William Hoset and another, he proceeded thither; and this being known, Robert, bishop of Bath, thinking to triumph over the king's enemies, marched cautiously and in battle array to meet them; whereupon two of them took to flight, and Geoffrey was made prisoner. The garrison of Bristol being incensed thereat, approached Bath in hostile fashion with their lord, the earl's son; they despatched an envoy after the prelate, and threatened that unless their fellow-soldier, Geoffrey, were set free, they would hang the bishop and his companions. Hereupon the bishop, like a timid hireling, brought forth Geoffrey out of prison and delivered him up to them. When this reached the king's ears, his anger was hot against the bishop, regarding him as the abettor of his enemies; and had he been influenced by anger rather than by the love of peace, he would have deprived him of his pastoral staff. But since the bishop had thus acted under constraint and against his own will, the king gave not place to his wrath, upon which, according to the rule of the apostle, it is sinful to let the sun go down. The king, however, afterwards did what he had resolved on in council, for he sent a large army to Bath, that they, by strengthening the city, might defend it from the enemy. Not long afterwards the king marched against Bristol, where, at that time, there had sprung up, as from hell, a series of cruelties worthy of the days of Nero or Decius, through the means of a certain kinsman of the earl, Philip Gay by name. By his agency there were invented there various cruel torments, which thence were disseminated far and wide throughout England, and reduced the whole island nearly to nothing. The king, therefore, having wasted and burnt the surrounding lands and towns of the earl of Gloucester, laid siege to the castle; but at length, weary of the tedious blockade, he diverged to besiege the earl's other castles, Cary in Dorsetshire, and Harptree in Somersetshire; and then, having thrown up and manned castles in front of them, he departed and marched with the whole of his army to Dudley castle, which Ralph Paignel held against him. There he set fire to the surrounding country, and took and carried off much cattle; and then went by sea, together with a large body of his soldiers, to besiege Shrewsbury castle, which William Fitz Alan held against him. This William, however, having heard of the king's approach, secretly took flight with his wife, his sons, and some others, leaving in the castle those who had sworn to him that they would not surrender it. After a siege of many days, a machine was prepared to assault it, constructed in the following fashion, as was related by those to whom it was known. A large mass of timber was heaped up and brought forward, the castle moat, by the king's command, was filled, fire was kindled, the smoke rose in the air and smothered all. The royal gate was forced open. The wretched defenders, falling from or creeping out of the castle, all sought safety in flight, and by the king's orders they were pursued and all put to death. Five of the most noble men among them were hung. The enemy being thus vanquished, the king departed thence and marched upon Wareham. A treaty having been entered into, Ralph Paignel was reconciled to the king for a time.

In the meantime a conspiracy was set on foot against the king by the aforesaid earl of Bristol and Milo the constable. They abjured the fealty that they had sworn, and despatched messengers to the city of Anjou, to summon the ex-empress, king Henry's daughter, promising her that within the space of five months she should be the mistress of her father's kingdom, as it had been sworn unto her during the lifetime of her father. This was the beginning of evil. This grievous breach of faith, yea almost the last, brought ruin upon the whole country.

While this was going on, David, king of Scotland, issuing for the third time with a great multitude of men and horses from the fastnesses of the confines of his kingdom, began to burn fields, towns, and castles round the borders of Northumberland, and to devastate nearly the whole country. As he now threatened to march as far as York and the Humber, Thurstan, archbishop of York, summoned a meeting of the province, and caused them by common assent and counsel to promise by oath that they would resist the king. The king of Scotland was still more irritated herewith, so much so that he would be restrained by no dissuasions, but marching as far as the river Tees, on the 8th day of the Assumption of St. Mary [22d Aug.], which fell on a Monday, he gave orders to surprise our men, there being a thick fog on the morning of that day. And thus, hoping to steal upon us unawares, he left many towns untouched, and contrary to custom forbade his men to set fire to any place. Our forces, meanwhile, being tardily warned by a certain esquire, were nearly taken by surprise, but they armed and arrayed themselves with the greatest haste, and sent out archers to the extreme van, by whom the Scottish army suffered much loss. Then the royal barons themselves marched with the soldiers, for they had all dismounted and placed themselves in the front ranks, and so they fought hand to hand with the enemy. Whereupon in the very first charge victory crowned their efforts; for the Scots, giving way immediately, either fell, or fled in the greatest terror. Our men, however, being on foot and all their horses at a distance, were unable to pursue them long, otherwise they had either captured or slain the king himself, his son, and all his host. As it was, nearly ten thousand of his men fell in different places, and fifty of the flower of his army were made prisoners. He himself escaped by flight, but with the greatest fear and dishonour. His chancellor, William Comyn, was captured by the bishop of Durham, but being freed from his chains he gave thanks to God, heartily hoping he should never again fall into such peril. The king's son, also, attended by one knight only, came on foot to Carlisle, his father barely escaping by woods and thickets to Roxburgh. His army, which consisted of French as well as of English, Scotch, and Galwegians, and men of all the isles which belonged to him and his realm, was innumerable. Out of two hundred of his mailed warriors only nineteen carried back their armour, for each had thrown away nearly all that he had, which became a prey to the enemy; whereby immense spoil both of horses, arms, and clothing, and many other articles, was pillaged from his army. Eustace Fitz

John was his companion, and came to the same end with himself, escaping wounded with his bare life to his castle. These were the brave men who fought in the name of Christ for king Stephen: the earl of Albemarle, Bernard de Balliol, and many others, the earl himself behaving with great valour in the fight.

The king of Scotland, after this reverse, in order to comfort his people and console himself, laid siege with all his forces and many and various engines and inventions to Wark castle, or Carram, belonging to Walter de Spec, and from his former investment of which he had been driven by the earl of Mellent ; but owing to the obstinate defence by the garrison, his efforts were but of little avail. For they made frequent sallies from the castle, and either cut down or burnt his engines, slaying many men. Wherefore he now despaired of being able to take it.

On the seventh of October, on the 29th day of the moon, in the twilight of the night before Saturday, the whole firmament towards the north appeared of a red colour, and rays of divers blended colours appeared and vanished. These things were significant perchance of that mighty shedding of blood which we have mentioned as having occurred throughout Northumberland and many other parts of England. A man of great religion, a monk of the cell of Eye, by name William, who had already been elected by Simon, bishop of Worcester, was ordained abbot of Pershore on Sunday, the 12th of the kalends of December [20th Nov.]. Roger, bishop of Salisbury, a mighty builder of castles, walls, and houses, being borne down and brought to the close of life by sorrow and grief, died at his episcopal see on the 2d of the nones of December [4th Dec.], and was buried in that church, leaving in his castles an immense sum of money, which he bequeathed to the use, not of God, but of king Stephen. There are those who say that more than forty thousand silver marks were there found, and that he had likewise hoarded up an enormous amount of gold with a variety of ornaments, and knew not for whom he had amassed them. He adorned with magnificent decoration a church in honour of the holy Mother of God.

In the year 1138 from the incarnation of our Lord, and in the ninth of the pontificate of pope Innocent, being the third of king Stephen's reign, a synod was held at London in the church of St. Peter, at Westminster, on the 13th day of December, in which, after many causes had been discussed, chapters were published and confirmed by all to the number of sixteen. Over this council presided Alberic, bishop of Ostia, the papal legate in England and Scotland, with the bishops of divers provinces to the number of seventeen, of abbots about thirty, and an immense multitude of clergy and the people.

A.D. 1139. The solemnization of Christmas being over, and the Purification of the holy Mother Mary [2d Feb.] at hand, the venerable father Walter, abbot of Gloucester, in the ninth year and a half of his preferment, and about the third hour of the day, gave up the ghost, and was buried by the venerable abbots, Reynold of Evesham and Roger of Tewkesbury, on the 6th of the ides of February [8th Feb.]. After his burial two friars are despatched to the monastery of Cluny, on the business of our elect Gilbert; on whom king Stephen, having heard the fame of his extraordinary goodness, had at the petition of his constable Milo conferred at London the church of Gloucester.   Theobald, archbishop of Canterbury, Simon of Worcester, Roger of Coventry, Robert of Exeter, and Reynold, abbot of Evesham, having been unanimously elected, went, at the pope's command, to the shrine of St. Peter. Having arrived there, they were received with honour by the apostolic see, and admitted to the Roman council, an event without parallel for many past ages.   After having fully discussed their cause, they returned joyfully to their own country, bringing with them the synodal decrees, now enrolled far and wide throughout England.   The two friars also who had been despatched to fetch the lord abbot Gilbert, returned in peace, after having presented him to king Stephen, by whom he was honourably received, and the government of the church of Gloucester was freely bestowed upon him; he arrived at Worcester on the holy day of Pentecost, which was then celebrated on the 3d of the ides of June [11th June], and he was ordained by Robert, the venerable bishop of Hereford, with great rejoicings and thanksgiving; and afterwards, on the following day, with the good wishes of many people of all conditions, he was established in his see with joy and gladness, as befitted such a man in the Lord.

In the octave of Easter, which was on the 2d of the kalends of May [30th April], Stephen, the magnificent king of the English, coming with a royal retinue to Worcester, was received by a festive procession of all the clergy and people of the surrounding country. When prayer was concluded and the accustomed blessing pronounced, the king offered on the altar the royal ring which he had taken from his finger, and on the morrow it was restored to him by common consent.   Therefore, the king, filled with admiration at the humble devotion of the monks of Gloucester, yea rather of God's flock, took back the ring as he had been adjured by the love of Mary, the holy Mother of God.   Thence, departing from Worcester, the king encamped at Ludlow, where a double fortification was erected for the storming of the castle which held out against him, and returning through Worcester, he marched towards London.   Certain of the soldiers, caring little for the horrors of war, in their presumption demanded to try their strength on Ludlow; and in the furtherance of this enterprise a large army of men began to flock together.   Truly it was a misery to behold one brandishing his spear in the face of another, and piercing him with the lance, and thus deliver him unto death, regardless of the judgment which the spirit would have to undergo.   But king Stephen struck terror into these designs by his threats, for he marched a second time from Ludlow through Worcester, and reduced all to peace, and quietly marched to Oxford, which means The ford of the oxen.   During his stay there, he was justified in arresting Roger, bishop of Salisbury, his nephew, the bishop of Lincoln, and also Roger his chancellor, as conspirators against his royal crown, and committing them to custody.   Upon hearing this, Nigel, bishop of Ely, fearful for himself and his people, fled with an army to Devizes, that he might there find protection, the cause for which has been fully treated of in the foregoing pages, yet seems this year to have been repeated over again. A council being afterwards held, an order was issued that all towns, castles and fortifications whatever, in which secular affairs were mainly transacted, should yield to the right of the king and his barons; but that churchmen, the bishops, namely, (God's watch-dogs I call them,) should not cease to bark in defence and protection of their flock, and keep vigilant watch lest the invisible wolf, their malignant foe, should scatter and seize upon the sheep.

In the month of October, the earl of Gloucester, bastard son of Henry, formerly king of England, with his sister, by the father's side, formerly empress of the Romans, and now countess of Anjou, returned to England with a large army, and arrived at Portsmouth before the Feast of St. Peter ad Vincula, on the kalends of August [1st Aug.], the king being then engaged in the siege of Marlborough; by whose arrival terror pervaded all England. Upon hearing this, king Stephen was angry, and his wrath broke out upon those whose duty it was to have guarded the sea-ports. He is the king of peace, and would also that he were the king of vigour and justice, treading under foot his enemies, weighing all things in the equal balance of justice, and preserving and strengthening in the bonds of fortitude the friends of peace. When, however, he knew that the ex-queen had received the ex-empress with her large retinue at Arundel, he marched thither in displeasure. But she, dreading the king, and fearing she should lose the dignity which she held in England, swore that none of his enemies had reached England by her means, but that, saving her dignity, she had granted hospitality to men of authority as to persons once in her service. Whereupon the king, having dismissed her, commanded the ex-empress to be conducted to Bristol castle, to his brother the bishop of Winchester, with such honour as befitted his kinswoman; but he himself followed in pursuit of the earl. Hearing no certain news of him, however—for he had betaken himself into certain by-paths for a time—he marched his forces according to his previous determination. Milo the constable, after having sworn an oath of fealty to the king, went over with a large military force to his lord, while the earl of Gloucester promised him that he would faithfully assist him against the king. The misfortunes, however, which now sprang up throughout England, from this quarter, namely, the town of Bristol, are beyond the knowledge or eloquence of man to describe. For of those who resisted or obeyed the royal authority, as many as could be taken are made prisoners, and the captives all given up to chains and frightful torments; a variety of cruel punishments is devised, troops of soldiers are being hired on every side for the consummation of this work of destruction, and to these the husbandmen and the inhabitants of villages and towns, with all their property and substance, are given and sold for pay.

The queen remained in this place for more than two months, receiving homage from all, and dispensing the laws of the kingdom of England according to her pleasure. Departing thence, she came on the 18th of the kalends of November [15th Oct.] to the town of Gloucester, where she assumed the command and took the homage of the citizens and the surrounding districts. But upon those who refused to submit to her, and preferred to remain faithful to the king, torments worthy of the age of Decius or Nero were inflicted, and death in many cases ensued; and the city, glorious in past ages, became filled with direful howlings and tortures, shocking to those who dwelt within it. In the midst of all these miseries the king laid siege to the hostile castle of Wallingford. Tired of the protracted blockade, after having erected castles against it, he marched thence and encamped at Malmesbury, where he enacted the same part against his adversaries, the workers of discord.

In the midst of these events, sad tidings came to the ears of the citizens of Worcester; and it was generally reported that their city was to be sacked, pillaged of its wealth, and destroyed by fire. When the citizens heard this, they were terrified, and consulted as to what were best to be done. Whereupon they put themselves under the protection of God, the most High Father, and his most holy Mother, and under the tutelage of the confessors Oswald and Wolstan, bishops of that city, and thus committed themselves and all belonging to them to the divine protection. Any one there present might have seen the whole furniture of all the citizens carried into the church. Oh! miserable sight! Behold, the house of God, which should have been entered with sacrifices, where the sacrifice of praise should have been offered up and the loftiest vows recorded, seems now but a warehouse for furniture. Behold the mother church of the diocese converted into an inn and council-chamber of the citizens! By reason of the number of chests and sacks, but little space remained to the servants of God in such an hostelry. Within chanted the monk, without might be heard the sobbing of the infant, and the wail of children at the breast, and cries of sorrowing mothers mingled with the voices of the singers. Oh! misery of miseries to behold! The high altar stood robbed of its decorations, the cross pulled down, and the image of Mary, the most holy Mother of God, removed from sight. Curtains and palls, albs and copes, stoles and other vestments, were hidden within the shelter of the walls. At the celebration of divine service on saints' festivals, dignity, honour, and all the wonted magnificence were wanting. Out of fear for the enemy, everything was so arranged, lest the foe, stealing upon them unawares, should bear off whatever he could find, and thus iniquity should prevail. At daybreak one morning in the beginning of winter, namely, on Tuesday, the 7th of the ides of November [7th Nov.], whilst we were engaged in divine service within the church, and had already chanted our primes, behold, our apprehensions were realized,—a great army, strong and valiant, marched from the south. The city of Gloucester, having furnished itself with a countless host of horse and foot soldiers, marches to invade, sack, and burn the city of Worcester. We, however, in our apprehension for the ornaments of the sanctuary, clothed ourselves in our albs, and carried the relics of ·Oswald our most benignant patron, we tolled all our bells, and marched in humble procession out of the church; and as the enemy were rushing in from gate to gate, we proceeded through the cemetery. Our enemies hasten to make their first united attack upon a certain fortification of great strength, situated in the southern portion of the city near the castle, which was manfully and courageously resisted by our people. The foe were repulsed at this point; but a beacon opposite the north was set on fire, and then they stormed the north side of the town; here, meeting with no resistance, an excited and unbridled rabble rush in and fire the buildings in many parts. Woe is me! much of the town was destroyed by the flames, though the larger portion remained standing and uninjured. An immense booty of various furniture was carried off from the city, and of oxen, sheep, cattle, and horses, from the country. Many people were taken in the streets and courts; they were bound in couples like hounds, and carried away unto a miserable captivity. Whether they possessed the means or no, whatever sum was fixed by their cruel captors for their ransom, that they were compelled upon their oath to promise to pay, and to pay. The deeds done on the first day of winter were very grievous. And now the prey being secured, and numbers of buildings destroyed by fire, the maddened and drunken rout retrace their steps, never to return on a like depraved errand. On the 30th day of November, the earl of Worcester came to the city, and when he had beheld the ravages of the flames, he grieved and felt that the blow had been struck for his own injury, and wishing to revenge himself for this, he marched with an army to Sudely, for he had heard that John, the son of Harold, had deserted from the king, and had gone over to the earl of Gloucester. If it be inquired what the earl did there, the answer must be such as should hardly be handed down to memory; for he returned evil for evil, by seizing and carrying off from the men there great booty of their goods and cattle, with which, on the morrow, he returned to Worcester.

After these things, the king with a large army marched from Oxford to Worcester; and what he had previously heard of its misfortunes, he now beheld with his eyes; and he grieved thereat. Having stayed there for three or five days he bestowed the honour of royal constable, of which he had deprived Milo of Gloucester, his enemy, upon William, the son of Walter de Beauchamp, sheriff of Worcester. A lying report reached the king that his enemies, having violated their sworn promises of peace, had invaded Hereford, and penetrated into the monastery of St. Ethelbert, king and martyr, as if it had been a fortified castle. Whereupon, setting out thither, he encamped at Little Hereford, or Leominster, where certain of the inhabitants swore fealty to him advisedly, while others refusing, thus spoke, " If the king will not believe our oaths, he may at least, if he will, rely upon our faithful words." When the solemn days of the Lord's Advent were at hand [3d Dec.], a treaty was made and confirmed on both sides, after which the king returned to Worcester, where a certain clerk, (a man of exemplary piety,) Maurice by name, had been elected by the clergy and the people to the church of Bangor, and was presented to the king in the castle by the bishops Robert of Hereford and Sigefrid of Chichester; these made oath that he had been canonically elected, and would be worthy of the see, and the king confirmed their election. Being urged by the bishops to do fealty to the king, Maurice answered that he could in no wise do so. "There is a man of religion amongst us," said he, "whom I hold for my spiritual father, and who was archdeacon to my predecessor David, and he forbade me to take this oath." To which they made answer, "Reason requires that you should do what we demand." Then he exclaimed, "If you, who are men of great authority, require this, far be it from me to delay doing so," and so he swore fealty to the king.

From Worcester the king went to Oxford, and thence, with his court, to Salisbury, where he intended to celebrate his Christmas, and, as was the royal custom, to wear his crown. The canons offered two thousand pounds to him on his arrival, upon which he conferred upon them the entire exemption from all taxes upon their land; moreover he gave them twenty marks for their own use, and forty for roofing the church, and he promised that if he should obtain peace, he would refund to them what they had bestowed upon him.

A.D. 1140.   A few days after Christmas the king came with his court to Reading, where fate gave a lesson teaching us of what value is the kingly dignity. There by advice of his attendants he provided two abbeys, Malmsbury and Abbotsbury, with their own pastors. These bishop Roger in his lifetime had held, after having stripped them of their honour and privileges. Malmsbury he bestowed upon a monk called John, a man of great probity, and the abbey of Abbotsbury he gave to Gosfrid. Then for the purpose of securing peace and tranquillity he marched his forces to Ely, a measure which in my opinion was entirely unnecessary, and which at the same time was a deplorable business, thereby sanctioning the thirst of vain glory among his soldiers, by permitting them to harass his army. They all agree to the proposal, they array themselves for war, the conqueror takes from the conquered everything specified in the detestable bond of avarice, and, if I may compare great things with small, they whisper to one another like Juda and his brother Jonathan dwelling in the land of Gilead, to Joseph and Azarias,—"Let us also get us a name, and go fight against the heathen that are round about us." They slaughter one another with sword and spear, little heeding what will become of the wretched souls of the slain! During the rebellion of the king's opponents, many on both sides were wounded, taken prisoners, and consigned to captivity. The bishop of Ely, perceiving the valorous charge of the king and his troop, gave ground, yea, fled like a hireling, and he taking himself to the neighbourhood of the town of Gloucester, went over to earl Robert. Nor is this wonderful, for it had been to him as the loss of his right hand when his uncle Roger, bishop of Salisbury, died. The king, however, got possession of Ely castle, and posted his men therein. Thurstan, archbishop of York, the twenty-sixth in succession, a man of advanced age and full of days, having laid aside the old man put on the new; for bidding farewell to secular pursuits he dons the monkish habit at Pomfret, on the 12th of the kalends of February, [21st Jan.], and on the nones of February [5th Feb.], he departed this life in a good old age, and there he was buried. Milo, the ex-constable, having collected a great army, invaded Winchcombe on Thursday the 2d of the kalends of February [31st Jan.], burned the greatest part of the town, plundered it, and carried off the spoil, the mammon of unrighteousness being (albeit unjustly) required of them. Thence he marched to Sudely. Whilst he was in mind to attack it, the troops which were in the town made a stand and compelled him to retreat, leaving, as it is said, two of his men killed and fifteen taken prisoners. The king and the earl of Worcester came with a great army to Worcester, and after the lapse of a few days, first the earl and afterwards the king advanced with a vast host to Little Hereford, purposing to drive out their enemies. During the king's stay in these parts the earl, remembering the injuries inflicted upon his townsmen, invaded Tewkesbury with a large force of armed men, and burned the magnificent house of the earl of Gloucester, and everything in its vicinity, together with those of some other persons within one mile's distance of Gloucester; but at the supplication of the lord abbot of Tewkesbury and his brethren, the conqueror spared their goods. Having taken no small booty, both of men and their apparel and cattle, he mercifully commanded that the prisoners be speedily released from their fetters, and return to their own houses; and on the morrow he set out for Worcester, protesting to all that he had scarcely ever either in Normandy or England accomplished such a burning. But the king on his return to Worcester hastened his march to Oxford. The before-mentioned Maurice and Uhtred were consecrated bishops of Bangor and Landaff, by Theobald, archbishop of Canterbury, in the presence of the bishops of Hereford and Exeter. The king, on his arrival at Winchester, by advice of his barons, bestowed the bishopric of Salisbury upon his chancellor Philip, and the abbey of Fescamp upon Henry, a monk, his kinsman. An eclipse of the sun takes place while the moon occupies the tail of Draco, the sun itself illuminating the head. By advice of the barons of Philip king of France, and Stephen king of England, it was settled that the son of the latter should take to wife the French king's sister. The betrothal took place abroad in the month of February, in the presence of the queen mother of England, and before a large number of the barons of both kingdoms. A certain knight, by name Robert, was the son of a nobleman named Hulbert. He, fearing neither God nor man, but relying entirely on his own strength, with his many cunning devices, assailed the castle of Malmesbury. Whereupon many of the king's troops which were within fled to the church of the holy bishop Aldelm, as to a sanctuary. In pursuit of these he one day entered the chapter of the monks with his armed knights, terrifying them with threats, and commanding them to give up to him the king's men with their horses if they valued the safety of their own wealth. But they, fearful of infringing the peace of God and their blessed patron Aldelm, refuse to obey these commands, till at length, (though unwillingly, and in order to appease his fury,) they deliver up the horses. After they had remained for a long time in the castle and had laid waste the surrounding country, the king came up with his army and besieged it for nearly three days. William de Ypres, as it is reported, a kinsman of this Robert, acted as the mediator upon both sides for the surrender of the castle, and at last obtained the king's consent that the castle should be delivered up upon the condition that everything should be surrendered to the king, and this was done. Robert therefore joined the earl of Gloucester, and remained for a while with him, all the while meditating treachery. Unknown to the earl, shortly afterwards, (for he was untaught by experience and bent on revenge,) he repaired with his men to Devizes, where an agreement having been first made between himself and his followers that the castle once taken should never be surrendered, he scaled the wall with cruel cunning, and giving the signal of victory to the king's soldiers who were within, he penetrated the outer defences unobserved, and acted the tyrant upon all. On the fourth day afterwards, by force and subtlety he gained possession of the inner tower, and in the pride of his heart he continually ravaged the whole neighbourhood everywhere, and whatever evil he could do he ceased not from doing. At length he went to John, a man illustrious in war, who was then the governor of the castle of Marlborough for the king's service, and he demanded with threats that he should be guided by his advice, yea, rather his instigation, and do the work of Satan against not only the king but the earl and every one else, assuring him that if he would not comply, he should immediately lose his head. John replied,—"By God's help I would sooner take a man than be taken by him," and immediately seized him and consigned him to prison, where turn for turn he caused every description of torture which he in his cruelty had inflicted upon others to be applied to himself. When all these things became known, the earl of Gloucester and Milo the ex-constable, with many men, came to the said John, to whom the earl promised to give five hundred marks, with the agreement that he should deliver up to him the said Robert on an appointed day, and give good hostages for himself. John being pacified with the promised money and hostages, gave up Robert to him, with the understanding that within fifteen days he should be restored to him. This agreement completed, the earl returned to Gloucester, carrying the said Robert with him, and a discussion followed touching the surrender of the castle of Devizes, which he demanded should be freely given up to him ; but Robert refused, lest he should break the oath which he had sworn to his comrades, to wit, that the castle should not be surrendered. But being terrified by threats of the gallows, he answered that he would yield to his request, provided he might only escape death.   Within the time appointed in the agreement this malignant Robert was led back to the presence of John, to whom the earl told everything which had happened, and how Robert, under the fear of his menaces, had promised to deliver up the castle.   He also asked him again to permit Robert to accompany him to Devizes, with the understanding that if he should succeed in making himself master of the castle it should be placed in John's command under him; and upon his prayers being acceded to, the earl returned immediately to Devizes with Robert.   In the meantime the said John despatched letters to all, both within and without the castle, swearing that neither he nor the earl would do any injury to Robert, provided only they would firmly keep their oath in not surrendering the castle to any one.   Leaving the ex-constable and a certain powerful personage named Humphrey, with some others, behind him, the earl returned to Gloucester, after giving directions to all that in case Robert refused to deliver up the castle of his own accord he should be hung.[1]   Robert did refuse, as did his comrades also, lest they should appear perjured.   In short, he was taken and hanged as a warning to others, after his two nephews had shared the same fate.   Glory be to God Almighty that He has delivered up the wicked!

Before the Assumption of St. Mary [15th Aug.] the earl of Gloucester marched against Bath; but the king had long before this sent out spies to entrap the enemy, and defend themselves and their possessions to the uttermost.   A hostile meeting consequently took place; on the one hand the soldiers of the king, among whom were two knights, John and Roger, both valiant and warlike men; on the other, the retainers of the earl.   Many were taken prisoners, and more were wounded and killed, among whom a certain knight named Geoffrey Talbot, valorous but crafty, now with the king, now with the earl, subtle in every action, was mortally hurt, and dying of his wounds on the 11th of the kalends of September [22d Aug.] was buried along with the canons at Gloucester.   The royal troops however gained the victory.   Before the Nativity of St. Mary [8th Sept.], Robert, son of king Henry, at the instigation of Ralph Paganel, having associated with himself the knights of the earl of Warwick along with those whom he had brought out of Gloucester, and many other common soldiers, suddenly assaulted the town of Nottingham, and finding it unprovided with military defence, commenced sacking it, while the citizens on every side fled to the churches.   One of these, who had the reputation of being wealthier than the rest, having been taken prisoner, was led strongly bound to his own house and compelled to give up his gold.   For this purpose he led the greedy pillagers into his cellar, where all his furniture was stored up.   As soon as he perceived them intent upon pillage, and occupied in breaking open doors and locks, he craftily slipped away, and escaping through the chambers and hall, he closed all the doors behind him and fastened them with bolts.

[1] Here ends the MS. in Corpus Christi College, Oxon.   The remainder is translated from the editions, fol. Francof. 1601, p. 675, and of the E. H. S. ii. 127.

After this he set fire to the place, and consigned his houses and all his goods, together with the robbers, to the flames. It is said that upwards of thirty of the men who had entered the cellar perished in that fire, by which, as it is also reported, the whole town was burnt; for the knights and the whole army swore that they were innocent of having set fire to it. By this means the whole city was destroyed by the flames, and those inhabitants who were captured outside the churches were carried away prisoners, some even as far as Gloucester. The rest of the mob, men, women and children, who had entered the churches, fearing to sally forth lest they should be taken by the enemies, nearly all perished as the churches fell a prey to the raging conflagration. A cruel spectacle and most wretched, even to the enemy themselves, to behold the temples of God, which even the heathen would have spared, consumed by fire! In like manner was Nottingham destroyed, a most noble city, it having continued from the period when the Normans subdued England down to the present time in the enjoyment of the greatest peace and tranquillity, besides being populous and wealthy. The government of the abbey of Malmesbury was conferred by Henry, bishop of Winchester, legate of the holy Roman church, upon a certain monk, by name Peter, nobly endowed with learning and science. Having donned the garb of religion at Cluny, he had for some time held the Priory de Caritate, being removed from which he was appointed to the monastery of St. Urban the pope, in the diocese of Catalonia; but calamities increasing upon him, he was compelled to abandon that place, and at the persuasion of the above-mentioned bishop of Winchester he came to England, and this year undertook the rule of the church already mentioned.

A.D. 1141. Stephen, king of England, after prolonged labours in besieging castles in which (for the peace of the kingdom) he had toiled five years and six weeks, at last at the siege of Lincoln castle, on the day of the Purification of St. Mary, being Sexagesima Sunday [2d Feb.], was surrounded and taken prisoner, by the just judgment of God, by Robert, earl of Gloucester, the son of his uncle, and Ranulph, earl of Chester; and was carried first to Gloucester on Quinquagesima Sunday [9th Feb.], and then to the town of Bristol, and there consigned to prison. Many of his adherents were captured along with him and loaded with chains. In the meantime the empress, king Henry's daughter, was staying in the city of Gloucester, and rejoiced exceedingly at this event, she having now, as she thought, obtained possession of the kingdom which had been promised to her by oath; and having taken counsel with her followers, she departed out of the city on the fifth day after Ash-Wednesday [17th Feb.]; and accompanied by two bishops, Bernard of St. David's, and Nigel of Ely, Gilbert abbot of Gloucester, with many barons, knights, and attendants, she advanced to the city of Chichester, in which she first rested after the joyful intelligence, and of which she also assumed the dominion. Departing thence, when she had come nigh to the city of Winchester, there advanced to meet her, with magnificent state and pomp, the prelates of nearly the whole of England, many barons and chief men, knights innumerable, and divers abbots with their retinues, two convents of monks of the city, and a third of nuns, all chanting processional melodies and praises, and the clergy of the town with the citizens and much people. The most noble city of Winchester thus surrendered to her empire, and the crown of the realm of England was delivered to her dominion; by the legate himself those were accursed who curse her, and those blessed who bless her; they who oppose her were excommunicated, and those who obey her command were absolved. Departing from Winchester with her attendants, she went to Wilton, where Theobald, archbishop of Canterbury, was present to welcome her. So great a concourse of people flocked together, that the gates of the town barely sufficed for the multitude who entered. Thence, after the celebration of the festival of Easter, she came within the Rogation days [4th May] to Reading, where she was received with honours, the principal men and people pouring in from all sides in submission to her. One of these leading men, Robert D'Oyley, was there summoned by her touching the surrender of Oxford castle, and upon his consenting to it she came thither and received possession, and the homage of the whole city and surrounding districts. Setting out thence with great joy and exultation, she was received in the monastery of St. Alban's with processional honours and rejoicings, and many citizens from London visited her there, and held divers discourses touching the surrender of the city.

In these days a certain horrible event befel in Worcester, which we deem worthy of relation. On Wednesday before the octave of our Lord's Ascension [11th May], about the ninth hour of the day, at the town called Walesburn, distant one mile from Hampton, the bishop of Worcester's town, a violent whirlwind and most dreadful darkness arose, reaching from earth to heaven, and striking the house of a priest named Leofrid, which it prostrated to the ground and shattered to atoms, together with its offices; the roof of the church also was torn off and cast across the river Avon, and nearly fifty houses of the country people were in like manner thrown down and ruined. Hailstones of the bigness of a pigeon's egg fell, by the blows from which one woman was killed. At this sight all present were struck with terror and dismay.

The empress, as we have before related, after a treaty with the Londoners, hastened in security to the city, attended by many prelates and nobility, and was received with processional honours at Westminster, where she remained for a few days to set the affairs of her kingdom in order, having first, as was meet, provided for the interest of God's holy church, pursuant to the advice of good men. She gave the bishopric of London to a venerable monk of Reading, Robert by name, in the presence and by the orders of his reverend abbot Edward. God's affairs being thus accomplished, the queen of England interceded with Matilda for the king her husband, who had been taken captive and committed to prison. The first and greatest nobles of England pleaded the same cause, offering to place at her disposal many hostages, castles, and great riches, in order that the king might be restored, not to his kingdom, but simply his liberty, promising also that they would persuade him, after he had been dismissed from the kingdom, thenceforth to serve God alone as a monk or pilgrim; but she heard them not. The bishop of Winchester, too, petitioned that the government which belonged to his brother should be given to his nephew, that is, to the king's son, but neither would she hear him. The citizens also requested that they might be permitted to observe the laws of king Edward, which were excellent, and not those of Henry her father, which were severe. But she refused good advice, being influenced by a spirit of too great severity, and so she would not consent; in consequence of which a great commotion arose in the city, and a conspiracy was formed against her, so that she whom they had received with honour was now ordered to be disgracefully apprehended. Being warned however by some of the citizens, she betook herself with her attendants to an ignominious flight, leaving all her own and their apparel behind them. Perceiving this, the bishop of Winchester, who was also legate of the holy Roman church, busied himself for the deliverance of his brother; and in order to effect this he secured the courage and good will of the Londoners in his behalf. In the meantime the fugitive lady came to Gloucester, where, having taken counsel with Milo, the ex-constable, she returned with him immediately to Oxford, intending to remain there until she could collect her scattered forces. And because she had chiefly been influenced by the advice, and been supported by the assistance of Milo, insomuch as up to that time she had neither eaten one day's meals nor had any provision for her table, except through his munificence or forethought—as we have heard from Milo's own mouth—in order that she might the more straitly bind him to her service, she bestowed upon him in reward the earldom of Hereford.

On the approach of the Festival of St. Peter ad Vincula [1st Aug.], her troops having now increased in valour and numbers, she came, unknown to her brother, the earl of Bristol, to Winchester, but finding that city already revolted against her, she took up her abode in the castle. Wondering at her unlooked-for arrival, and exceedingly troubled thereat, Henry, bishop of that city, escaped out at another gate, and then and there escaped. Discord now broke out among themselves, and this wealthy city, so long famous through all lands, was encompassed with a sudden blockade, in consequence of domestic quarrels, and was drained of its inhabitants and property, while common soldiers and destructive mercenaries rage furiously to and fro. Nor was even this sufficient for the pontiff's wrath, for, goaded by fury and wishing to strike terror and dismay into their minds, he gave orders that the whole town should be set on fire and burnt; and this he accomplished. Thus, on the second of the month of August, having fired the city, he reduced to ashes the monastery of the nuns with its buildings, more than forty churches, together with the larger and better portion of the town, and lastly, the monastery of the monks dedicated to the service of God and St. Grimbald, with its buildings. There existed in this church of St. Grimbald a great cross and a holy, formerly made by order of king Canute, and by him most handsomely adorned with gold and silver, gems and precious stones. Now, wonderful to relate, this cross, on the approach of the flames, as if conscious of the danger which threatened it, in full view of the brethren who were present, began to sweat and grow black, thus typifying the blackness of the incendiaries, while in the very instant of its catching fire a horrifying crash of mighty thunder thrice roared from heaven. The city having been thus made a prey to the flames within, and beleaguered by enemies without, the bishop is said to have addressed the following words to the earl of Northampton:—"Behold, lord Earl, I have commanded these things, do thou study to terminate them." Which words lay bare the inmost feelings of the speaker's heart. Seven weeks after the siege had been in progress, the bishop, weary at last of its protracted duration, on the evening of the day preceding the Festival of the Exaltation of the Holy Cross [14th Sept.], commanded peace to be proclaimed throughout the city, and the gates to be thrown open. The empress had already mounted her horse, accompanied by, and under the guidance of her brother Reginald; more than two hundred of her knights were left behind as guards, under the command of the earl of Hereford; and then the bishop suddenly ordered his men to arm themselves, to make a violent charge upon the enemy, and take as many prisoners as they could. Many were thus captured, and very many here and there slain; among whom, a knight named William de Curcell, with six of his companions, was put to death, and buried at St. Grimbald's. The empress, hearing of this, was much terrified and disturbed thereat, and in consequence she repaired to the castle of Luggershall, where she arrived sorrowing and downcast; but she found no fit resting-place there, on account of her dread of the bishop. By the advice of her followers, she once more mounted her horse in male fashion, and was conducted to Devizes, but fearing that she could not find shelter there from her pursuers, she was placed already nearly half dead on a litter, and being bound with bandages after the manner of a corpse, and borne upon horses, was carried ignominiously enough into the city of Gloucester. Her brother Robert, earl of Bristol, having sallied out in another direction, was hard pressed by the pursuers and captured at Stolibridge by the Flemings, with earl Warren, and after being presented to the queen, who was staying in the town, was by her command committed to the care of William de Ypres, and imprisoned in the city of Rochester. But Milo, the earl of Hereford, hemmed in by his enemies, after having cast away his arms and furniture, and glad to escape with life alone, came in disgraceful flight, half naked, weary and alone to Gloucester. The pursuing forces of the bishop having followed John, the aider and abettor of the fugitives, to the monastery of Wherwell, when they could by no means expel him therefrom, they, on the day of the Festival of the Exaltation of the Holy Cross

[14th Sept.], set fire to and consumed the church of St. Cross, and with it the nuns' houses and property there; but after despoiling them of their vestments, books, and ornaments, and cruelly shedding very much human blood before the holy altar, yet could they neither capture the said John, nor drive him from his place of refuge. Alfrida, during the reign of her husband Edgar,[1] the glorious king of the English, erected this monastery in honour of St. Cross in remorse for the murder of her step-son. In this state of affairs the bishop Henry, his anger being in some degree appeased, but his covetousness much increased, at the suggestion of the prior of Newminster, (which had been just burnt down,) recovered from the ashes of the cross five hundred pounds of silver, thirty marks of gold, three crowns, and as many footstools of the purest Arabian gold and most precious stones, fashioned with surprising and fairest workmanship, and stored them up among his own treasures.

In the meantime the king and. the earl were kept in durance, but the queen, busying herself exceedingly for the king, and the countess labouring earnestly for the earl, after employing divers mediators and trustworthy friends in this behalf, the result of their mutual deliberations resolved itself into the following condition :— namely, that the king being restored to his kingdom, and the earl raised to the government of the whole of England under him, they should both direct their efforts to secure the tranquillity and peace of the realm, as they had hitherto been the authors and promoters of all its dissensions and troubles. But the earl, refusing to act without the consent of his sister the empress, dissented altogether from the terms of this agreement, and spurned all hints of reconciliation with the king. Whence it came to pass that they parted mutually unpacified, and during the whole of the ensuing year the whole kingdom and country were torn to pieces with rapine, murder, and sacrilege.[2]

[1] A note in the margin of the MS. C. states, in reference to the monastery of Wherewell, that "Aelfdryth, the wife of king Eadgar, influenced by remorse for the murder of her stepson, erected this monastery in honour of Holy Cross," thereby avoiding the error of the text. See Dugd. Monast. i. 256.

[2] Here the printed copy ends abruptly. The continuation from A.D. 1152 to 1295, will be given hereafter in its own appropriate place.

THE END OF THE CONTINUATION OF

FLORENCE OF WORCESTER.

Also published by Llanerch:

CONTEMPORARY CHRONICLES OF THE MIDDLE AGES. Sources of twelfth-century history: William of Malmesbury, Richard of Hexham, and Jordan Fantosme.

MEDIAEVAL CHRONICLES OF SCOTLAND. The Chronicles of Melrose, and Holyrood.

SIMEON OF DURHAM. A history of the kings of England.

A HISTORY OF THE CHURCH OF DURHAM. Simeon's account of the monks of St. Cuthbert.

LIFE OF SAINT COLUMBA. English translation of the Reeves edition of Adamnan's famous work.

THE LEGENDARY XII HIDES OF GLASTONBURY. Ray Gibbs. History, archaeology, and the legends of King Arthur and Joseph of Arimathea.

From booksellers, or direct mail-order from the publishers. For details of these, and other books, write to:

Llanerch Enterprises,
Felinfach,
Lampeter,
Dyfed.
SA48 8PJ.